The Bullying Epidemic

THE PSYCHOLOGY, INCIDENCE & PREVENTION

G.A. MOHR, PHD

WORLD HONS MULT., CEO OF TRI
(TRANSWORLD RESEARCH & INNOVATION)

G. A. Mohr
The Bullying Epidemic
The Psychology, Incidence & Prevention

TRI

Transworld Research & Innovation
9 Hampstead Drive
Hoppers Crossing VIC 3029
AUSTRALIA

Contents

PREFACE

> *The psychological observer ought to be more agile than the tightrope dancer in order to insinuate himself under the skin of other people,* Søren Kierkegaard, *The Concept of Dread,* 1844 (tr. W. Lowrie, 1957).

We are, strictly speaking, simply one of many kinds of animals, but what sets us apart from other species is the enlarged cerebral cortex required to store the semantic memory needed for our advanced and complex languages. Thus Part I (Introduction) briefly discusses the evolution of the human brain, language and learning, skill learning, how memories are stored, and the key subject of this book, bullying.

Part II, Bullying in Families, Schools, Workplaces and Society, discusses family life, the education system, hierarchical organizations and psychopaths in which these abound, and social life.

Part III, Attitude Formation and Measurement, discusses the psychology of attitudes, the mass media, advertising and the psychology of habits.

Part IV, Psychology and Psychiatry, discusses the psychology of attitudes, personality, the psychology of conflict, psychological assessment, and treatment of mental disorders.

Part V, Conclusions, discusses how we can improve our lives and deal with bullying, then drawing some bottom lines.

Appendix A presents the Mohr Psychological Inventory (MPI).

Appendix B gives the Mohr Checklist for Psychopaths.

1

Appendix C discusses the 'reverse evolution' that is, sadly, all too evident in a deteriorating world with overpopulation, resource depletion, war and terrorism in many nations, and mankind deteriorating too, both physically and mentally with new diseases etc., and evidence of decreasing IQ over the last 50+ years.

Many examples of bullying reported by the media are given in the book, along with a few pages recounting some of my more notable personal experiences of bullying, most of these in the workplace, and with considerable personal consequences which, on reflection, incline me to hope that this book will encourage some victims of bullying to deal with it and reduce its impact on their lives.

Finally, once again I am grateful to the publishers for yet again doing an excellent job of promptly publishing this book.

Geoff Mohr, Melbourne, 2019

PART I
INTRODUCTION

Chapter 1

TRIBAL HOMO SAPIENS

Tribalism is the strongest force in the world today.
Vine Deloria, U.S. Native American leader,
Custer Died for Your Sins: An Indian Manifesto (1969), ch. 11.

Introduction

Humans are animals, of course, but simply with an enlarged cerebral cortex to store the semantic memory needed for our advanced languages. Nevertheless, we evolved from animal origins and, therefore, possess the same physical and behavioural characteristics as most of the larger land-based animal species.

Physically, we eat, we sleep, we defecate, and so forth. Behaviourally, besides our language, which we take so long to learn in infancy, we make various other communicative noises, we still encourage the despicable alpha-male phenomenon (for example in such animalistic sports as rugby), our male sports stars still bare and beat their chests after victory, just as apes might do, and, of course, we have a sorry history of conflict ranging from interpersonal conflict to world wars.

Indeed, our history of wars and other disasters is such that we might, indeed, wonder whether we are not, perhaps, in many ways the most stupid of animals.

3

Evolution of tribal man

Chimpanzees, with which we share circa 96% of the same genes, are sociable animals that live in groups of 20 to 60, forming into subgroups of adults (male and female), all-male groups and groups of mothers and offspring. African gorillas also live in bisexual groups of between 2 to 30 but which do not comprise smaller subgroups.

The best known studies of chimpanzees were conducted by Jane Goodall and associates in the Gombe National Park on the edge of Lake Tanganyika in Tanzania (Goodall, 1971).

Ultimately, Goodall was quite disillusioned to find that *tribes* of chimps were led by an alpha male and would occasionally have small wars with neighbouring tribes, these resuming at intervals over periods of many years. She concluded that they were all too much like humans!

Comparisons of blood proteins and the DNA of the African great apes with that of humans indicates that the line leading to modern people did not split off from that of chimpanzees and gorillas until comparatively late in evolution, perhaps 6 million to 8 million years ago.

Fossils of the first *hominines,* the *australopithecines,* dating to 5 million years ago have been discovered. This genus seems to have become extinct about 1.5 million years ago, but before doing so one of seven species of australopithecines, *Australopithecus africanus*, evolved into the genus *Homo* between 1.5 and 2 million years ago.

The earliest evidence of stone tools comes from sites in Africa dated to about 2.5 million years ago. These tools seem to be associated with all hominine species.

Around 1.7 to 1.9 million years ago two new species of large brained, small-toothed hominines emerged, *Homo ergaster* in Africa and *Homo erectus* in Asia.

Later *H. erectus* skulls possess brain sizes in the range of 1100 to 1300 cc (67.1 to 79.3 cu in), within the size variation of *Homo sapiens*.

A number of archaeological sites dating from the time of *Homo erectus* reveal a greater sophistication in tool making than was found at earlier sites. Evidence found at the cave site of "Peking Man" in northern China, suggests that *Homo erectus* used fire.

The remains of the foundations of an oval structure built by a *Homo erectus* group were found at the Terra-Amata site in France, and within this structure, there was a fireplace (Weiss and Mann, 1978).

The *Homo* species spread widely and by 350,000 years ago planned hunting, fire making, wearing of clothes, and probably burial rituals, were well established.

Between 200,000 and 300,000 years ago, *Homo sapiens* evolved.

The Neanderthals or *Homo sapiens neanderthalensis* had similar DNA to modern man and occupied parts of Europe and the Middle East as early as 120,000 years ago. They lived only in family groups, the men being hunter-gatherers to feed the family.

The Neanderthals left cave paintings that were an important evolutionary advance. These often depicted a simple activity, perhaps a precursor to the highly pictorial hieroglyphic script of the ancient Egyptians (Egerton-Eastwick, 1896).

Though Neanderthals had 10% larger brains than modern man has, there is some evidence that the part of the cerebral cortex devoted to language and thinking in modern man was underdeveloped in Neanderthal man, casting some doubt on whether Neanderthal man was capable of modern spoken language.

Thought by some to be a different evolutionary branch, the Neanderthals disappeared from the fossil record about 30,000 years ago.

Differing in appearance, modern humans or *Homo sapiens sapiens* evolved in southern Africa or the Middle East perhaps 90,000 to 200,000 years ago and 70,000 years ago began to spread to all parts of the world, reaching Europe about 40,000 years ago, soon outnumbering, perhaps interbreeding with, and finally supplanting the local, earlier *Homo sapiens* populations.

Like chimpanzees, Homo sapiens sapiens formed tribes and there is evidence of religion, recorded events and art dating from 30,000 to 40,000 years ago implying the advanced language and ethics required for the ordering of social groups.

Evolution of religion

Around the same time Homo sapiens developed cave art, about 100,000 years ago, he would have developed language and, eventually some form of 'pictorial' communication which eventually evolved into hieroglyphic script, then cuneiform script, and finally the symbolic writing we now use.

Typically, each tribe had a leader, a religion, and a common language and culture.

The first forms of religion involved such beliefs and practices as:

(a) *Animism*, belief that plants, inanimate objects and natural phenomena had souls or spirits.

(b) *Polytheism,* belief in multiple Gods, sometimes attributing certain acts of nature to each.

(c) *Ancestor Worship* teaching that a tribe's people were descended from a common ancestor.

(d) *Immortality* or belief that the dead live on as spirits, promises of immortality to the faithful still being amongst the 'blackmail' tactics preachers use today.

Eventually these religions evolved into the *monotheism* that dominates the world today.

Thus, at the outset it was the tribal elders who passed on tribal beliefs from one generation to another, a situation that still exists amongst a few primitive people today. Along the way *shamans* or 'witch doctors' claiming some special connection with the spirits appeared, along with religious rites and ceremonies.

In groups of hunter-gatherers, just as with many other species of animals, the 'dominant' males were, of course, responsible for protection of the group from external threats which, just as with chimpanzees, often took the form of other 'tribes' or groups.

At the same time, however, the supposedly wiser elders still indoctrinated the young into religion and had considerable influence, if not control, over the 'dominant males.' Their weapons for control ranged from rhetoric to dire threats of a vengeful spirit or God.

Thus, from the ancient Greeks through to the middle ages a study of *rhetoric* was considered important because of its use to bullshit people into doing as political and religious leaders wished. Francis Bacon (1561 - 1626), for example, studied Elizabethan logic and rhetoric at Cambridge University for two years, leaving at the age of 14 (note that people got married at this sort of age then).

Conflict

No doubt there was occasional conflict within the family groups that Homo sapiens lived in, perhaps, for example, over decisions about where to search and hunt for food.

Indeed, such arguments may have led to conflict over who leadership of the group should be trusted to.

There may, of course, have also been occasional conflict with other family groups over territorial issues or, in effect, 'hunting and searching rights' in certain areas which more than one group lived near.

Once tribes were established, questions of leadership may have become more important. No doubt the stronger males were likely to be chosen as leaders in both regular hunting and occasional conflicts between neighbouring tribes.

Indeed, tribal conflicts are 'war' and, of course, some American Indians still ceremonially perpetuate the practice of covering their faces with 'war paint' that traditionally preceded a tribal conflict.

In addition, the elders would often, at least, have had some influence, whilst their role in passing on tribal folklore would certainly have involved tales of conflicts past with other tribes and thus encouraged acceptance and continuance of such conflicts.

In addition, tribal witch doctors or shamans would have had considerable influence, their superstitious view of things no doubt causing other tribes to be considered 'heathen' and viewed with suspicion, if not hostility.

Thus they increased the 'differences' between their tribe and others, an important factor in ethnic conflict which is further discussed in Chapter 17.

Indeed, it was often supposed that the Neanderthals were wiped out by invading Homo sapiens sapiens from the South, but is now believed that, in fact, the two closely related species interbred and thus those of us with European lineage have some Neanderthal DNA.

No doubt the invaders also killed a great many Neanderthals as well, perhaps mostly the more threatening males. In other words, in war kill the men and rape the women, something that has not changed since then in the brutality of war.

Conclusion

Primitive man was not far different from modern man, having large groups sometimes in conflict, supposedly stronger leaders to lead or dictate those conflicts, religious leaders to create ethnic differences to encourage mistrust and tribal conflict, and elders to keep alive and thus help continue a history of conflict.

An example of the latter today, some people call one of the major Australian TV channels 'The Hitler Channel' because it so often airs documentaries about Hitler and his associates to keep us reminded of one of the greatest villains in relatively recent history, and keep us mentally prepared to blindly accept the political propaganda and bullshit that will precede the next war some of us are ordered to participate in.

Thus, when I saw repeated pictures of Saddam Hussein holding a rifle in the media in the months before the post 9/11 US invasion of Iraq, I knew that the US would go to war with that country, however mistakenly. As usual, they did far more harm than good and, in effect, lost because, of course, they certainly didn't win anything but lost a great deal of money yet again, as they did in Vietnam and Korea.

The US also lost WW2 (to Joseph Stalin) but made a great deal of money using Lend Lease to sell badly needed weapons to several countries including England, France, the Netherlands, and Russia.

Finally, and farcically, humans still perpetuate the absurd tribal practices of sports with a conflict connotation, for example shooting, archery, and rugby (do as told and charge the enemy as in the trench warfare of WW1).

Primitive tribal man did likewise but with spears and perhaps knives and rocks.

Modern man, thanks to advanced technology, has far more brutal weapons and thus could be argued to have become far more brutal, just one factor in our 'reverse evolution' which is discussed in Appendix C.

The bottom line for this chapter, of course, is that tribalism is has always been a major factor in human conflict and still is, for example:

➢ The roots of most of our team sports lie in primitive man's 'team hunting' practices, and also, no doubt, primitive practicing of spear throwing etc. while the tribe's women sat around dealing with their children.

➢ Sadly, the 'conflict' so evident in many team sports such as rugby, which was developed to condition young English men for the 'charge the enemy when ordered' required in trench warfare etc., World War 1 involving many notable examples of this primitive, stupid practice.

➢ Sadly too, the 'conflict' evident in these team sports often overflows into the crowd of spectators, sometimes resulting in serious injuries, and sometimes fatalities.

➢ Sadly as well, such stupid sports are taught at schools, of course, encouraging divisiveness and thence bullying.

➢ School sports also encourage competitiveness, and help exaggerate and/or emphasize physical and ability differences between students, in turn contributing to bullying practices.

➢ 'Religious tribalism', of course, has been a major cause of many conflicts and wars throughout history, the present *World War 3* between dozens of Islamic jihadist terrorist organizations in the Middle East, Africa and Asia and non-Muslim people's continues to this day (Mohr et al., 2015; Mohr et al., 2018g).

➢ Political parties also involve, of course, a good deal of tribalism, and a great deal of verbal conflict in parliament and in campaigning, especially in the weeks leading up to an election. And politics, of course, has always been a major factor in wars throughout history, for example the protracted Cold War between the USSR and the USA and its closest allies in the 20th century, and which has resumed to some extent of late.

➢ The *War of The Sexes,* that is, the ongoing battle by feminists etc. for women to have equal job opportunities, equal pay, to be respected and treated fairly without discrimination, and to prevent workplace bullying and sexual abuse continues, the latter part of the battle being made very evident by the ME TOO movement of late (Mohr, 2012b; Mohr, 2018c).

☺☺☹☺☺☹☺☺☹☺☺☹☺☺☹

1. Tribal Homo Sapiens

Chapter 2

THE HUMAN BRAIN

> *We must, however, acknowledge, as it seems to me,*
> *that man with all his noble qualities . . . still bears in his bodily*
> *frame the indelible stamp of his lowly origin.*
> Charles Darwin, *The Descent of Man* (1871), ch. 23.

Evolution of the human brain

Bacteria were the first organic life form on the planet. There are two theories as to how they first appeared:

(a) Nitrogenous rains formed the first organic compounds in warm vents at the bottom of the ocean, these developing into bacteria.

(b) Dormant bacteria came to the Earth on meteorites, springing to life in these warm vents. The author favours this theory in the recent book *The Evolving Universe* (Mohr et al., 2014; Mohr et al., 2018a – 2nd edn).

Next plants developed in these hot springs, eventually making their way to the land. Around this time fungi developed, presumably from bacteria (there seems no other possibility), some scientists believing that bacteria can also transform into viruses (Cantwell, 1990).

Then bacteria merged somehow to form larger organisms in the sea, this process of evolution continuing to produce larger and larger creatures in the sea, brains developing in such creatures as fish to allow them to control their bodily functions.

Then the fins of some fish species developed in such a way as to allow them to move onto the land, beginning the evolution of land-based animals.

The remarkable process of evolution continued to allow birds to take to the air, their two-legged nature placing them on the same early branch of the tree of evolution as man.

With the evolution of apes came chimpanzees, with which we share 96% of the same genes and somewhat similar social and other behaviours such as that of alpha males and tribal conflicts.

Comparisons of blood proteins and the DNA of the African great apes with that of humans indicates that the line leading to modern people did not split off from that of chimpanzees and gorillas until comparatively late in evolution, perhaps 6 million to 8 million years ago.

Fossils of the first *hominines,* the *australopithecines*, have been discovered dating to 5 million years ago. This genus seems to have become extinct about 1.5 million years ago, but before doing so one of seven species of australopithecines, *Australopithecus africanus*, evolved into the genus *Homo* between 1.5 and 2 million years ago.

The earliest evidence of stone tools comes from sites in Africa dated to about 2.5 million years ago. These tools have not been found in association with a particular hominine species.

Around 1.7 to 1.9 million years ago two new species of large brained, small-toothed hominines emerged, *Homo ergaster* in Africa and *Homo erectus* in Asia. Later *H. erectus* skulls possess brain sizes in the range of 1100 to 1300 cc (67.1 to 79.3 cu in), within the size variation of *Homo sapiens*.

A number of archaeological sites dating from the time of *Homo erectus* reveal a greater sophistication in tool making than was found at the earlier sites. Evidence found at the cave site of "Peking Man" in northern China, suggests that *H. erectus* used fire.

The remains of the foundations of an oval structure built by a *Homo erectus* group were found at the Terra-Amata site in France, and within this structure there was a fireplace (Weiss & Mann, 1978).

The *Homo* species spread widely and by 350,000 years ago planned hunting, fire making, wearing of clothes, and probably burial rituals, were well established.

Between 200,000 and 300,000 years ago, *Homo sapiens* evolved.

The Neanderthals or *Homo sapiens neanderthalensis* had similar DNA to modern man and occupied parts of Europe and the Middle East as early as 120,000 years ago. They lived only in family groups, the men being hunter-gatherers to feed the family.

The Neanderthals left cave paintings which were an important evolutionary advance. These often depicted a simple activity, perhaps a precursor to the highly pictorial hieroglyphic script of the ancient Egyptians (Egerton Eastwick, 1896).

Though Neanderthals had 10% larger brains than modern man, there is some evidence that the part of the cerebral cortex devoted to language and thinking in modern man was underdeveloped in Neanderthal man, casting some doubt on whether Neanderthal man was capable of modern spoken language. Thought by some to be a different evolutionary branch, the Neanderthals disappeared from the fossil record about 30,000 years ago.

Differing in appearance, modern humans or *Homo sapiens sapiens* evolved in southern Africa or the Middle East perhaps 90,000 to 200,000 years ago and 70,000 years ago began to spread to all parts of the world, reaching Europe about 40,000 years ago, soon outnumbering, perhaps interbreeding with, and finally supplanting the local, earlier *Homo sapiens* populations.

Like chimpanzees, homo sapiens sapiens formed tribes and there is evidence of religion, recorded events and art dating from 30,000 to 40,000 years ago implying the advanced language and ethics required for the ordering of social groups.

The structure of the human brain

In the human brain the upper layer, the cerebrum, is the largest part of the brain and its external layer is called the cerebral cortex. The outer portion is grey because it contains billions of nerve cell bodies, and the inner portion is white from the tangle of axons coated in myelin sheaths.

The cerebral cortex makes up 76% of the human brain and provides the information processing necessary for language, reason, and creative thought. It is the larger frontal cortex of man that gives him greater intelligence and far more complex language than other animals.

There are only two main types of cells in nerve tissue:

[1] The actual nerve cell is the neuron, the 'conducting' cell that transmits impulses and is the structural unit of the nervous system.

[2] Neuroglia, or glia for short, the word 'neuroglia' meaning 'nerve glue'. These are nonconductive and maintain homeostasis, form myelin, and provide support and protection for neurons in the central and peripheral nervous systems. Homeostasis is the metabolic equilibrium actively maintained by several complex biological mechanisms that operate via the autonomic nervous system to offset disrupting changes.

The human brain has circa 10 billion neurons and circa 50 trillion neuroglia. Each neuron has three basic parts: the cell body (soma), one or more dendrites, and a single axon. The soma is from 10 to 25 micrometres in diameter and is often not much larger than its nucleus.

Neurons are complex and very numerous, and are the core components of the brain and spinal cord of the central nervous system (CNS), and of the peripheral nervous system (PNS).

Dendrites branch many times into a complex 'dendritic tree' with thousands of 'spines'. An axon, also called a nerve fibre when myelinated, may branch hundreds of times. Axons and dendrites in the CNS are about one micrometer thick and sensory neurons can have axons that run from the toes to the posterior column of the spinal cord, or more than 1.5 metres in adults.

In the brain messages are transferred from the axon terminals of one neuron to the dendrites of another via connections called synapses, memories being stored in the dendritic spines.

Neuron structure and size varies considerably, for example unipolar neurons having a single 'tree' for the axon and dendrites, whereas multipolar neurons have several tree-like structures to accommodate the axon and numerous dendrites.

Neurons can also be classified by function:

(a) Afferent neurons or *sensory neurons* transmit information from tissues and organs to the CNS.

(b) Efferent neurons or *motor neurons* transmit signals from the CNS via nerve fibres to the effector cells of muscles or glands to stimulate contraction or secretion.

(c) Interneurons connect neurons in different regions of the CNS.

The nervous system

Figure 2.1 shows the structure of the nervous system (Sweeney, 2009). The central nervous system consists of the brain and the spinal cord and it interprets sensations and issues commands in the form of motor responses, which are based on current sensations, reflexes, and experiences.

The peripheral nervous system comprises the axons that branch from the spinal cord and carry nerve impulses to and from the brain.

The autonomic or 'involuntary' nervous system is based in the midbrain's pons and medulla and it regulates the functions essential for life, such as heart function and breathing.

The sympathetic branch puts the body on alert and supplies it with energy in response to fear or excitement. The parasympathetic branch relaxes the body, lowering heart rate, breathing rate, and blood pressure.

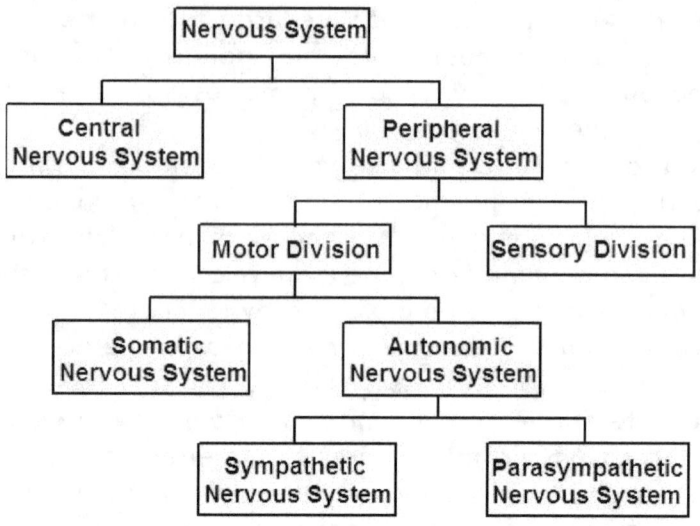

Figure 2.1. Divisions of the nervous system.
Each division is responsible for the collection of and
response to different stimuli.

Chemical effects

Neurons release neurotransmitters that bind to chemical receptors of which there are three types:

[1] Excitatory, causing an increase in firing rate.

[2] Inhibitory, causing a decrease in firing rate.

[3] Modulatory, causing long-term effects unrelated to firing rate.

Table 2.1 shows the key neurotransmitters, their location, and function.

The cell membrane of the axon and soma contain voltage-gated ion channels that allow neurons to generate and propagate an electrical signal or 'action potential'. These signals are generated and propagated by charge-carrying ions including sodium (Na^+), potassium (K^+), chloride (Cl^-), and calcium (Ca^{2+}). Several types of stimuli can activate a neuron by causing ion-specific channels to open, allowing ions to flow through the cell membrane and change its potential.

Table 2.1. Neurotransmitters.

Neurotransmitter	Location	Function
Acetylcholine	Nervous system parts associated with motion, including the brain's motor cortex	Makes muscles contract. Also plays a role in attention, memory, and sleep.
Dopamine	Brain and the peripheral nervous system	Body motion and reward experiences, including pleasure.
Endorphins	Brain, pituitary gland, and spinal cord	Powerful, natural opiates, that block pain
Gamma-aminobutyric acid (GABA)	Retina, spinal cord, hypothalamus, and cerebellum	Commonest neuro-transmitter – quiets neurons.
Glutamate	Brain and spinal cord	Activates cells for learning and memory.
Norepinephrine	Brain and peripheral nervous system	Regulates moods, blood pressure, heartbeat and arousal
Seretonin	Brain stem, cerebellum, pineal gland, and spinal cord	Crucial for sleep and appetite. Linked to depression and anxiety.

Thicker axons carry action potential more rapidly, many of them having myelin insulating sheaths to increase the efficiency and effectiveness of impulse transmission (Sweeney, 2009).

Conduction of nerve impulses in on an 'all or none' basis, that is, if a neuron responds at all, it must respond completely. Thus greater intensity of stimulation doesn't produce a stronger signal but can produce a higher frequency of firing.

Many drugs, besides pharmaceutical ones, affect the brain, for example (Sweeney, 2009):

[1] LSD "binds so tightly to serotonin receptors" that very small amounts greatly affect the brain, causing hallucinations and sometimes psychosis.

[2] Marijuana's active ingredient, delta-9-tetrahydro-cannabinol (THC) inhibits the release of glutamate and GABA, reducing communication between certain neural networks. In contrast, caffeine has the opposite effect, slightly raising cognitive function.

[3] Morphine affects the cerebral cortex without affecting the lower parts of the brain.

[4] Cocaine stimulates the whole brain, but particularly its emotional centres.

Storage capacity of the human brain

Each of circa 10 billion (10×10^9) neurons in the brain can have from 1,000 to 10,000 dendritic spines, so that, assuming 1,000 spines per neuron, there are about 10 trillion (10×10^{12}) spines. Assuming each spine can store 1 byte of information, the total brain capacity is 10 Terabytes (10×10^{12} bytes).

Because of the level of 'noise' in the brain, however, each bit of information must be stored redundantly in as many as 100 spines, so if the average 'redundancy' is 10 spines, the effective capacity of the brain is 100 Gigabytes (100×10^9 bytes).

The brain must have 'spare capacity', however, so that only part of the brain is used, so a conservative estimate of 'effective' brain capacity might be about 50 GB.

Note, however, that some estimates of the number of neurons in the brain are as high as 100 billion, giving an effective brain capacity of 500 GB.

This we might compare with a fairly good, but not top of the range, PC which today would have at least 5 GB of RAM (random access memory), and a hard disk storage capacity of at least 500 GB.

The number of neurons in the brain varies greatly between species, the nematode worm having only 302 neurons, whereas the fruit fly has circa 100,000 neurons.

As might be expected, some studies have found a correlation of 0.40 or more between brain size (measured by MRI or CAT) and IQ, the correlation being higher in adults than in children (Mackintosh, 2011).

It is generally assumed that the humans have evolved with relatively large brains in order to provide the large amount of semantic memory required for our advanced languages. Animals, of course, rely largely on 'visual memory', and one might expect that visual memory requires more storage capacity than language. We learn and remember language, however, in a largely visual fashion, thus recognizing both letters of the alphabet and words or 'word parts' in visual fashion, so that, indeed, a substantially larger brain is required for the semantic memory required to store language.

The memory system

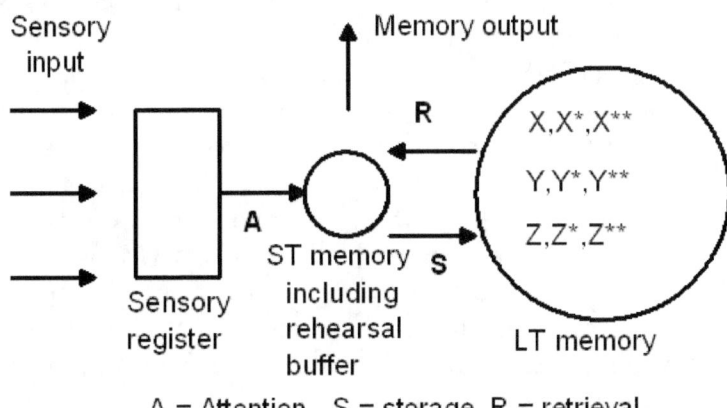

A = Attention, S = storage, R = retrieval

Figure 2.2. Information processing model of memory.

Figure 2.2 shows the multi-store or Atkinson-Shiffrin information processing model of memory (Atkinson & Shiffrin, 1968). In this, the *sensory register*, located in a part of the brain called the thalamus, processes information from sensory channels associated with vision, hearing and other senses.

The visual sensory register can hold 10 - 20 bits of information for only about 1 second, whereas the auditory sensory register can hold information for up to 4 or 5 seconds.

Of the up to 20 bits of information that our visual registers can accommodate with a brief glance, for example an array of letters of the alphabet, we can only remember four or five of them, this number being called the *span of apprehension*.

As a consequence most information in the sensory registers is lost but that to which sufficient attention is paid is transferred to the *short-term-memory* (STM), located in a part of the brain called the hippocampus. Here it is held for about 20 - 30 seconds and some of it is processed by being rehearsed in the *rehearsal buffer*, the rest being lost.

This model fits everyday life fairly well. For example, when somebody tells you a phone number and you are interrupted while dialing it you are likely to forget it because it will be lost from STM. This is because the STM holds only about 5 - 9 items and, under certain conditions, as few as two or three.

Sternberg (1966) conducted an experiment that illustrates how memory, in this case STM, works. He showed a group of people sets of from 1 to 6 digits and seconds later asked them if the set contained a particular digit. Response times were closely proportional to the number of digits shown, demonstrating that the coding of the set in STM was searched serially or one digit at a time.

In the rehearsal buffer such processes as repetition of the information link it to information already stored in memory and then pass it to *long-term-memory* (LTM) where it remains for periods of days up to a lifetime. In LTM information is *consolidated*, a process that may take from half an hour up to months. If consolidation is somehow interrupted some memory loss occurs.

An important part of the process of LTM processing is *long-term potentiation* (LTP) in which chemical 'dosing' strengthens neural connections.

Thus the strength of a memory depends upon the type or amount of attention paid to the stimuli. Attention to physical characteristics is encoded less than the sounds of words, whilst emotional content enhances encoding, sometimes leading to 'flashbulb' memories which may include minute details of extremely emotional moments.

Similarly, memories that in LTM that have recently been accessed are 'dosed' chemically so that they are easier to recall again in the near term, whereas memories that have not been accessed for a long time are difficult to recall, taking from a few minutes up to several hours to recall.

Most LTM information is stored in the cerebral cortex, the 'thinking' part of the brain which is much more developed in humans than in other species.

Simple passive repetition of information, or *maintenance rehearsal,* is not sufficient to ensure that items are passed to LTM. The active process of *elaborative rehearsal,* involving reorganization of the material and attaching meaning to it is more likely to pass information to LTM.

There are four types of LTM:

[1] *Procedural memory* or implicit memory is 'knowing how' to perform some skill, often learnt by procedural or implicit learning.

[2] *Declarative memory* is 'knowing that' or memory of data or facts and events.

[3] *Episodic memory* of prior life experiences is a type of declarative memory. 'Flashbulb' memories are clear episodic memories of unique and highly emotional events, an example being the movie footage of the 'twin towers' collapsing after the 9/11 attacks.

[4] *Semantic memory* such as words and language rules is another type of declarative memory which involves more 'preprocessing' in STM than episodic memory.

In such processing, even inherently organized material is *subjectively organized* by the learner into categories. Up to a point, it is found that the more categories used the better the material can be recalled.

Semantic memory uses *constructive processes* to store information in an organized manner, often into a hierarchical structure of categories and sub-categories.

Recall of the information then occurs by *reconstructive processes.* With these, speed of recall depends upon the hierarchical level at which information is recalled, more general 'heading' information being recalled more rapidly than specific information.

Thus, when we have difficulty remembering a person's name, for example, we often can only remember one or more names similar in some respect such as their first letter and then finally remember the required name anything from seconds to days later.

Memory processing also makes much use of images and *concrete* images are easily formed for words like 'cat' whilst *abstract* images for words like 'mercy' are more difficult to form.

Australian aborigine elders, for example, remember centuries of tribal history by associating important events with environmental features and recall and pass on this history by 'walking through' these places.

Information stored in LTM is easier to recall if it is stored with *retrieval cues* which are associated with 'blocks' of information. Individual items within these blocks are then stored with 'tags'.

How easily information is recalled later depends much upon how well it has been associated with images, categorized and provided with cues.

An example of how images affect information recall from LTM occurs if witnesses who saw a speeding car crash are asked:

"How fast do you think the car was going when it _ _ _ _ _?"

with the final verb having such variations as *contacted, hit,* and *crashed.*

Speed estimates will increase in the order of these three verbs by as much as 25% because the new information in the wording of the question conflicts or *interferes* with the memory and associated images of the event in LTM.

Information that has been stored in a well-organized fashion can sometimes be recalled by *redintegration*, the process by which some event such as a 'leading question' unlocks a rapid sequence of memories that may be connected by a chain of associations.

This is the ideal situation when we read an exam question. One or more words in the question quickly trigger recall of a stream of relevant information. If the exam is the usual written answer one we tend to forget part of the answer before we can write it down.

Conclusion

Humans make a wide array of tools, we cook food, we build houses, roads and bridges, we heat and cool our buildings, we build ships, cars and aircraft, and man has walked on the moon. It is advanced language, in particular, that sets us apart from other animals and allows us to do these things, communicating our ideas to successive generations so that our knowledge and skills have advanced for many thousands of years. Language and learning, therefore, are discussed in the following chapter.

In the foregoing chapter the basic structure of the human brain was discussed, showing that our senses transfer and store information in the dendritic spines of the neurons, perhaps in the synapses at the ends of these spines.

It was estimated that our brain capacity was comparable to that of a modern PC, though some writers estimate human brain capacity to be an order greater than this, if not more.

☺☻☹☺☻☹☺☻☹☺☻☹☺☻☹

2. The Human Brain

Chapter 3

LANGUAGE AND EARLY LEARNING

> *Some people have argued that language is what makes the human species different from other species.*
> Roger Bell & Ralph Hall, *Impacts: Contemporary Issues & Global Problems*, The Jacaranda Press, Milton QLD, 1991.
>
> *Language is the autobiography of the human mind.*
> Friedrich Max Müller,
> Quoted in *Scholar Extraordinary* (Nirad Chaudhuri, 1974).

The development of language

Despite his larger brain size, there is some doubt whether Neanderthal man had developed language. Doubtless the roots of language lie in the 30 different vocal sounds made by vervet monkeys (Insight, 1982), no doubt related to *lallation* or meaningless mumbling in infants. Given some encouragement they are then ready to learn such 'baby talk' as

da da, ma ma, wee wee
gee gee, puff puff, bow wow

The messages in any language are built up from a small catalogue of elementary speech sounds which are combined to form words from which sentences are built up.

Generally, these words are *arbitrary* and do not sound like or have any other relationship with the things they represent but there are a few exceptions such as some of the words for animal noises, a phenomenon called *onomatopoeia* (using words that imitate the sound they denote).

27

Language involves a *duality of patterning* (Foss & Hakes, 1978) in which it relates two different forms of representation: an external *phonological system* for sound and an internal *semantic system* for meaning. These two systems are related by a language's *syntactic system*.

We understand a sentence spoken to us because our brain stores it temporarily in our short-term-memory (STM) and compares it to the word and language rules stored as *semantic memory* in our long-term-memory (LTM). If we *rehearse* the message in STM it may be stored in LTM.

How we understand language

The way in which text is remembered provides an insight into why key words are important in the memory process. It is believed that text is not stored in memory literally but as a number of *propositions*, each of which has a *relational* term for which there are *arguments* (using the latter word in the same way it is used in connection with mathematical functions, especially when they are used in computer programs).

The sentence "Tom hit Jack", for example, is remembered as

(HIT, TOM, JACK)

If later "Tom apologized for hitting Jack" this is stored as

((APOLOGIZE, TOM), (HIT, TOM, JACK))

with the simple proposition of the original memory embedded in a complex one. Here the 'strong' word HIT acts as a key word and it is linked directly to the word TOM in long-term memory.

There is no doubt that a deer can remember events such as, "Lion killed deer" as a visual memory stored in *episodic memory*. As a result the *declarative memory* 'danger' would be added to the neuron in LTM storing the image of a lion, or perhaps to a newly formed adjacent neuron.

Some clue to how humans developed language is found by observing that howler monkeys have massively developed larynxes and hyoid bones (the bone that supports the tongue) so that their spectacular howls can be heard for miles.

Somehow, somewhere, humans gradually evolved with the physical attributes required to produce a variety of sounds and began to associate these with objects, passing this knowledge on to following generations.

As noted in the penultimate section of the present chapter, Krech's remarkable environmental enrichment experiments with rats demonstrated vividly that the gradually growth in the development of human language was undoubtedly largely responsible for the evolution of the large cerebral cortex that distinguishes modern man from other species.

The spread of language

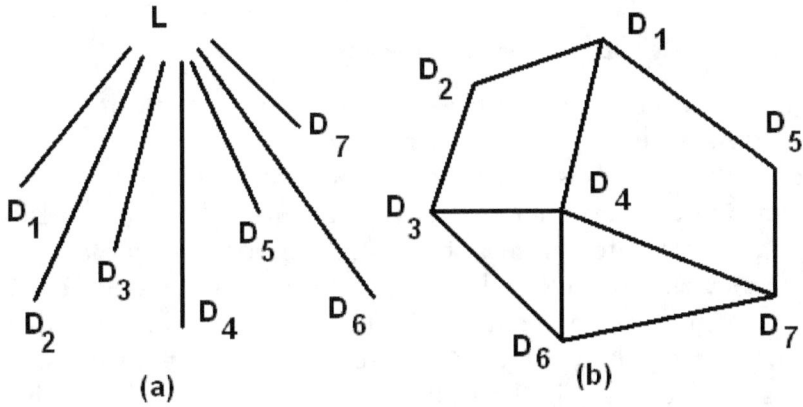

Figure 3.1. Language and dialects: (a) according to the notion of pure language; (b) a more accurate representation.

Somehow language spread with the migration of early humans, perhaps during the Agricultural Revolution, so that some languages have similar words, for example for father:

pater (Latin), padre (Italian), pere (French)
vater (German), father (English)

Just as European languages are rooted in Greek and Latin, oriental languages have roots in ancient Chinese and languages in the Middle East have roots in the ancient Babylonian and Egyptian languages.

There are now, of course, many languages and many more dialects. As a rule of thumb, two people speak the same language if they are mutually intelligible. Two exceptions are the Chinese dialects Mandarin and Cantonese which are not mutually intelligible. Another is that Norwegians can usually be understood by Swedes.

Language, however, is not a 'pure' thing such that any variation from it is impure or substandard, as depicted in Fig. 3.1(a). From the point of view of modern linguistics Fig. 3.1(b) is the more nearly correct picture and it avoids linguistic chauvinism, a notion that has often led to one group of people trying to impose their language on another. This view also corresponds to way in which language spread globally.

Language development in infants

At birth the human brain is relatively large compared to the body. Almost all the neural cells that will ever be available are present but only a basic network of the *axons* and *dendrites* that connect *neurons* together exists. At the outset these connections develop as the infant learns basic perception and motor skills, the long *axons* that extend from the brain cells then receiving signals from *receptor cells,* such as the small hair cells in the inner ear, or sending signals to *effector cells* in the muscles.

This development in the bulk of the brain parallels that in all animal species and is that necessary for basic functioning and survival.

What sets humans apart, however, is the considerable development of the *cerebral cortex*, the envelope of brain cells that covers the brain. This is where our thinking and storage of abstract memory information such as language occurs.

Development of the articulatory mechanisms required for controlled speech and the cortical mechanisms that control them is a slow maturational process that occurs in *Broca's area* of the frontal cortex. It has been suggested that babbling, however, is a sub cortical process.

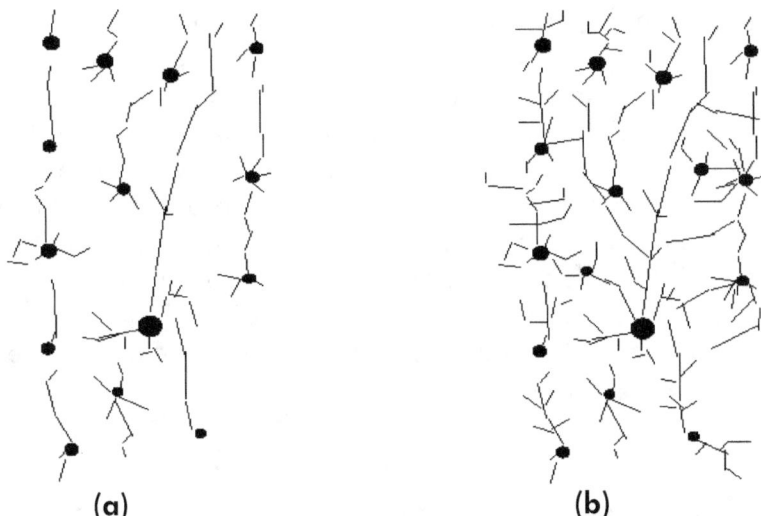

(a)   (b)

Figure 3.2. Postnatal development of the human cerebral cortex around Broca's Area (language related): (a) newborn; (b) 1 month.

Semantic memory of language is stored in *Wernicke's area* of the temporal lobe of the cerebral cortex.

Figure 3.2(a) shows a small part of the cerebral cortex of a newborn child in which long *axons* extend from the neurons and form branches. Fine *terminal arbors* at the end of these branches connect at *synapses* to the short *dendrites* surrounding other neurons. Figure 3.2(b) shows considerably more dendrites and branching of the axons at the age of one month (Foss & Hakes, 1978). At the age of 24 months the neural network is a good deal denser.

The network continues to develop in following years and the neurons, while not increasing in number, do increase in size.

In addition, the motor nerve pathways that control such activities as speech production must gradually develop sheaths of the protein *myelin* that prevent 'short-circuiting' of impulses between nerve tracts.

As a result of this gradual brain development each human characteristic is developed at a different rate.

Eye coordination, for example, develops much more rapidly than speech. Nevertheless, for the first few months the infant may smile at any moving object such as a dummy head whereas later it may be upset by the faces of strangers.

Packard (1978) cites an example of the importance of timing in which two Harvard researchers studied the way kittens learnt to recognize shapes and patterns, a physiological ability that develops in the fourth week. If the kittens were blindfolded for this week they effectively became blind for life. Thus there appear to be periods when the infant's brain is highly receptive so that it is easiest to change a child's intelligence for better or worse before the age of four.

Imprinting

Imprinting is an important part of the early learning process in higher animals that plays a significant part in brain development.

Konrad Lorentz, an Austrian ethologist, demonstrated this by being the first moving object seen by ducklings after hatching. He waddled in a squatting position and quacked and soon the ducklings assumed him to be their mother and followed him about and flew to him when he quacked.

In other famous experiments baby monkeys have been persuaded to accept a foam-rubber dummy monkey complete with feeding bottle as their mother and kittens have been imprinted to accept as fellow kittens rats placed in their cage.

It has been suggested that the most critical period for imprinting in humans is from six weeks to six months and in this period the human infant develops attachments, particularly to its mother.

As the experiment of blindfolding four week-old kittens demonstrated, neural links in the brain close at certain ages for every function. Similarly, it is difficult to become a top musician if you start late.

Imprinting occurs, at least to some extent, in the learning of languages, so that becoming truly bilingual gets more difficult as one gets older. When older it is well nigh impossible to master a second language with the same ease, fluency and accent as the first.

Much of our language learning is stored as *semantic memory*, one of four basic long-term-memory types discussed earlier in this chapter. Semantic memory is very stable so that the meanings of words or the rules for their use may never be forgotten.

Some experiments have shown that semantic memory stores information in logical hierarchies which go from general categories to specific ones, so that clusters of words with related meanings are stored in the same location in the brain.

Much of this stable memory base for language and other knowledge is founded by imprinting at a very early age and it is important to take advantage of this in educating young children.

Modeling

According to some experts the critical period in a child's intellectual, social and emotional development is between eight and eighteen months.

During this period, in particular, much of a child's learning is by *modeling* or *imitative learning,* also referred to as *learning by observation.*

It is desirable, therefore, for parents and others to use controlled modeling with infants in order to give them a head start in learning language and other skills.

After only four weeks babies begin to mimic the mother's mouth movements in speech and babbling begins at about two months, followed by laughter at about three months.

At six months *lallation* begins, that is, the baby utters repeated sounds such as 'ma ma' or 'ba ba'. At 10 months the baby begins to try to copy sounds made by the parents and by the end of the first year it may have learnt one or two real words.

3. Language and Early Learning

In the first years much of the effort in training children is directed at development of survival skills such as eating, learning to walk and potty training. Modeling plays an important part in this, for example in the process of learning to walk, where the infant has had plenty of opportunity to watch the actions of adults.

Learning in a child's first year could be much advanced, therefore, by conscious and careful use of modeling, that is, demonstration of skills to be developed such as development of effective and clear speech.

In these early efforts use could be made of pictures and objects with which to associate the baby's first word efforts, for example the mother pointing to herself when vocalizing ma-ma.

Much of the time we also instinctively use *conditioning*, that is, repetitive presentation of items associated with simple skills to be learnt, often followed by praise when satisfactory progress is made.

At this early stage the cot can become the infant's first learning centre and objects that might be helpful to its learning can be placed within the infant's field of view, for example a picture of a dog in order to teach the word 'bow-wow'.

Here advantage might usefully be made of a TV set to play tapes or DVDs of simple movies, for example involving objects the words for which are to be learnt, perhaps including the numbers 1 to 4.

Demonstrating the possibilities for abstract learning at an early age, chimpanzees have been found better able to recognize the symbols for the numbers 1 to 4 than groups of objects up to four in number.

The important point, however, is that a good deal of patience is needed in the education process, particularly at the outset. Time is taken for memories to develop and fix and it is perhaps best to be a month or two ahead of the child's expected capabilities in trying to inculcate knowledge and skills for, as we all know, in later life it can be years after getting a certain idea that we actually get around to acting on it.

What is certain, however, that the sooner a mother begins to talk to her baby the better and, to a lesser extent perhaps, the same no doubt applies to many other areas of early learning.

Group modeling

At around the third month the baby recognizes the mother and smiles at her. Before this point it will be amused by many objects, including strangers, but now attachments have been formed by imprinting and it may be upset by strangers.

Within the first year, therefore, it would make good sense to involve the infant in *play groups* involving small groups of mothers and infants. In these early efforts at group activities can be attempted and the child can begin its social development.

Packard (1978) raised the interesting possibility of the use of professional people to teach by modeling.

These people would be trained to know the periods during which learning of various areas of knowledge areas can best be commenced and in how best to use modeling techniques to initiate that learning. Such people would then visit the home or attend play group sessions.

Packard cited an experiment with a form of group modeling was undertaken at New York Medical College. This began with twenty pairs of mothers and babies when the babies were only four weeks old and lasted three years at the end of which the children were compared with those of a control group. The children in the experimental group were a good deal more advanced in language and other skills than the control group.

Indeed, some experts doubt the competence of the modern family for child rearing and believe that more professional efforts are essential to help develop emotional stability and intellectual development in infants.

Vocabulary growth in early childhood

When children reach the age of one the pace at which learning can take place greatly increases.

Much of what has already been learnt will have been learnt by modeling, for example the ability for form words. Other skills like that of standing upright and then walking will have been learnt in part by conditioning and the associated reinforcement of praise as progress towards the objective is made.

Now learning can be accomplished with a host of aids such as pictures, simple books and educational toys.

In addition, more formal processes such as those of rote learning of words can be used. At the outset the words to be learnt should carefully chosen, for example objects within the child's everyday environment to allow associative processes to help fix the words in long term semantic memory.

By this formative age the child has been out and about a good deal and optimistic attempts have been made to teach it many words of which it will have learnt only a few.

Table 3.1. Words learnt with age.

Age (years)	Words learnt
1	3-5
1.25	15
1.5	25
1.75	100
2	250
2.5	450
3	900
4	1550
4.5	1900
5	2100
5.5	2300
6	2550

As shown in Table 3.1, however, word learning occurs at a quite rapid rate from here on, to the point at which a basic command of language has been obtained at age five.

Whilst the first year is instrumental in learning to begin to talk, in the second year a comparatively massive growth in vocabulary occurs. Thereafter the rate of increase is approximately linear but slows down as the child comes to grip with a widening range of subjects at school.

By the time they have learnt to read a little, however, children are able to learn things by *cognitive* learning which *processes* and stores *abstract* information.

Latent learning occurs when subjects are exposed to a body of information, rather than in small parts, and they then apply that information later on, perhaps in a test.

A laboratory example of this is that an experimental group of rats allowed to roam a maze will then do better in learning to get through it for a reward than a control group with no prior experience of the maze.

At school children are taught by presenting them with visual and verbal information to learn subjects in discrete 'blocks'. Here cognitive and latent learning occur and revision exercises and tests are used to reinforce and correct their knowledge.

The effect of environment

Modern man is distinguished from other creatures by having a larger cerebral cortex, the centre for our thinking and language. This larger cortex must have evolved by the adaptive processes inherent in Darwin's theory of natural selection.

Clues to just how this occurred were given by the work of social psychologist David Krech and his group at UC Berkeley (Packard, 1978).

In this they provided a group of rats with an "enriched environment" of large cages with various things rats enjoy such as slides, wheels and the like. Then a maze with a sugar reward at the end was added. This had a dark and a lighted alley and the rats soon learnt which led to the sugar.

Then the maze lighting was reversed regularly so that the rats had to relearn the 'sugar route'.

A second control group of rats lived normally and a third group was kept in a deprived dark and noiseless area.

After 90 days it was found that the 'enriched' rats had developed thicker cerebral cortexes.

This was perhaps the first evidence that the brain is modified by experience. The enrichment conditions caused the following changes (Atrens & Curthoys, 1982):

[1] The size of the cerebral cortex was increased.

[2] The size of the cortical neurons increased.

[3] The size and number of synaptic contacts increased.

[4] The quantity of acetylcholinesterase, the compound responsible for breakdown of the neurotransmitter acetylcholine, increased.

Therefore, the rats which had experienced environmental enrichment were apparently anatomically and biochemically superior to those which had endured a deprived environment.

This result provided laboratory evidence that environmental enrichment could physically and chemically alter the brain. This ability of neural tissue to change because of its activation is called *plasticity*.

It seems likely, therefore, that as early man discovered fire, began to make tools and advanced in many other ways his brain gradually evolved into that of *Homo sapiens sapiens* or

Conditioning

Much early learning occurs by:

(a) Imprinting, that is selection of a person to imitate.

(b) Imitative learning, that is, imitation of others.

Parents and teachers also use a good deal of *conditioning*, that is, repetitive presentation of information to be learnt, accompanied by occasional doses of positive and negative reinforcement. Conditioning, therefore, is discussed in more detail in the next chapter.

Chapter 4

Conditioning, Memory and Learning

> *If education is always to be conceived along the same*
> *antiquated lines of a mere transmission of knowledge,*
> *there is little to be hoped from it in the bettering of man's future.*
> *For what is the use of transmitting knowledge*
> *if the individual's total development lags behind?*
> Maria Montessori, *The Absorbent Mind*, ch. 1 (1949).

Introduction

The preceding chapter dealt briefly with modeling which plays a crucial part in the early learning of infants. Mention was also made of how we also instinctively use *conditioning*, for example repetitive presentation of items associated with simple skills to be learnt, often followed by praise when satisfactory progress is made.

Conditioning is a fundamental learning process but it also has applications in psychotherapy, for example behaviour modification using *aversion therapy,* and thence more sinister ones in 'brainwashing' prisoners of war or crime suspects to obtain information from them or to make them 'switch sides'.

In the modern era, however, it is more relevant to everyday life than ever as conditioning is used to some extent in advertising to repetitively expose people to a brand name. They quickly develop recognition of the brand and, before long, some degree of acceptance, if not approval.

Much of the excessively long and drawn out education process is also conditioning for obedience and routine. Military training, of course, is one of the more extreme examples of conditioning.

Some understanding of the mechanics of conditioning is therefore well worthwhile in an age when we are confronted with it almost at every turn.

Classical conditioning

Classical conditioning, or learning by association, was first demonstrated by Ivan Pavlov's celebrated experiments with dogs in the 1890s.

In these he noted that a caged dog's mouth salivated when it saw food on a pan swung within its reach. Here the food is the *uncontrolled stimulus* (US) and salivation is the dog's *uncontrolled reaction* (UR)

Next, a bell was rung shortly before presentation of the food and the dog's saliva collected in a cup to measure the amount. Here the bell is the *controlled stimulus* (CS).

It was found that the after a few repetitions of the paired stimuli of bell and food the dog would begin to salivate with the ringing of the bell alone, this being the *controlled reaction* (CR).

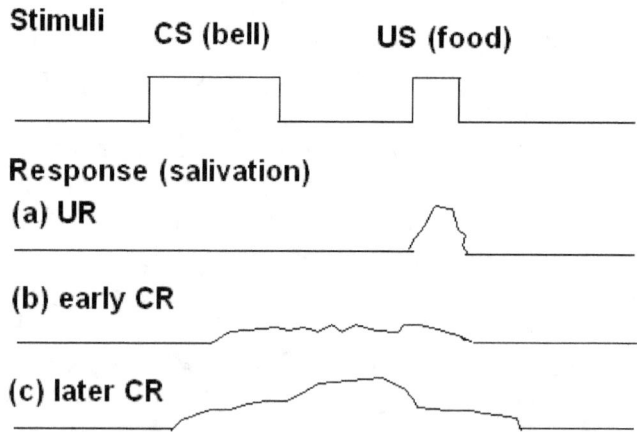

Figure 4.1. Pavlov's classical conditioning experiment:
(a) Bell precedes food presentation.
(b) Bell the only stimulus.
(c) US resumed temporarily - then only CS giving result shown.

Similar results can be obtained with almost any stimulus that consistently evokes a reflex response such as electrical shock.

For example, a dog or a human given a mild shock to a leg will quickly withdraw the leg.

If the electrode giving the shocks is attached to the leg, on the other hand, flexion of the leg will occur in response to shock, the US. Then when a prior conditioned or 'neutral' stimulus is given as warning conditioned response is developed and remains after the US is removed.

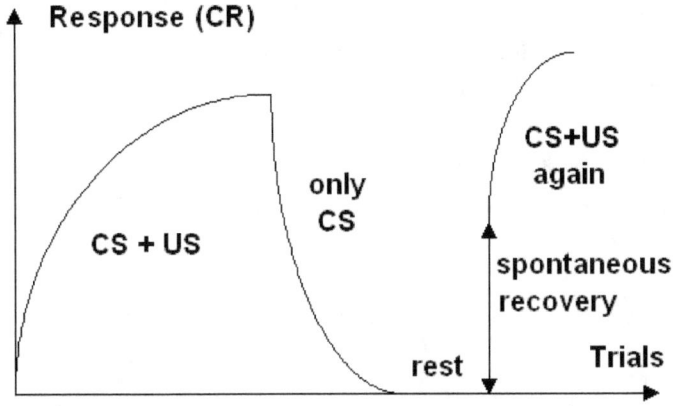

Figure 4.2. Conditioning, extinction and recovery.

After many trials the results can be graphed as a *learning curve.* Typically this takes the form shown in Figure 4.2 where the curve gradually flattens as the number of trials increases.

Here the US and CS remain paired. If the US is removed, however, *extinction* occurs and the response (the CR) decreases. Then, if the US is again added after the CS, the response recovers, the initial amount of response being called the *spontaneous recovery.*

Advertising often uses classical conditioning by repeatedly associating a product with positive ideas and images, thereby encouraging people to have positive feelings towards the product itself.

Operant conditioning

Operant conditioning, or learning by consequences, is characterized by the use of *reinforcement* which encourages a response in which the subject *operates* in some way, rather than just exhibiting a passive reflex response as in classical conditioning.

The classical experiments in operant conditioning were conducted in the 1940s by Skinner, a Harvard psychologist. In these he placed a rat in a box in which there was a lever that delivered food to it when pressed.

Initially the lever was operated from outside and soon the rat learnt the association between seeing the lever move and the appearance of food.

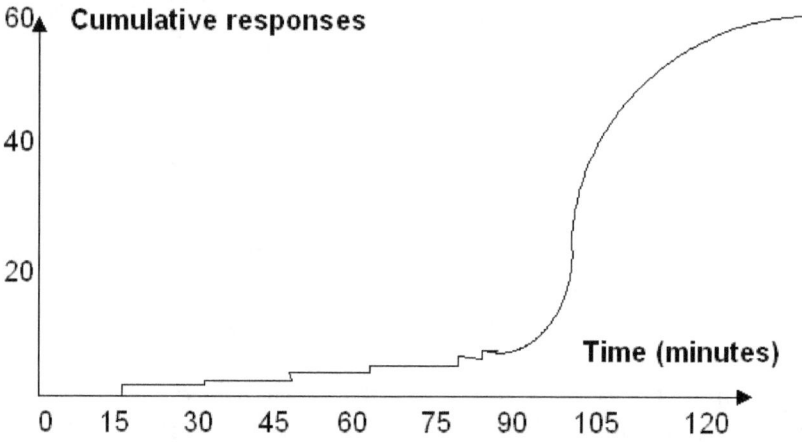

Figure 4.3. Operant conditioning responses by rat in Skinner Box. First response at 15 minutes, second at 30, third at 45, but after 75 minutes the rate of response becomes high.

After a while it operated the lever itself to obtain food and continued to do so with increasing frequency as it became more familiar with the routine, as shown in Figure 4.3.

In the result of Figure 4.3 the rat in the 'Skinner Box', as it came to be called, took 15 minutes to successfully operate the feed lever.

Four more intervals of about 15 minutes occurred before following operations when, the rat having fully learnt the procedure, the rate of operation accelerated markedly.

We instinctively use operant conditioning in bringing up children, the reinforcement to encourage desired actions being smiles and vocal approval.

Note that the timing of reinforcement is important. In a Skinner box, for example, the greater the time delay between the rat pressing the lever and the delivery of the food the longer it will take the rat to associate the two events and thus learn the feeding operation.

As with classical conditioning, *extinction* occurs when reinforcement ceases. This 'unlearning' process may be stronger still when *negative reinforcement*, typically some form of punishment in the educational context, is used.

Conditioned physical responses may be accompanied by emotional feelings or responses and many of our feelings are developed by conditioning.

In the case of classical conditioning *conditioned emotional responses* (CERs) may develop. Indeed, our feelings about many people and other things in our lives develop in this kind of way.

Advertising is also a case in point where an ad reminds us of a familiar product, evoking feelings of recognition and approval whilst the implications for education are all too obvious.

Generalization and discrimination

When alternative conditioned or 'signal' stimuli are used in classical conditioning the subject may learn to *discriminate* between them and respond more strongly to one than the other.

In Pavlov's classical experiments, for example, he found that dogs also responded to a buzzer as a CS instead of a bell, but less strongly.

This is called *generalization* and the more similar the alternative CS the better the response. Sometimes, however, the conditioned responses occur when a new but similar CS is used that has never been paired with the US previously.

In this way a child can develop a fear of dogs after being bitten by a black dog. It may then generalize that fear into a phobia about other harmless black objects.

When two stimuli are used but pairing of the US or 'reward' is not maintained with the second stimulus the subject develops *discrimination* and begins to learn to ignore the second stimulus.

Behaviour shaping

In operant conditioning *shaping* can be used to speed up the process. In Skinner's rat experiment, for example, shaping might begin by remote operation of the 'food lever' only when the rat gets close to it, gradually decreasing the distance of the rat from the lever before the lever is operated.

Then the lever is only operated when the rat touches the lever. Next the lever is only operated when the rat attempts to depress it.

Thus behaviour shaping involves reinforcing *successive approximations* to the desired behaviour pattern.

In this way conditioning can be accelerated and quite complex patterns of behaviour can be taught, a familiar example being circus bears that have been taught to ride bicycles in this way (Lindzey, Hall, & Thompson, 1978).

Packard (1978) reported that up to 20% of teachers in the eastern USA were systematically using behaviour modification techniques that involved systematic use of rewards and punishments in their classrooms.

Two teachers in Montana went too far by extending the 'Skinner box' idea to a four-foot high box for miscreant students. It had no lighting and no ventilation other than two small holes for observation. The relatives of a retarded child that had been locked in this box complained and the teachers were sacked.

A better example of 'behavior-shaping' was tested by University of Kansas researchers. They had the teacher divide the class into two teams, and the team which incurred fewer violations of several rules for good class behaviour was given various rewards. The researchers reported good results.

Objections to such applications of behaviour shaping are that they focused on restricting behaviours such as talking in class whereas advocates of 'open' classrooms encourage a freer learning environment.

The advent of the PC in schools, however, has brought a highly mechanized learning process, some aspects of which progressive educators are pleased with.

With the use of appropriate teaching software, PCs become a 'teaching machine' with which students can learn at their own pace and receive instant reinforcement for correct answers.

Skill learning

Learning some skills requires a large number of repetitions n, for example 'touch' typing where when fully proficient we do not have to consciously think of which key to associate with each letter of the alphabet to be typed. Such memory is called *procedural memory* or implicit memory.

Skill learning has three stages:

[1] The cognitive stage in which the requirements and components of the skill are learnt.

[2] The association stage in which the components are performed together and the skill is perfected.

[3] The automation stage at which the skill is completely remembered.

In learning skills *feedback* is important in stage [1] to help perfect each component of the skill and again important in stages [2] and [3] to help assess which components require further learning.

If the requirements of a new skill overlap those of one previously learnt *positive transfer* makes the new skill easier to learn. Conversely, if some parts of the new skill contradict those of an 'old' skill then *negative transfer* may make learning the new skill more difficult.

An example might be riding a bike where turning the handlebars to the right steers to the right. Used to this, in yachting one might have some difficulty becoming accustomed to pushing the tiller to the right to steer left.

Reinforcement schedules

To this point we have assumed reinforcement, when used, was applied on a continuous basis, that is, after each response.

In operant conditioning reinforcement can also be made according to some fixed schedule. Examples include:

[1] The *fixed-ratio schedule* gives reinforcement after a certain number of responses.

[2] The *fixed-interval schedule* where reinforcement is given after a fixed interval of time, regardless of how many responses are made.

[3] In *variable-ratio* schedules reinforcement might come, for example, after three, then six responses, then three again. Similarly *variable-interval schedules* vary the time intervals between reinforcement.

Another obvious alternative is *random interval reinforcement,* that is, choosing an average interval and multiplying it by a random number between 0 and 1 produced by successive applications of a random number generator such as the RND( ) function of BASIC and other computer programming languages.

As might be expected, extinction is slower after cessation of scheduled reinforcements. This is the situation in human life where, for example, parents can only occasionally reward or punish a child's behaviour.

The result is that we may continue doing things we were shaped to do early in life long after reinforcement has ceased.

Primary and secondary reinforcement

A primary reinforcer, or unconditioned reinforcer, is effective for an untrained subject, for example food as a positive reinforcer or electric shock as a negative reinforcer.

A secondary reinforcer, or conditioned reinforcer, must be learnt by being paired with a primary reinforcer.

In a Skinner box, for example, a gong could be sounded every time the primary reinforcement of food was obtained. As in classical conditioning, the subject would associate the gong with the food and soon it would become an effective secondary reinforcer.

A better example occurs in child rearing where parents typically reward children for good behaviour with food treats or presents as primary reinforcers, accompanied by praise as secondary reinforcement. Ultimately the secondary reinforcement of praise may become the most frequently used and important form of reinforcement.

Contiguity of reinforcement, that is the time interval, is also important. The smaller the interval in time between the two reinforcements to be associated, the sooner the secondary reinforcement is learnt.

Repetition and learning

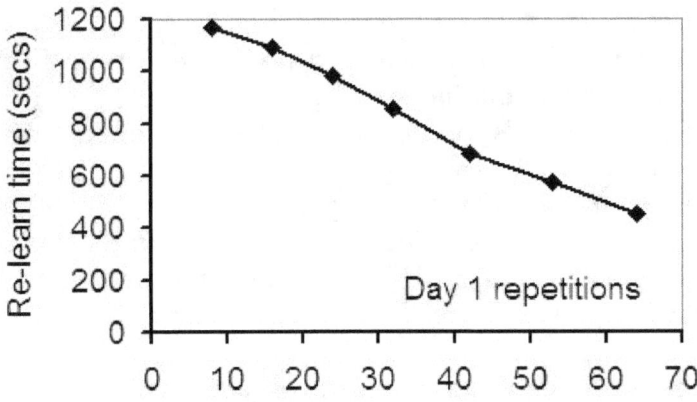

Figure 4.4. Influence of number learning repetitions on retention 24 hours later.

In a classical experiment Hermann Ebbinghaus found that after reading through a list of 16 syllables for 0, 8, 16, 24, 32, 42, 53, or 64 repetitions, and then 24 hours later assessing how many further repetitions were needed to re-learn the list, the result was the almost linear relationship shown in Figure 4.4.

This result shows that more practice (on day 1 here) gives greater learning. More important, it shows that each learning trial on day 1, which takes about 7 seconds, saves about 12 seconds on day 2. Thus it is better to spread learning trials out over time and this phenomenon is known as *distribution of practice* (Baddeley, 1990).

One trial of distributed learning had four groups learning to type with (Baddeley, 1990):

1. One session of one hour/day.
2. Two sessions of one hour/day.
3. One two-hour session/day.
4. Two two-hour sessions/day.

It was found that the first group learnt the keyboard more efficiently than the other groups. That is, the rate of learning per hour of practice was greater for the group with greater distribution of learning.

Learning curves

Suppose the degree to which a person or group has learnt something or been conditioned is given by the probability $p = 0$ to 1, and p depends on n, the number of repetitions of the learning process.

If we assume that the learning process is hyperbolic so that the degree of learning gradually increases towards 100% or the asymptote $p = a$ with $a = 1$, then this is represented by the hyperbola of Figure 4.5(a), the equation for which is $p = an/(b + n)$

This equation can easily be rearranged to give

$n/p = (b + n)/a$

so that if we plot n/p against n the straight line of Figure 4.5(b) is obtained and the magnitude of the intercept with the n axis = b whilst, of more interest, the inverse slope of the line equals the horizontal asymptote a of the hyperbola.

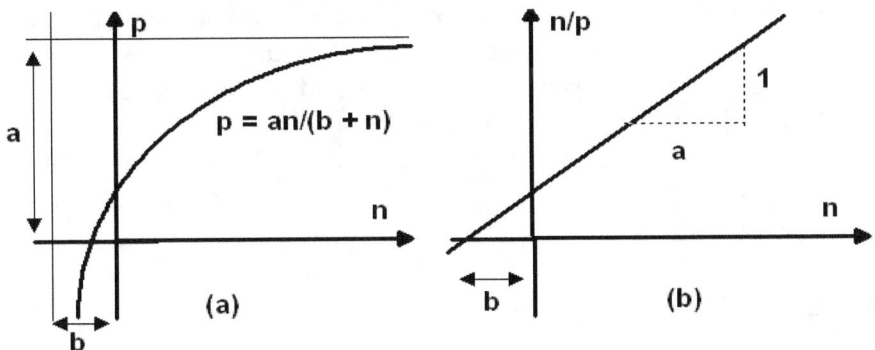

Figure 4.5. Mohr Plot for learning.

This equation can easily be rearranged to give

$n/p = (b + n)/a$

so that if we plot n/p against n the straight line of Figure 4.5(b) is obtained and the magnitude of the intercept with the n axis = b whilst, of more interest, the inverse slope of the line equals the horizontal asymptote a of the hyperbola.

In experimental situations this plot is useful in testing whether results are indeed hyperbolic and, if so, estimating the 'ceiling' value towards which some variable is converging.

Applied to the memory of a single person we set $a = 1$ and a typical result might be $b = 3$, $n = 3$, giving $p = 0.5$, or 50% memory retention after three repetitions. Here p is either:

(a) How well an item is learnt. People's names might be a good example of this. Myself, I often think one needs about three repetitions of such things to remember them.

(b) How much of a 'block' of information is learnt. An example might be a list of names where, because of *interference*, words at the beginning (the *primacy effect*) and end (the *recency effect*) are remembered best.

For a slower learner, on the other hand, b might double to 6 so we need $n = 6$ to get $p = 0.5$ or 50% learning.

Applied to conditioning of the populace by advertising, *p* is the proportion of the population affected and larger values of the asymptote *b* which flatten the curve might occur when there are two or more competing advertisers in the market. In politics this highlights the advantage of dictatorship.

In education it perhaps highlights the importance of avoiding conflicting messages so that it is often best to learn one subject at a time.

Forgetting

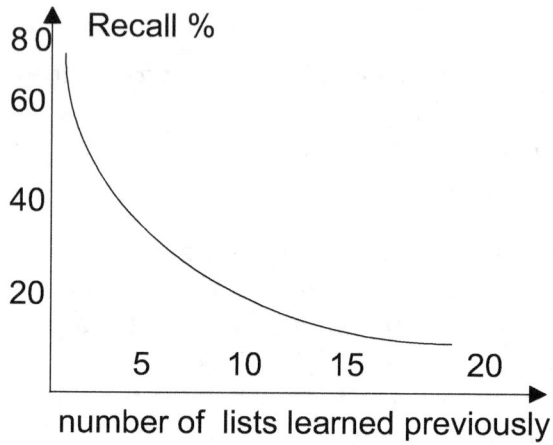

Figure 4.6. Decrease in recall of a list with increasing number of lists learnt previously.

Figure 4.6 shows an example of *proactive interference* in which the accuracy with which lists are remembered declines as the number of lists learnt previously increases (Morgan et al., 1979).

Here the increasing number of previously learnt lists interferes with the learning of the last list. At the same time *retroactive interference* will occur so that learning of further lists reduces recall of the earlier lists.

A similar effect, called the *serial position effect,* applies to the items of a single list so that items early in the list are remembered better than those in the middle (the *primacy effect)* whilst items late in the list are remembered much better than those in the middle (the *recency effect).*

Interference is one of the major causes of forgetting and forgetting curves generally take roughly the same form as that of Figure 4.3 where the curve is hyperbolic like those of Figure 4.2, but 'upside down.'

Interference is *trace-dependent* forgetting because of physical changes in memory traces when something new is learned.

Memory traces can also be changed by *decay* or by *motivated forgetting*, for example when we deliberately *repress* a memory.

Retrieval failure is when we lack or fail to use the right cues to retrieve stored memories. This is called *cue-dependent* forgetting.

Pseudoforgetting is when we fail to recall something, not realizing that it was not stored in LTM in the first place.

Generally, memory can decline with age, for example with the onset of senile dementia of the Alzheimer type (SDAT), Alzheimer's disease, or brain damage caused by injury, alcohol or other drugs.

Improving memory

Sometimes *mnemonic* techniques are used to improve memory.

The *method of loci* associates items to be remembered with physical objects in one's environment.

The *word peg method* typically uses a list of ten number-word pairs, for example one-sun, two-shoe and so on. Then to remember a list of food items the first two of which are bread and butter one might visualize:

[1] White bread as being bright like the sun,

[2] Our shoes slipping on butter on the floor.

The method may only be useful for one or two very important lists and can fix many items of a short list for many years.

An example of the *link method* is *narrative chaining* in which a list of words is remembered by inventing a story involving each item in the list.

The *method of word associations* uses a phrase with the first letter of each word corresponding to each item of a list, for example:

My very energetic mother just sits up near pop is used to remember the names of the planets in order from the sun, that is Mercury, Venus, Earth, Mars, Jupiter, Saturn, Uranus, Neptune, Pluto.

This method is often used by medical students to remember anatomical names.

Acronyms are another useful mnemonic in which words are formed from the first letters of a group of words, for example WHO for World Health Organization. Abbreviations of the names of companies (e.g., IBM) and mathematical and other methods (e.g., MIS = Management Information Systems) are also formed in this way.

Memory structure

Figure 4.7 shows a proposed structure in which the brain stores information about animals as categories and sub-categories with properties attached to each 'node' in the structure (Collins et al., 1969).

Some experimental results do not fit this model, for example Ripps et al. (1973) found that people were quicker to agree to the truth of the statement: *A cat is an animal* than they were to the truth of the statement: *A cat is a mammal.* They argued that MAMMAL should be closer to CAT than ANIMAL in the hierarchy.

More important, however, is that the word ANIMAL is much more frequently used than the word MAMMAL and frequency of reference to a memory certainly does enhance the speed of recall.

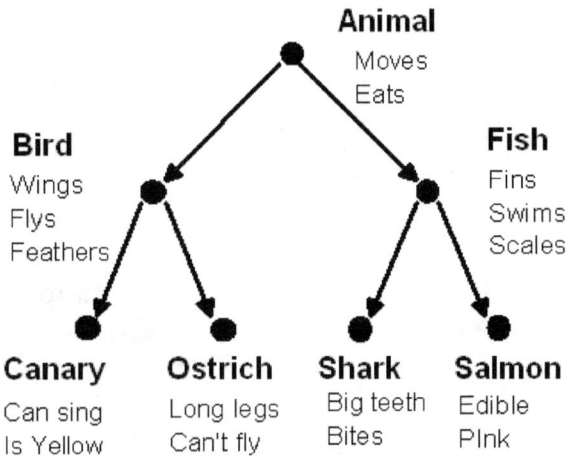

Figure 4.7. Hierarchical organization of the mental lexicon.

The present author would also argue that the brain almost certainly must store memories in a *precedence network* based on the order in which learning occurs.

In such a network a memory search that succeeds in finding a 'connection' or *common* property shared by a 'new' item in short term memory and an item in long-term memory might then store the data on the new item in the same physical area.

For example, the first animals that most children encounter are domesticated cats or dogs so that they will begin forming the memory structure shown in Figure 4.8.

Here four memories have the *common property* 'animal' and cat is the first animal encountered by an infant and thence the first memory stored (at node 1, perhaps one or more brain cells). The second memory is dog, the third lion, and so on. Then cat and dog are associated by the property *domestic* (in the child's language perhaps 'house' or 'home') whilst lion and elephant are associated by the common property *jungle*.

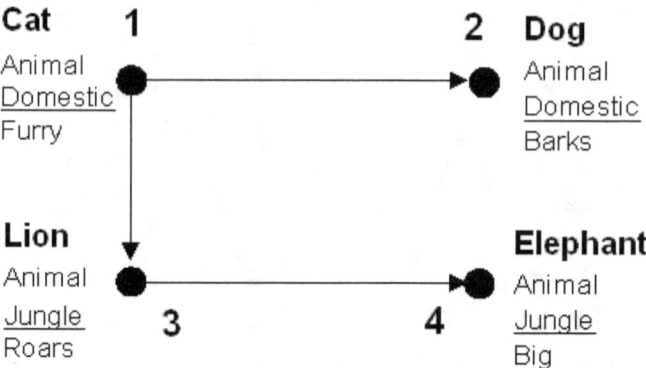

Figure 4.8. Precedence memory network.

Such memories have a considerable visual 'content' and the ease of recall of a memory will depend its 'strength' which will depend on such factors as the degree of elaboration with which it was committed to long-term memory and the frequency and recency with which the memory has been revisited.

Long-term potentiation

In practice a signal between two neurons is an electrical impulse passed along the axon of the first to the dendrites of the second via a synaptic junction. At this junction neurotransmitter chemicals pass the signal across a 'synaptic gap.' Evidently these chemicals react with RNA or peptide macromolecules in the neurons that play a role in memory *coding*.

In the case of classical conditioning, therefore, with frequent 'dosing' in this way the storage of a memory is made more permanent, an effect called *long-term potentiation* (Vander et al., 1994).

Thinking

In education the four elements of thinking should be used:

[1] Images. We often use *visual imagery* in thinking. For example, we often find it easier to describe the shape of something by sketching it or a physical operation by demonstrating it.

[2] Symbols. Language involves the spoken and written use of symbols. These symbols can be words, mathematical formulae, pictures (including diagrams, maps and graphs) or gestures that represent either *objects, operations, relationships* and *qualities.*

[3] Concepts. Concepts can be defined as categories that represent a class of objects, events or qualities wherein each item has a number of common features. A simple example are birds which 'mentally' are a concept and these have common properties such as two legs, wings, flying and the ability to fly and lay eggs.

Such categorization is important for both efficient learning and memory storage and efficient recall and thence thinking.

Learning of concepts is made easier by *transfer* when they are similar to already familiar concepts.

When driving, for example, when you see a set of traffic lights (a concept) you note which colour is 'on' and quickly decide (a thinking process) what action to take.

[4] Rules. Rules involve connections between features of a concept and between different concepts.

In the example of traffic lights we should know the rules and have only to choose 'yes' or 'no' as to whether we follow the appropriate rule.

The rule for traffic lights might be represented as:

(green = go) OR (amber = slow down) OR (red = stop)

and the rule for driving might be written:

(accelerator = go) OR (no accelerator = slow) OR (brake = stop)

so to stop at a red light we have to connect the two rules, a process probably carried out in short term memory.

Creative thinking

Creative thinking to obtain new ideas often involves *divergent thinking* (Morgan et al., 1979) and typically occurs in three stages:

(a) Preparation: define the problem and resources needed.

(b) Incubation: acquire information and think or dwell on the problem.

(c) Assembly: combine information to form the solution.

In a much too drawn out education system endless classes with a lecture format should occasionally be replaced by sessions with a seminar format. Sometimes these could involve *brainstorming* to solve a problem, for example devising an effective advertising campaign for a product.

Group brainstorming has been found effective because:

[1] People tend to have twice as many ideas in the group situation because of the more stimulating environment, 'cross fertilization' of ideas and arousal of competitive spirit.

[2] Alternation of individual and group thinking improves results.

[3] As more ideas are produced they tend to improve.

[4] Second sessions a few days later improve results because of the 'incubation' process so important in creative thinking.

[5] The group uses *critical thinking* to evaluate the ideas.

Conclusions

Conditioning, or at least some form and degree of it, is used in many areas of life, for example, in training infants in the basics of life, educating young children, and in 'brainwashing' the public through repetitive advertising to become "consumer zombies", as discussed in Chapter 13.

Behaviour shaping, essentially for form of conditioning, is also much used in training and educating young children, also requiring reinforcement to be effective.

It has been found that the use of small learning groups with a specialist teacher can give children a head start in life, and increase their IQ (Mohr et al., 2017; 2019a).

Figures 4.4 and 4.5 remind us that deliberate learning requires some repetition, whilst Figure 4.6 reminds us not to try to learn too much new material at once, but to spread learning efforts over time.

Learning curves can remind us that bullies will have taken some time to learn and copy bullying behaviours from parents, siblings, fellow students, or fellow workmates, whilst forgetting curves remind us that, of course, it takes some time to 'unlearn' errant behaviours.

4. Conditioning, Memory and Learning

Chapter 5

BULLYING

> *I didn't know what the word "bullying" really meant*
> *until it started happening to me. I thought it was being beaten up*
> *or being threatened. Sometimes it is, but really bullying*
> *is when someone hurts or upsets someone else on purpose.*
> *Some children pick on people to make themselves feel better, because*
> *bullying is about power. Sometimes they are actually bigger or*
> *stronger, but sometimes they just know how to make themselves*
> *popular. They pick on people using this power so that*
> *they can feel more powerful, usually because they don't feel*
> *that they have power in other parts of their lives.*
> Helen Cowie, Harriet Tennenbaum & Ffion Jones,
> *Emily Is Being Bullied: What Can She Do?* (2019).

The bullying epidemic

A 2016 "anti-bullying conference" in Melbourne reported that "children as young as three are being identified as bullies amid concern many childcare centres and kindergartens aren't doing enough to stamp out the problem" (The Herald-Sun, 6/8/2016).

Recent research also shows that young bullies at school are likely to become anti-social adults, whilst a 2006 survey found bullying in the Victorian public sector to be "frequent", with almost 24% of staff saying they frequently thought of leaving the public sector. Similar findings have been made in Australian hospitals.

Now with the advent of the ME TOO movement, it is clear that we are experiencing a global epidemic of bullying, ranging from miscreant school students to 'bastard bosses' and political and religious leaders (or 'Little Hitlers') who abuse people both verbally, physically and sexually.

5. BULLYING

Several examples of the serious consequences that can arise from bullying are cited by Coloroso (2016), just a few examples being:

➤ In Invercargill, New Zealand, in August 1997, a 15-year-old boy committed suicide, the coroner's report stating: "Bullying and victimization were a significant factor in the boy's life in the months leading up to his suicide".

➤ In Victoria, British Columbia, in November 1977, a 14-year-old girl died after being attacked and beaten unconscious by two girls, her arm and neck being deliberately broken, and her body dumped in the Gorge Inlet. It was reported that she had tried to "fit in and had wanted desperately to belong to their group, but she was regularly mocked and taunted about her brown skin and her weight", that one of the attackers had been angry because she believed the girl had been spreading rumours about her, and that the other attacker was "mad" at the victim because she believed that the victim had been "involved with her boyfriend".

➤ In Littleton, Colorado, on April 20, 1999, two boys "used assault weapons and homemade bombs to lay siege to their school". They killed 12 classmates and a teacher, injured 18 other teenagers, and then killed themselves.

   Friends said the two perpetrators were "constantly ridiculed and taunted at school", and an anonymous classmate had falsely accused the two boys of bringing marijuana to school, prompting a search of their property.

   More humiliating, it was reported that:

   People surrounded them in the commons and squirted ketchup packets all over them, laughing at them, calling them faggots. That happened while teachers watched. They couldn't fight back. They wore ketchup all day and went home covered in it.

   In a suicide note left by one of the perpetrators, it was noted that he felt targeted and alienated, and in their (the two perpetrators) minds it was "payback time".

What is bullying?

Bullying happens when:
➤ A person upsets or attacks another person verbally, physically and (sometimes) sexually.
➤ The errant behavior is repeated once or more over time.
➤ The perpetrator has, or thinks they have, more power over the victim.

There are different types of bullying including:
➤ **Emotional/psychological bullying (teasing):** for example, name-calling, making fun of someone, or commenting on a person's appearance in some negative way.
➤ **Threats of harm.**
➤ **Indirect bullying:** for example, leaving a person out of group activities, not inviting them to family events, or telling others to avoid the victim.
➤ **Physical attacks:** for example, a child hitting, kicking, pushing or pulling the hair of another child.
➤ **Physical attacks on a person's property:** for example, a child stealing another's lunch money, damaging their books, throwing their school bags around, drawing on their clothing, or hiding their equipment such as pens etc.
➤ **Rumour mongering:** spreading negative, often untruthful, rumours about the person.
➤ **Mean messaging and cyberbullying:** mean phone calls or notes, or using an electronic device such as a mobile phone or tablet.

According to Moore (2012) the physical attributes of physical bullying in schools include hitting, spitting and punching, whilst the verbal attributes include teasing, ridicule, sarcasm and 'scapegoating', noting that bullying usually occurs in areas with minimal adult supervision such as bathrooms and hallways.

She also notes that bullying may be between just two individuals, or there may be many people indirectly involved such as bystanders and witnesses, and that there may also be "assistants" or "reinforcers" (e.g. those who observe and laugh).

Moore (2012) also lists a number of "elements that generally characterize bullying":

➢ A power imbalance that favours the perpetrator(s).
➢ Perpetrators may be supported by a group of peers, some of them encouraging the bullying, and others who watch but do nothing to help the victims.
➢ Victims get "negative attention" from their peers and are excluded from the group of peers and isolated, such exclusion and isolation fortifying the "power" of the perpetrator(s).
➢ The bullying is "uninvited" and "unwanted" by the victim.
➢ The bullying is "deliberate, repeated, and often relentless".

What roles do people play in bullying?

When bullying occurs people play different "roles", and sometimes people play more than one role, for example being a victim sometimes to people higher in a workplace hierarchy, and bully to others lower in that hierarchy.

The different roles include:

➢ That of bully. Bullies raise their own self-esteem by putting others down, and bullies often have strong 'social intelligence' and realize what will humiliate and hurt their victims.
➢ That of victim, whose self-esteem is damaged by psychological bullying, and they are likely to develop anxiety symptoms as a result of physical bullying or their possessions being damaged or stolen.
➢ Bully-victim, i.e. both victim to some and bully to others.
➢ Defender: a person who 'steps in' to help and protect the victim.
➢ Assistants to the bully: people/friends who help the bully.
➢ Reinforcers of the bully: people who encourage, praise etc. the bully
➢ Outsiders/bystanders: people who watch the bullying but do nothing about it.

Who is at risk of bullying?

Anyone somehow 'different' from most of the others, in the class/group/section or division of an organization, or simply lower in the hierarchy of that group of people, may be at risk of bullying, for example (Cowie et al., 2019):

➢ People/children with special needs or disabilities.

➢ People/children of a different race or ethnicity.

➢ People/children who are perceived by bullies as weak, sensitive, having low self-esteem.

➢ People/children who are less popular with others and who therefore have few, if any, friends.

➢ People/children who are passive, quiet etc., who may be perceived by bullies as weaker etc.

The 'Makeup' of a bully

Bullies are not born as such but "inborn temperament is a factor, but so too are what social scientist Urie Bronfenbrenner called 'environmental influences': children's home life, school life, and the community culture (including the media) that permit or encourage such behavior" (Coloroso, 2016).

In other words, what is now commonly called 'nature and nurture'. Indeed, David Galton, grandson of Francis Galton, the pioneer of the theory of evolution and friend of Charles Darwin, believes that about 50% of personality is inherited genetically, the rest coming, of course, from imitative, social etc. learning (Galton, 2001).

According to Coloroso (2016), there are:

Four things we should know about bullies:

1. *They are taught to bully.*

2. *They bully because they can.*

3. *They choose to bully.*

4. *They choose whom to bully.*

In other words, they choose to use their position, strength etc., and power that comes with it, to manipulate, control, dominate, and humiliate those they deem to be 'less' than themselves, or as a threat to their status.

Indeed, even politics is an example of the latter point, leaders of governing parties in the antiquated Westminster system often raving abusively at and about opposition leaders in parliament, particularly when a full election is imminent.

The roles bullies play

According to Coloroso (2016), bullies can choose from 7 kinds of bullying roles:

1. **The confident bully** with a big ego that "swaggers" onto the scene and has "a penchant for aggressive behavior, and no compassion for his target.

2. **The social bullies** who use "rumour, gossip, verbal taunts, and shunning" to isolate their targets and effectively exclude them from social activities. They are of the positive qualities of others, may have a poor sense of self, but hide their insecurities in a "cloak of exaggerated confidence and charm". They are devious and manipulative in getting people on their side, and against their victim.

3. **The "fully armoured" bully** is detached, showing little emotion and seizing opportunities to bully when no one will see or stop them. They are vicious and vindictive to their victims, but charming and deceptive to others.

4. **The "hyperactive bully"** is weak intellectually, with less than average IQ, and has poor social skills, often reading hostile intent into the innocent actions of others, and reacting aggressively to slight provocation.

5. **The bullied bully** is both a bully and a victim, and is less popular than other bullies, viciously striking back at those who bully them, and at weaker/smaller targets.

6. **The bunch of bullies**, a group of friends that collectively bully their victims.

7. **The gang of bullies** in pursuit of power, control, domination, subjugation, and territory.

The common traits of bullies

Generally, bullies have the following traits Coloroso (2016):

1. They like to dominate other people.
2. They use other people to get what they want.
3. They don't see "the other person's vantage point'.
4. They are only concerned with satisfying their ego etc., not with the rights and feelings of others.
5. They usually bully when there are no witnesses.
6. They view weaker siblings or peers as prey.
7. They refuse to accept responsibility for their actions.
8. They lack the foresight to realize the consequences of their behavior.
9. They crave attention.
10. They enjoy inflicting pain on their victims.

The top 10 conflict starters

A national survey in the US of more than 2,100 students in grades 3-6 found that the top 10 'conflict starters' that were reported were (Drew, 2010):

11. Being teased or made fun of.
12. Rumours and gossip.
13. Name-calling.
14. Being blamed for something.
15. Someone being unfair.
16. Being left out.
17. Being picked on for being different.
18. Cheating at games.
19. Threats.
20. Mean notes or text messages.

5. BULLYING

The incidence of bullying in schools

Coloroso (2016) cites a 1991 survey of 211 students in 14 classes from grades 4-8, their teachers, and their parents, that compiled the following statistics:

➢ 35% of students were involved in bullying incidents.
➢ 38% of special education students were bullied, compared to 18% of other students.
➢ 24% reported that race-related bullying took place sometimes or often.
➢ 23% of students engaged in bullying.
➢ 71% of the teachers reported that teachers intervened often or "almost always".

A 2007 study reported that 87% of staff believed they had effective strategies to deal with bullying, 97% saying that they would intervene if they saw bullying occur, but only 21% of students involved in bullying said that they reported it to a staff member (Coloroso, 2016).

A 2011 National Education Association survey of 2,163 K-12 teachers and 2,901 Education Support Professionals (ESPs) obtained the following results (National Education Association, 2011):

➢ 43% thought bullying to be a problem at their school.
➢ 62% had witnessed bullying 2+ times in the last month.
➢ Bullying was reported to 45% of teachers and 35% of ESPs in the last month.
➢ Parents had reported bullying to 16% of both groups in the last month.
➢ Staff thought verbal, social & physical bullying worse than cyberbullying, and were more likely to report these forms.
➢ They reported concerns about bullying based on weight (23%), gender (20%), perceived sexual orientation (18%), and disability (12%).
➢ 93% reported implementation of a bullying prevention policy in their district.
➢ Only about 50% had had training related to the policy.
➢ Only 58% said their school had implemented formal anti-bullying policies.

➤ 42% of teachers and 27% of ESPs had direct involvement in anti-bullying activities.
➤ Staff involvement in high schools was only 24%.

What are the effects of bullying?

Victims of bullying often do not want to tell anyone about being bullied because they are afraid of making matters worse.

Often there are no obvious indications that a person is a victim of bullying, but there are some signs that might help identify a victim (Cowie et al.):

➤ The victim loses confidence in socializing and becomes nervous and withdrawn.
➤ The victim may become apprehensive about going to school or work.
➤ The victim's work performance decreases noticeably in some way.
➤ The victim comes home upset and perhaps injured, or having had belongings lost or damaged.

In a survey of 1,000 children and teenagers Lovegrove (2006) found these examples of bullying and its effects:

➤ 75% of young teenagers said that teasing or bullying about their appearance was what they were most afraid of at school: *I spend my whole life trying to look prettier and thinner so that no one can call me fat* (Eleanor, aged 16).

➤ Almost 50% said they felt uncomfortable being around people who looked different from them: *Of course we don't like them – they look weird* (Ryan, aged 18).

➤ A third said they kept quiet in class because they felt bad about how they looked: *You don't want people to laugh at you when you don't look right, so you don't put your hand up to answer the teacher* (Lottie, aged 14).

➤ 20% said their families were critical of their appearance: *I have hardly any friends and my mum says that's down to how I look. She calls me a freak* (Andrew, aged 17).

Dealing with bullying

To deal with bullying a few key measures are often recommended:

- ➢ "Just ignore it and act like you don't care" one young schoolgirl was advised. She reported: "It seemed to work for a while. They didn't seem to be laughing at me as much - - and I still felt very upset. In some ways, the whispering was worse than the laughing and the names" (Cowie et al., 2019).
- ➢ Make friends with the bully. According to Lovegrove (2006) this will not help: "Great. Now not only do they make your child's life miserable at school, they also feel that they have you on their side!"
  According to Lovegrove, "people who bully feel insecure in some way" so paying them a compliment may make them feel better about themselves.
- ➢ "I'd also heard that instead of crying or hitting back, being assertive can help. I knew that being assertive wasn't the same as being aggressive – I'd already found out that made things worse. So one lunch break I gave it a try" (Cowie et al., 2019).
- ➢ If the victim's appearance is the excuse for bullying then they should try to improve their appearance by wearing different clothes, changing their hair style, and by losing weight if necessary.
- ➢ Victims should tell their friends and enlist their help to deal with bullying. If they have no friends, or very few, then they should try and make sure they have a few from whom to select a couple of 'good friends' who might be of help to them.
- ➢ Tell the teacher or boss, in the case of workplaces, for example: "She (the teacher) was so nice, I felt OK about telling her what was happening. She said the same thing as Mum – that it wasn't my fault and that it needed to be stopped" (Cowie et al., 2019).

➢ If the bully says their bulling was only meant to be a joke, it should be strongly pointed out to them that their bullying was wrong and should be penalized.

➢ If the bully says their victim was 'asking for it', again they should be told their actions were wrong and should be penalized.

According to Lovegrove (2006), however, ignoring bullies won't help because: *Bullies require your attention. Ignoring them means that they have to try a whole lot harder to get it!*

How to stop bullying in schools etc.

In some countries schools are legally required to have an anti-bullying policy incorporating a set of measures to discourage bullying. These measures may include requiring schools to:

1. Listen to students, carers and parents with complaints about bullying.
2. Encourage students to respect all types of people with different ethnicity, appearance, ability levels etc.
3. Actively discourage discriminatory language and behavior.
4. Help students understand what bullying may involve, and how to deal with it, for example the measures noted in the preceding section.

Note that some of the common measures taken to punish bullies may have negative effects and, indeed, resemble relational and verbal bullying, for example:

➢ Threats of physical isolation: e.g., "If you do that again you will be confined to your room for the rest of the day."

➢ Threats of embarrassment and humiliation: e.g., "If you act like a one-year-old I'll dress you like one in a nappy.

➢ Emotional isolation: e.g., "I won't talk to you because you hurt your brother".

➢ Grounding: e.g., "You can't go out tonight because you bullied your sister."

Cyberbullying

According to recent Press reports cyberbullying is an increasing problem, WordWeb 6 defining **cyber-** as: *Relating to information technology, computers or the Internet.*

According to Moore (2012):

"Cyberbullying can occur as hateful, hurtful, and harassing messages sent or posted via SMS/text messages, wall comments on social networking sites, chat rooms, blog posts and the like. But it can also take the form of uploading or distributing embarrassing videos or images or other media: it need not be limited to 'written' or 'verbal' communications."

Characteristics that make cyberbullying different from schoolyard bullying include (Moore, 2012):

> ➤ *Cyberbullying does not stop at the front door,* so that people can be bullied via their internet connections to PCs, tablets, and mobile phones via Facebook etc.

> ➤ *A single instance of digital harassment can be repeated indefinitely and spread globally* to "invisible audiences", sometimes becoming 'viral'.

> ➤ *"Once posted, hurtful or embarrassing information is virtually impossible to delete"* and even if the information is deleted, it is likely that Google or another search engine will have found and 'cached' it so that it can be accessed in the future.

> ➤ *"There is a greater potential for anonymity"* for the perpetrator, cyberbullies being able to use false names.

> ➤ *Cyberbullying is a "preferred mode" for girls,* girls being more likely to take part in "psychological and covert" types of bullying that allow them to gossip and spread malicious rumours about others, whereas "typically, boys are involved in more physical and outwardly aggressive forms of bullying".

> ➤ *Cyberbullying may involve 'sexting',* that is, sending/posting sexually explicit photos or messages which may sometimes 'go viral'.

When parents discover their child indulging in cyberbullying they should intervene immediately, subsequently monitoring the child's TV viewing, video game playing, and computer activities, also encouraging more constructive and healthier activities.

Parents should also realize that victims of cyberbullying often feel ashamed and afraid to retaliate for fear of raising the 'level' and frequency of conflict. Thus they should encourage their children to tell them ASAP if they experience any kind of bullying, whether by another child, a teacher etc.

Conclusion

Bullying is also known as *"predatory aggression* - a scary term, to be sure, but not as scary as the actual behavior it defines" (Coloroso, 2016).

Bullying in schools and workplaces has now become a major issue, having been found commonplace in a wide variety of organizations ranging from schools to government organizations and private companies.

For example, in a national survey in the US of 2,100 students in grades 3-6, 44% (963) students reported that bullying happens often, every day, or all of the time in school and other places (Drew, 2010).

Bullying harms everyone, hurting the victim psychologically, and sometimes physically or materially, upsetting the victim's parents, friends, teachers etc., and perhaps reducing the performance of individuals in the 'host' organization, or at least some part or section of it.

Some ways of coping with and dealing with bullying have been discussed in the foregoing chapter. In addition, of course, in serious cases bullies can be reported to the police and/or legal action threatened or taken.

☺☺☺☺☺☺☺☺☺☺☺☺☺☺☺☺

5. BULLYING

Chapter 6

FAMILY LIFE

*Nobody has ever before asked the nuclear family
to live all by itself in a box the way we do. With no
relatives, no support, we've put it in an impossible situation.*
Margaret Mead, quoted in: *New Realities*, June 1978.

*The striking point about our model family is not simply the
compete-compete, consume-consume style of life it urges us to
follow. The striking point, in the face of all the propaganda,
is how few Americans actually live this way.*
Louise Kapp Howe, *The Future of The Family* (1972).

Mohr's Law of Politics

Making marriage, or an equivalent relationship, work is less than easy. Mohr's Law of Politics is that build a 'fence' of any kind and there will be people in substantial numbers on either side of it as potential competitors (Mohr, 2018e).

Some political divisions are comparatively arbitrary compared to the considerable differences between men and women, some of which are discussed in the present chapter (Mohr, 2012b, 2018c – 2nd edn).

Women's ability to bear children is a very major difference, one that men are somewhat in awe of. Women, on the other hand, are sometimes in awe of men's greater strength and, indeed, sometimes in fear of it. The latter difference we evolved with and it was the basis of our survival in our troglodyte hunter-gathering days.

There are usually, however, many other differences between two marriage partners. As Baker (2004) points out:

Gender aside, the potential for conflicts continues to abound. We come from difference places and are affected more than we understand by our family of origin.

Then, for example only, there are differences in personality, habitual behavioural differences, differences in educational and work background, and differences in likes and dislikes.

Communication

Lack of effective and constructive communication is the great problem of the human race. What makes us unique amongst animals is our enlarged cerebral cortex that stores the semantic memory required for our advanced languages.

Yet throughout history we have continued to behave just like the chimps that Jane Goodall (van Lawick-Goodall, 1971) was so disillusioned by, we have periodic conflicts with other groups of people, be it tribes, nations or followers of another religion.

This is largely because of a lack of *effective* communication and thence *understanding* of other people.

Such understanding is, of course, made more difficult when people speak a different language, but men and women also, in effect, speak different languages to some extent at least, in part because of their different upbringing, and thence different issues and related vocabulary.

As a result of their different, somewhat socially stereotyped, upbringing, men and women have different values. Women, of course, care more about children, in part owing to the powerful 'maternal instinct'. Men, on the other hand, care more about the football team they follow winning, and such comparatively trivial pursuits tend to alienate them from many women.

There are many more minor differences. Women care much more about their appearance, having been brought up supposed to look beautiful. Men's business suits, on the other hand, relate to army uniforms and are designed to make them look stupid, not hard to do.

These differences, of course, make communication difficult. As a somewhat tongue-in-cheek test of this, try sending a member of an all-male board to a meeting dressed as a woman!

In a marital-type relationship, however, I would recommend that the partners have some sort of discussion every day or two. In this they can air their respective gripes about each other, if any, and it is far better to bring them out in the open in this way than risk the other partner complaining to other people as this may result in rumours which may ultimately cause considerable damage to the relationship.

Perhaps more important, the partners should discuss any problems they may be having at work as these may pose a risk to a partner's career. Problems with their children should, of course, also be discussed.

Finally, financial matters should be discussed occasionally to make sure that the family financial situation is sound.

Partnership

A marital-type relationship should, of course, be a partnership and the work should be shared. In the traditional male breadwinner scenario housewives would always complain that they were still busy cooking and dealing with children after the man had finished work, giving rise to the old saying:

"A woman's work is never done."

Today, a high proportion of wives are also employed at least part-time, often requiring expensive day care for children, and this places a considerable financial stress on many families that are also struggling to pay substantial rents or mortgages.

Even when both partners work full-time, however, most women find themselves doing most of the housework, leading to continuing complaints:

Women still do around 80 per cent of home chores and caring tasks, despite their increased workforce participation. (Helene Couprie, Time Allocation within the Family, *Economic Journal*, 2007).

It found single working women spent an average of ten hours a week doing housework and single men seven hours. After becoming a couple, women's housework time shot up to 15 hours a week, while the average male contribution dropped to five hours, even when both spouses work outside the home (Caro & Fox, 2008).

The problem relates to the traditional housewife role of women, of course, and the solution is that men should be encouraged to spend more time helping with both housework and caring for and teaching children.

If the working woman-cum-housewife then has a little more spare time, that can be spent relaxing and talking with their partner, thus helping keep the relationship working congenially and effectively.

Healthy life

Healthy lifestyle should be a primary objective in every family, this including sound diet, watching one's weight, getting enough exercise, getting plenty of quality sleep, and getting enough relaxation time.

A healthy diet should, of course, include plenty of vegetables and a little fruit, limit fat (particularly saturated and trans fat) and thence meat (especially red meat), limit fatty fast food, limit fatty and salty snack foods, and limit sugary confectionary and drinks.

Children should limit sugar, of course, to protect their teeth, also brushing them soon after eating. Indeed, I find it lamentable that there is no provision for this at school.

Watching one's weight and exercise, of course, go together, and it is important to keep one's weight fairly close to that recommended for one's height and sex (Mohr, 2012c, 2013a, 2015, 2018a, 2018b).

To help build strong bodies children should have about an hour of exercise daily, including walking, and when old enough they should be encouraged to do an average of half an hour of more strenuous exercise daily.

For good health the same exercise requirements apply to adults, regular medium intensity exercise being required for a healthy heart and circulation system, for example.

A few hours of relaxation time is also necessary and this, of course, can include such entertainments as TV, music and reading.

For adults circa 8 hours of good quality sleep is necessary for good mental and physical health. Here the shared double bed can be a problem. If, for example, one partner snores, as is often the case, this can pose serious problems. Lonely young children invading the room in the middle of the night is another problem lessened (roughly halved, in fact) if the parents have separate rooms.

Sexual intercourse is merely an act of breeding which humans, being in most respects the most stupid creatures on the planet, as our always troubled history suggests, attach much too much importance to.

On the issue of satisfactory sex, according to the landmark Kinsey report, 10 percent of married women had never had orgasm during sexual intercourse, and 25 percent had not had orgasm during the first year of marriage (Lindzey et al, 1978).

Some people think that a couple's sex life might be better if they slept in separate beds, if not separate rooms, especially if one partner snores. Then, refreshed by sleeping well each night, a little 'mucking around' could be done on a more occasional basis if both partners had a double bed, even if in separate rooms, but perhaps with a shared bathroom between them.

The bottom line is that sharing a bed for life with the same ultimately 'rotting' thing is arguably somewhat insane, and certainly physically unhealthy, if not distasteful, if one had half one's wits left, that is.

Bullying in families

Bullying in families follows the characteristics discussed in Chapter 5, measures needed to deal with it also having been discussed in that chapter, in particular advising children to report any instances of bullying.

6. FAMILY LIFE

Personal experiences

Fortunately, I recall only a few instances of bullying when I was growing up, for example:

➢ At around age 5 I recall being on a family holiday staying in a Guesthouse in the hills area outside Melbourne. When we were walking up a steepish (to me) hill one day I said that I was tired and my father rebuked me for being weak and 'whining' etc.

➢ At a similar age, and taken on a ride on the scary (and eventually removed because it was deemed dangerous) "Big Dipper" rail-ride at Melbourne's amusement park "Luna Park", I complained about it being scary etc. and my father derided me for being weak and complaining, calling me: *"Old misery guts"*.

➢ When I was about 10 my mother had me help her do some of the family ironing, and I recall my approximately 6 years older eldest brother one day bullying me by insisting I had not done a good enough job on a couple of his shirts, and making me do them again.

➢ At around the same age, I recall my other brother, who was approximately 3 years older, pushing my head down into the toilet basin a couple of times because I had "told on" him about his bullying behavior to my parents.

➢ At about age 10 or 11 I suffered sexual abuse at the hands of an older person, but am not preferred to say who or where. I was a choir boy at the time, that being a possibility, but I'm not saying who/where etc., not liking talking about sex etc. much, believing humans usually make a farce, bad habit, fools of themselves etc. over it.

In later life, there were a few further instances of bullying by my eldest brother (BB), for example:

➢ Soon after moving to New Zealand to a new job in 1980, BB rang me impatiently one evening and abused and threatened along the lines of: *If you fuck this up* - - because I had not finished the structural engineering consultation work for a building project of his.

➢ Soon after I'd returned from New Zealand, having been bullied by a 'bastard boss' at the University of Auckland into resigning, my then wife got BB to visit me 'out of the blue' to tell me to get marriage guidance counselling (which he had recently got). I refused and he summarily had me committed for 2 days with the help of a 'shrink' he had used on his two eldest sons. In a bad position already, this was just about the 'last straw' in my 'academic/career crucifixion' and more details about bullying I suffered from my ex-wife and BB are given in Appendix B.

From early in our relationship my ex-wife bullied me on occasion, for example:

➢ One evening when I was happy and celebrating with her with a bottle of champagne, having graduated BE with 1st class honours overall, and thus obtaining a good postgraduate scholarship, she suddenly made a jealous, bullying insult. Shocked, I threw my glass in her direction. It missed but, upset, I stole a few of my mother's sleeping pills and ended up sleeping them off in a nearby hospital.

➢ From that day forth, unbeknown to me, she told one and all, including colleagues at work whenever possible (e.g., at faculty Christmas parties) that I was mad, an alcoholic etc., and this 'backstabbing' was a major factor in ruining my career.

➢ An example of this was one day in Cambridge when I was doing my PhD and her youngest sister and mother were visiting/staying with us. No doubt my wife had complained about her sex life for the sister piped up one day: *You can do it better with your finger.*

➢ As for sex-life, while I was slaving away at night in the Computer Centre, on Friday nights she had the Churchill College head barman visit her, rumour I heard being that he was 'getting into' a lady in the Churchill College married students' flats – she was the only person alone at night, so it must have been her! Indeed, when I returned to Melbourne a few weeks after her, she said: *"I didn't think you'd come back after what I did in Cambridge".*

➢ Part of my wife's bullying, of course, was 'backstabbing' gossip that extended widely and sometimes reached the ears of my University colleagues, contributing much to the ruination of my career noted a couple of times in this book (in ch. 8 and App. B).

➢ An example of the latter: interviewed by the Dean after I'd submitted my resignation in 1984, he said little else but: *"I admire your wife, she's coped"*, clearly demonstrating that her backstabbing had permeated my workplace.

➢ On one occasion early in my marriage my wife's mother said something along the lines of *"nasty German names"*, no doubt in part because her husband had lost an eye fighting with the Allies against Rommel in Africa in WW2.

➢ My wife said, when she was leaving me 'for keeps' in 1985 after my 'academic crucifixion' late in 1984: *"You'll be dead in a year"*, and I could not help but think that there was a degree of wishful thinking in that statement.

➢ Finally, to be fair, I should point out that on two occasions in the marriage I reacted badly to 'verbal assault' by my wife and pushed her so that she fell, on one occasion injuring her shoulder. After a couple of episodes with 'women friends' mentioned in Chapter 10, on balance I felt that, in the long run, I was the overall loser in arguments with women that got a little physical.

I believe my ex-wife had inherited the unpleasant personality that I encountered from her father, who was an unpleasant, obese, alcoholic with a bad temper at times, for example, smashing the top of my expensive record player one night when I was 'putting up' he and his wife so they could be near a hospital their youngest daughter was in after a bad accident.

Another factor was that she was the eldest of three sisters, resulting in what perhaps might be called 'big brother syndrome', that is, having the opportunity to learn controlling and bullying of siblings from an early age.

Perhaps another factor was that, as a kindergarten teacher, she'd become used to talking to parents about their children's behavior when they came to take them home, and she simply extended that habit to talking about other people.

A tragic example of family bullying occurred in my (now late) eldest brother's family. One day the eldest son, annoyed by #2 son being silly etc., threw a cutlery knife in his direction. It hit #2 son in the eye, and he lost it, no doubt suffering from PTSD every since. In the years that followed #2 son took up marijuana and alcohol aplenty, eventually developing quite serious schizophrenia. I doubt if he finished school, and guess he only had a job for a year or two, living for the most part in miserable solitude, despite somehow having two children with a woman he lived with for a few years. In the end he suicided at age circa 45.

As final personal example of family bullying, I should mention an instance in which I was the bully that I recall. This was one Saturday afternoon when I was working at Auckland University in the early 1980s. I suggested to my wife that she should mow the lawns because she needed the exercise and could 'stand to lose' a pound (in weight). Thus, on a nice sunny afternoon, I recall standing and looking out of the dining room/lounge area window watching 'the wife' mowing the back lawn while I was having a beer.

In other words, in line with the tenth law of the new religion Mohronism, one should judge things out of 10, not simply as 'black or white', and thence nobody is perfect etc., so on the bully scale I would score at least 1/10, 0 being impossible, as that would be 'perfection' in regards to that attribute/issue (Mohr & Fear, 2015; Mohr et al. 2018d).

Another admission I can make, in the interests of 'balance', is that all too often in life I have said the 'wrong thing', sometimes being needlessly critical or negative, or perhaps a little insulting.

On a couple of occasions (noted in Chapter 8 and Appendix B) I complained to the HOD in the wrong way, blurting out my complaint thoughtlessly, when much greater thought should have been given to the matter, and these incidents had a negative effect upon my career, with destructive results in the long run.

The bottom line here is that we all 'put our foot in our mouth' sometimes and, of course, usually end up regretting it.

Conclusion

One problem in marriage is that young men are not brought up thinking about children and romance. Often they are really just finding their way in the world a little when they have their first sexual relationship or two with women. When they all too often end up with unplanned for children they are completely unprepared for the situation.

Young women, on the other hand, have been brought up playing with dolls, and for them children are a raison d'etre.

In addition, they see getting married to some nice man and having children as being romantic. Indeed, much of the huge publishing and movie industries are based on this.

Thus, when the somewhat humdrum reality of marriage with wailing children emerges women are often quite disillusioned.

No doubt that is why we call that holiday taken after marriage the honeymoon, because reality will hit when the honeymoon ends, of course.

For marriage to work the relationship should be a carefully chosen one in the beginning. Then the marriage should only have been made after careful thought and advice, and after the relationship has endured for a substantial amount of time.

More important still, children should only be had if the relationship is likely to last, and after discussion, advice and counseling, along with proper career and financial planning.

Then one should also note that, with the world already overpopulated with humans, it is best to have only one or two children, also noting that only children and children from smaller families tend to have higher IQ (Vernon, 1960).

Then, to keep the partnership working well, frequent and effective communication and planning is required, along with optimism or 'hope' (GA, RS & PE Mohr., 2018), to ensure a healthy and happy life for the whole family.

A key part of this, of course, is avoiding bullying as far as possible, whether this is between siblings, or between parents, as all too often it results in violence, and sometimes family breakups.

☺☺☹☺☺☹☺☺☹☺☺☹☺☺☹

Chapter 7

PROBLEMS IN THE EDUCATION SYSTEM

*Whereas a rattle is a suitable occupation for infant children,
education serves as a rattle for young people when older.*
Aristotle, Politics book 8 (1340 BC).

*Indeed one of the ultimate advantages of an education
is simply coming to an end of it.*
B.F. Skinner, The Technology of Teaching (1968).

'It's never too early to start teaching our kids',
The Weekend Australian, Aug. 13-14, 2011.

Preschool education

It is important to take advantage of the rapid brain development in infants by providing them with a stimulating environment which should include a 'personal learning centre' (PLC) that includes educational pictures and toys.

By the second year they should be involved in small learning groups supervised by a specialist teacher so that they can begin real learning (Packard, 1978). In the third year they should begin kindergarten for at least a couple of days a week and these learning efforts should continue. By now they have a modest vocabulary and are capable of *cognitive learning* which processes and stores *abstract* information.

At this stage deliberate effort should be made at 'IQ building', noting that IQ tests include questions testing verbal, spatial and numerical ability. If a child has a problem with numbers, for example, early detection and correction of this will prevent far greater problems later.

Then, given a head start, they should commence school at age four, rather than the usual five in most countries.

Shortening the school program

No better example of *Parkinson's Law* exists than in education. Parkinson's Law is simply (Parkinson, 1980):

Work expands so as to fill the time available for its completion.

Leonardo da Vinci and Michelangelo were apprenticed at age 14 and Francis Bacon went to Cambridge University at age 12 and left at age 14.

The development of modern science from the 16th and 17th centuries is, perhaps, one of the reasons for the considerable growth in the number of years required at school.

Nevertheless, our system of 12 years at school is far too drawn out and should be reduced to 10 years for the 'average' student, this involving six years at primary school and four at secondary school.

Here the curriculum for the last four secondary years could remain much as now so that reduction to 10 years would be achieved by condensation of the first eight years of the 12 year system to six.

This might simply involve

(a) Making preschool education compulsory and thus removing the need for at least the first year at school.

(b) Acceleration of the learning of the three R's in the first few years and elimination of most unnecessary material.

The result should be better educated and brighter children who will be better prepared for life and the faster pace of tertiary courses.

Less fragmentation

Classes at both school and University are usually scheduled in a somewhat haphazard fashion so that hours of subjects A, B and C appear as A, B, C, A, B, C and so on. This results in a 'parade of clowns' effect that does more to confuse students than anything else.

The first author has always found it better to, for example, give two lectures consecutively, rather than at almost random times in the week a day or more apart.

This has the advantages of:

[1] Saving students &/or staff a good deal of inconvenience.

[2] It results in better learning because more *proactive interference* and less *retroactive interference* occurs (Morgan et al., 1979).

[3] A break of about 10 or 15 minutes is allowed in the middle and this provides a good opportunity for questions and discussion.

[4] The result is a more mature and friendly seminar approach and more motivated, inquiring and effective students.

Similarly, in the first years of school it might be better to tackle the 12 times tables, for example, by devoting a few weeks to it, rather than spreading it over years.

Then if the learning task is returned to a week or two later it should be found that *latent learning* has occurred and good progress has been made.

Indeed, it might be a good idea in later school years to fit classes into four days to allow students a fifth week day to do homework. If unnecessary activities were removed as far as possible then, for example, just half an hour more of formal classes per day might allow all the required class work to be fitted into four days.

Application of this less fragmentary approach is possible at University when students might have four or five subjects with one day of the week dedicated to each, rather than having them randomly spread throughout the week in bits and pieces.

University courses

There has been excessive proliferation in new University courses. My father, also an academic, used to joke about there being degrees in bee keeping in the USA. At the more reputable Universities there this may not, in fact, be the case. In Australia, however, this has come to pass with degrees where none were needed before, examples being journalism, marketing, nursing and viticulture.

There has also been a plethora of new postgraduate certificates and diplomas and Masters Degrees. Some of these, such as courses in Sexology, Puppetry or Citizenship studies are either lightweight, absurd or both.

Material that is really essential should have been included in undergraduate courses.

Some so-called postgraduate courses, on the other hand, introduce an entirely new vocational area. If these are all that is required in these areas then these courses should be offered as relatively short undergraduate certificate or diploma courses.

That we have masters "courses" at all is questionable. Mastership in Universities took its meaning from the Master status conferred by the craft-guilds of 500 or more years ago and was given after a relatively short period of teaching experience. Consequently, Cambridge and Oxford award Masters Degrees on completion of undergraduate courses.

Why then do 'latter day' Universities enslave their students for a couple of further years in usually redundant, if not frivolous Masters Degrees?

The answer undoubtedly comes in two parts:

(a) The education bureaucrats are ignorant.

(b) Simply money. The longer the education process, the more "products" and the more money to be made.

Research degrees may also be questionable. As just noted, Masters degrees as separate and additional courses are redundant. As for PhDs, historically these were awarded for further self-study, usually by academics. This involves no teaching so it is absurd that graduates are enrolled as "students" and then used as slave labour at the whim of supervisors for often impractical, if not useless, research topics.

TAFE

TAFE, an acronym for Technical and Further Education that originated in the UK, is an important alternative to University for school leavers. Here students are trained for the *real* occupations in the basic industries essential to human life, that is, food, clothing and shelter.

In contrast, and increasingly so, University courses are, strictly speaking, unnecessary. In other words we can usually live without a doctor or lawyer, house builders can usually do without an architect or engineer if need be. People used to run businesses without business degrees and we certainly don't need degrees in Sexology and Puppetry.

Many TAFE courses are part-time ones for apprentices. Unfortunately, many apprenticeships are unreasonably long and bordering on exploitation of a cheap labour source.

An example are hairdressing apprenticeships which take up to 6 years in Australia, certainly too long when most us would think a couple of weeks training would suffice.

Another looming problem is the introduction of diploma and degree courses in business to TAFE institutes when absurd numbers of people already do these in the Universities. Even MBA courses, let alone undergraduate business courses, are lightweight material that could and should be taught at school.

Problems in education

There are many problems in the education sector today, including: [1] Children being incarcerated in long-day-care centres which, cruelly, do little more than expensive babysitting almost from birth. This is an inhuman practice that reduces children to toys that amuse parents after work, a sick situation that must do more harm than good.

[2] As the discussion of brain development in infants in Chapter 3 points out, the early years are a critical time that should not be lost. Weiss and Mann (1978), for example, refer to a project in Milwaukee that found that children given more attention by the mother or a specially trained teacher, showed markedly higher IQ.

This is no doubt the reason that only children tend to have higher IQ and that, in families with more than one child, the eldest child has a slightly higher IQ on average (Vernon, 1960). The youngest child in larger families, on the other hand, does not do too badly compared to those 'sandwiched' in the middle and perhaps most deprived of attention.

[3] As noted earlier, 12 years at school is too long and 10 years would be a more sensible norm.

[4] There is far too much rote learning at school.

[5] Poor teacher training. Sykes (1995) reports widespread disillusionment with modern teacher training, much of which is a hotchpotch of psychology, sociology and history that cannot develop real expertise in any of these areas.
He cites several examples of recent doctorates in education being granted for dissertations with such titles as:
"The use of goal setting and positive self-modeling to enhance self-efficiency and performance for the basketball free-throw shot" for a PhD at the University of Maryland.
After such largely useless studies, Sykes laments, 'educrats' move into educational administration and oversee a decline in standards over the whole spectrum of education comparable to that evidenced by their largely irrelevant doctoral studies.

[6] Declining academic standards. A survey of 24,000 students in twelve countries by the Educational Testing Service in Princeton found that, compared to 40% of US students scoring at the 500 level in a standard test, the results were 78% for Korea, 73% for Quebec and 69% for British Columbia (Sykes, 1995). A similar decline in standards has occurred in Australia.

[7] In the USA outcome based education (OBE) has gone a long way towards disallowing fail grades, instead allowing students to retake tests until they pass. The idea of this is to avoid attaching negative labels to students, and much effort is also made to avoid attaching positive labels to the brightest students as well.

[8] Similarly, OBE eschews 'tracking' to permit accelerated learning for gifted students, despite conclusive evidence of its positive results, in this way ensuring that the overall standard of education is lowered further.

[9] In the USA new 'soft' approaches to teaching and grading reading and maths have led to a dramatic decline in literacy and numeracy skills.

[10] Drugs for school-age children. The overlong school education system should bore anyone with half a brain. To make matters worse increasing numbers of 'unruly' children are diagnosed with such doubtful disorders as Attention Deficit Hyperactivity Disorder (ADHD) and prescribed drugs such as Ritalin to sedate them.

In the USA and Australia in turn, increasingly large numbers of children suffer this fate. Reports of up to 15% or more children in some areas being on such drugs have not brought action to curb this disturbing trend as yet, but visions of a future society in which both parents and children have to be drugged to cope are unacceptable.

[11] Overgrown educational bureaucracy. In the US in 1960 one third of education employees were not classroom teachers. By 1991 46.7% were non-teaching staff and the teaching staff's share of the total payroll had shrunk from 54% to 41%. Much the same has occurred in England and Australia both in school and tertiary education.

[12] Growing up faster. Today's young, thanks to better nutrition grow faster than in the past. Da Vinci observed that children were half their ultimate height at age three. Now that figure is about 55%. Along with that, in part because of the ubiquitous media today, in many ways they mature faster than ever before.

Many children by their mid-teens, therefore, are becoming bored with school and drop out. Robertson (1981), for example, reported that 100,000 assaults against teachers occur in US schools each year. Doubtless this is one of several factors that contribute to the increasing discipline problem in schools.

[13] There are far too many assignments, tests etc. at school and University. When the first author was an undergraduate and teaching in Universities in Australasia there were 8 subjects in second year engineering, yet in Engineering Maths students were given sheets full of problems each week.

It should be all about showing *how* to do things and giving *answers*, not asking endless questions. At Auckland University these maths problem sheets often involved 2 or 3 different areas lectured by different people, an absurd situation.

Including the secretary who typed them, up to four morons helped fill their week redoing these sheets each year, a fine example of Parkinson's Law for both the staff and students.

Needless to say:

(a) The staff were simply a pathetic, mindless bunch of no-hopers who had never, and never will, achieve anything.

(b) The students were somewhat demoralized. Eight Uni. subjects in a year is too much, let alone being asked to spend up to several hours on the worse than useless homework for just one of them.

[14] Many University courses overlap with school. At Auckland University, for example, top school leavers were exempted from the first year of the course. Q: Why on earth, therefore, was that year needed at all? A: To employ a few more dumb academics.

[15] The ridiculous University courses like those in sexology were mentioned earlier in the chapter. MBAs etc. are not much better and are now so common that with an MBA one might now only be able to gain employment as a salesperson, if that.

To establish a coursework Masters Degree course that was efficient and fairly quick, in the mid-1990s I wrote an entire MBA course involving 14 subjects ranging from business finance, economics, maths and OR, IT and numerical methods, to the more lightweight areas of BP (business policy), business law, HRM, and advertising.

Each subject had 12 – 14 lectures in it, so the course could be done in as little as 14 weeks if one did one subject per week, though part-time study would take from 2 to 4 times longer.

The concise lecture notes came to about 400 somewhat cramped pages and I tried to publish this course with major publishers without luck, but was pleased that an editor at Heinemann agreed with my proposition that, a lucrative Harvard invention, MBA courses could now be found *"on every street corner,"* yet another example of how the USA has debased the education system.

A final edition of the course, however, was recently published as *The Scientific MBA* (Mohr, 2017).

[16] Once upon a time correspondence courses were poorly regarded. We are such slaves to fashion, and thence brainwashing, that the morons in Universities are happy to run courses by *distance education* over the Internet.

[17] There is insufficient emphasis on developing inquiring minds capable of finding answers to their own questions, rather than zombies so used to endless rote learning and tests that they have become too tired and bored to care about anything but going through the motions of life as perpetual consumers and slaves to big businesses that produce and sell mass marketed consumer products.

"Inefficiency" in schools

Australia's ABC Radio National "Life Matters" program at 4.45 AM on 27/3/2019 discussed the case of an 11-year-old schoolgirl who was doing well at school but felt that schools were "inefficient" etc., the problem being that being able to do her schoolwork quickly, she felt there was too much time left with nothing to do.

Her mother was thus worried about the difficulties she might encounter having to keep her daughter at school until year 10.

A psychologist and teacher advised that the girl be given extra-curricular activities to help make school more interesting for her, and that she be advised to consider ways in which she could "contribute" to the school.

Here then is an example of the boredom many students suffer in our excessively long and drawn-out education system, resulting in many of them indulging in harmful activities ranging from bullying to taking up smoking and experimenting with alcohol and drugs.

Indeed, the excessively long 12+ years at school, along with the plethora of sometimes ridiculous tertiary course, is an excellent example of Parkinson's Law that: *Work expands so as to fill the time available for its completion* (see Chapter 13 for further discussion of this), and also an example of 'job creation' for teachers and 'money making' for Universities etc.

Bullying in schools

The Australian SBS TV network Insight program at 8.30 PM on 26/3/2019, and hosted by Jenny Brockie, interviewed several school students in the audience about their experiences of bullying, some of the results being:

> ➤ A year 3 student said that she had been alone with no one to play with and that, when one group let her play with them, they bullied her by calling her "gross", "stupid" etc.

> ➤ A girl in year 8 said that a new girl had been "alone" and that a "group" had bullied her.

> ➤ One boy said that during years 3 to 5 he was "excluded" and called a "dog", "snitch" etc. Advised to "tell someone", he did so, and the bullying stopped.

> ➤ One girl reported that two years previously her cousin, aged 13, had "suicided herself", saying "bullying doesn't lead you to anywhere", that every life is precious, and people should stop bullying.

> ➤ Another young student said that one could "take away the power" of bullies by ignoring them.

> ➤ The principal of Yarra Valley School said: "All schools have an anti-bullying program".

The PBS Newshour shown on SBS TV at 1PM on 26/3/2019 reported on a school in the US where there had been two suicides, and it was reported that they had been victims of bullying and had "survivor guilt" and PTSD.

This raised the question of whether school shooting incidents were sometimes by victims of bullying, and an example of this was given in the first section of Chapter 5.

It was also concluded that victims of bullying should receive treatment for PTSD, depression etc.

Personal experiences

I recall being bullied a few times at the private primary school Grimwade House, a campus of Melbourne Grammar School. One situation was in 4th grade when myself and another student, both new to the school, finished regular arithmetic tests much quicker than the rest of the class, also getting top marks (the other student ultimately became a Rhodes scholar, whereas I did my PhD at Cambridge, getting special permission to submit in 2 years rather than 3 (in fact I submitted after 23 months).

As reward for finishing the tests quickly the teacher let us out to relax on the school sports oval while the rest of the class completed the tests. At the end of the lunchtime break one day another somewhat chubby student, obviously jealous, sat on me to stop be getting back to class on time.

He repeated this ridiculous exercise once or twice and, many years later, became a lawyer, ending up working at Melbourne University.

Another incident I recall easily was when playing an 'inter-house' cricket match. I took a good catch close to the stumps to catch a boy out when playing cricket. After the match had finished he came up to me in the locker rooms and arrogantly asked: "How tall are you?"

I told him, and he replied: "I didn't know they piled shit that high".

He also became a lawyer, ending up as a QC (Queen's Counsel).

Conclusions

Australia is probably the most Americanized country in the world and our education system, particularly in the Universities, has certainly become farcical. There it is no longer a matter of education but one of highly paid 'educrats' who have never done anything significant overseeing invention of increasingly ludicrous courses to advertise to increase the size of the University.

From birth to death it is all corporate stuff at the day care centre, school and University and, increasingly, those being brainwashed pay for the privilege.

With the invention of more silly courses students are expected to study longer and longer.

During the first author's undergraduate student days a lecturer explained that, owing to the *time value of money*, we would not in our lifetimes make as much money as a plumber who had started work at 15, even if we were paid substantially more. Plumbers make more money now than they did then!

If your parents spent a lot of money on a private school education the comparison is even worse. Unless they were rich they should have spent just a little of that money to give you the edge at a government school. The rest they should have invested at a good interest rate to buy you a shop in which to start up a lucrative business.

Then you might not need to go to University to study Accountancy, Architecture, Engineering, Dentistry, Law, or Medicine, businesses in which it really is best if you start up your own practice/business in any case.

As for postgraduate study, this is a form of slave labour. The first author recalls a physicist saying *"You're past your best at 26."* True of nearly all bludging academics who regurgitate from some text book they don't understand and sit on their backsides while graduate students do their research for them.

Perhaps the long drawn-out umpteen and excessive number of years at school, and the farcically excessive number of tertiary courses and degrees that now exists, most of them replacing far more efficient in many cases 'on the job training' and apprenticeships, could be summed up by the handwritten label I saw on a flagon of wine at a barbecue in Churchill College (Cambridge) one Sunday afternoon in 1975: the label read: *Regurgitation juice*, which I took to mean that lecturers 'regurgitated' from text books, and then students from notes etc. given by lecturers at exam time.

☺ ☺ ☹ ☺ ☺ ☺ ☹ ☺ ☺ ☹ ☺ ☺ ☹ ☺ ☺ ☹

Chapter 8

THE WORKPLACE

> *People ask the difference between a leader and a boss.*
> *The leader works in the open, and the boss in covert.*
> *The leader leads, and the boss drives.*
> Theodore Roosevelt, speech 24 Oct. 1910, Binghamton N.Y.

Introduction

In the workplace leadership or management style, and communication are important issues. The following chapter briefly discusses some of the key requirements for good leadership, and how good communication and group loyalty improve workplace performance.

Leadership

According to Bennis (1989), becoming a leader involves:

➢ Ongoing curiosity and learning.

➢ A motivational vision.

➢ Communicating that vision to inspire others to follow it.

➢ Being prepared to take risks.

➢ Maturity, honesty, and willingness to accept criticism.

➢ Searching for solutions to problems.

➢ Seeking success in small, incremental steps rather than waiting years for "Big Success".

In *The One Minute Manager* three keys to good management are proposed:

1. Agree on up to 6 goals with staff and put them in writing.

2. Staff should provide detailed records of progress to management.

3. When there is a lack of progress, management feedback should focus on any poor results, not the persons responsible, and should encourage staff to keep trying (Blanchard & Johnson, 1981).

Leadership and group performance

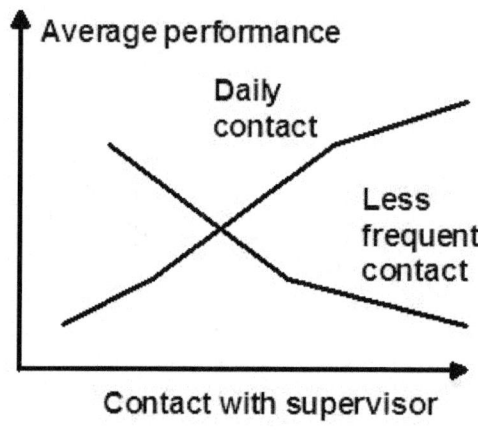

Figure 8.1. Communication with management.

Formal communication within a company will tend to follow the corporate structure. Effective communication can considerably improve productivity and morale.

Figure 8.1 shows the results of a study of the relationship between mean or average performance (or productivity) and amount of contact with the group supervisor. Clearly relatively frequent and regular management contact improves productivity as one would expect (Mohr, 2014b, 2018d).

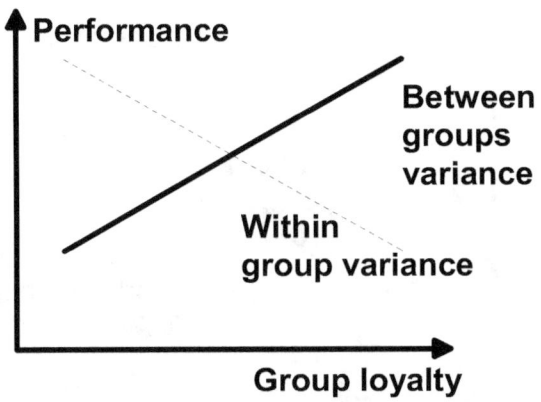

Figure 8.2. Performance and communication
with boss vs. group loyalty.

Figure 8.2 shows the type of result obtained in a correlation of worker performance and group loyalty, indicating that productivity improves if group loyalty is high. In part this improvement results from the (necessary) emergence of 'team leadership'.

The study of Figure 8.2 also found that correlation between the proportion of workers who took their complaints to the boss and group loyalty took the same form (that shown).

In addition, the correlation between how easy the group found communication with the boss and group loyalty also took the same (ascending) form shown in Figure 8.2.

Effective communication (and hence loyalty) within the group and with the supervisor, therefore, both lead to improved productivity. In addition group loyalty improves communication with the supervisor, that is, the factors of group loyalty, amount of supervisor communication, quality of supervisor communication, and productivity are all interwoven in such a way as to suggest that if communication is optimized considerable improvements in productivity might result.

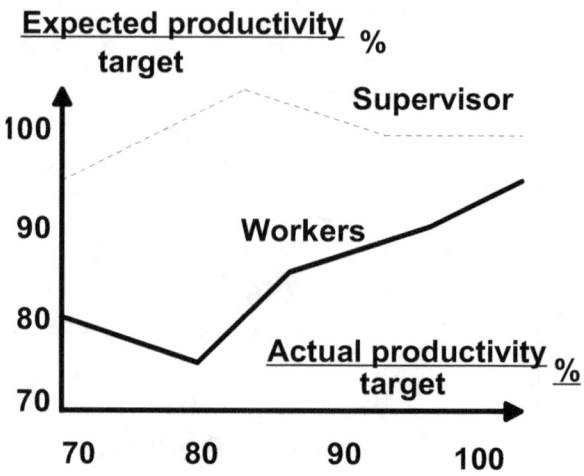

Figure 8.3. Expected vs. actual productivity

Figure 8.3 shows expected productivity compared to actual productivity for both the supervisor and the workers. Clearly the expectations of the supervisor are greater than those of the workers and are always fairly close to the target productivity.

The expectations of the workers, on the other hand, are for improvement when productivity is low and for slowing down when productivity is high, and are perhaps more realistic.

Unfortunately, however, there is no data from this study on the correlation between supervisor and worker expectations though this, of course, would depend on communications and, in any case, productivity variation is our main concern.

Figure 8.4 shows the results of a study of the effect of attitude of supervisor on productivity. There was a considerable spread in the results but there was sufficient correlation to support the finding that the more favourable the attitude of the supervisor (to both the workers and the job) the greater the productivity, as one might expect.

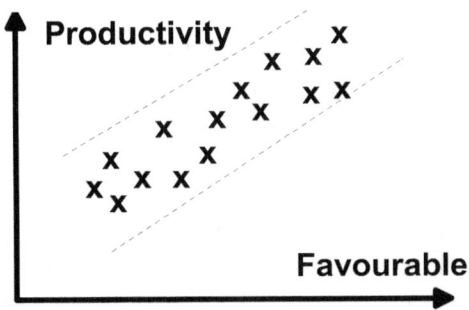

Figure 8.4. Dependence of productivity on supervisor attitude.

We might also expect that favourable supervisor attitude results in more favourable worker attitude and that the latter also results in greater productivity.

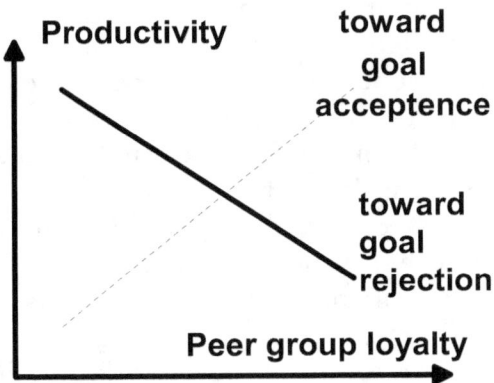

Figure 8.5. Loyalty towards company goals vs. productivity

Figure 8.5 shows the relationship of peer group loyalty to productivity when motivation is towards accepting versus rejecting company goals. Clearly peer group loyalty towards company goals results in greater productivity as one would expect.

The results of Figure 8.5 are related to those of Figure 8.2, showing that group loyalty is a very important factor in productivity.

8. THE WORKPLACE

Personal Experiences in Melbourne

Having graduated BE with 1st honours I spent 18 months doing a M.Eng.Sci. degree which was half coursework and half research, completing this in mid-1970.

Then in 1970 – 1971 I got two consecutive jobs doing consulting structural engineering (leaving the first because the boss said he was in financial difficulty), also doing part-time consulting for my eldest brother, an architecture and building graduate who had started his own business after losing his job with a building company on the grounds it was going 'broke'.

In mid-1970 I saw the boss of the 2nd/larger consulting biz I was then working in abusing one of his staff, I was told later because this man did part-time work for other people, and the boss resented this. Coincidence indeed, that day I had a job application in my briefcase, so at lunch time I posted it.

I got the job, this being as Lecturer at Caulfield Institute of Technology (CIT), and found lecturing easy once one had one's lecture notes written, leaving plenty of time for personal research, which I then began to do in various areas, including the Finite Element Method (FEM), in which I was eventually to 'make a name' internationally via 2 books on the subject.

At the end of 1971 the HOD hit 65, and a new HOD was appointed. He was a Queenslander with a PhD from Imperial College London, who I shall hereafter call Dillmer.

I recall no problems with him until after I'd taken a couple of years off to do a PhD at Cambridge, working very hard every night in the computer centre to get more work on FEM through the computer system.

Back at CIT in 1977 I began to suffer bullying, beginning with the Principal Lecturer raving at me that my work was "too theoretical". Then a senior lecturer assigned me the job of organizing the coffee for visitors to the college Open Day, clearly a dig at me because he'd heard I liked a drink via my wife's habitual gossiping behind my back.

Then one day in 1979 the HOD joked:

It must be hard having a Cambridge PhD and only being a lecturer, almost as bad as being HOD and having a PhD from Imperial College.

Another staff member at the same, competing for promotion, level (i.e., at the top of Lecturer scale) did two strange things that classify as bullying according to Chapter 5:

(a) I bought for the department a portable terminal to access the institute's mainframe computer via a phone line so that I could use it at home sometimes, rather than stay late at work to do computing, as I did many a night in my first year back from Cambridge, 1977. This colleague put this terminal in a locked cupboard in his office for ? reason, which I found odd.

(b) I lent him a book on the subject I had researched from 1972, and in Cambridge, namely the Finite Element Method (FEM). This too he hid in that locked cupboard. One day in 1979, when I was about to start work on what turned out to be the first edition of what came to be known (to me) as 'the tome' (a book I finally got out as 4th or 5th edn with OUP in 1992), I asked if I could have this book back. He replied that he had it at his home. A couple of days later I walked into his office and, because that usually locked cupboard was open at the time, could see that my book was, indeed, in it. Such hiding/stealing of my work materials was, of course, a form of bullying.

Another colleague, also on the top of the Lecturer scale and about 6 years older than me was, no doubt, impatient for promotion. A couple of months after I'd suggested to the HOD that I would joint my first FEM book effort with him (an offer which I later retracted, as noted below) I saw a note on this colleague's desk saying something about a "bribe" for promotion, which I took to refer to my offer of 'book-jointing' to the HOD. Sadly, that influenced me in changing my mind about it, as noted below, and this was, perhaps, a mistake.

For the sake of my career etc., I should have put the HOD's name on the book, as that would most certainly have helped get it published, and I had plenty of years ahead in which I could do another book, which indeed I did do a few years later (Mohr & M----, 1986/87), also getting the initial book idea done, although with an early almost doubling in size at the suggestion of a reviewer, then condensing it to almost half the size again, and then gradually expanding it to cover new areas and finally getting it out with OUP in 1992 (Mohr, 1992).

8. THE WORKPLACE

Personal Experiences in Auckland

Having had enough bullying etc. at CIT, in mid 1980 I took up a lecturing job in the rare, if not ridiculous, Theoretical and Applied Mechanics (TAM) Department at Auckland University.

There, the day before the University closed for Christmas, a staff member walked into my office and said:

What did you come to New Zealand for, to get away from your family and take drugs?

I'm sure this was payback via Dillmer back in Melbourne at CIT because the day before Christmas in 1979 I 'cancelled' a plan to 'joint' a book with him, and I recall his secretary then mumbling about there being a lot drugs in New Zealand.

The offender had an Irish surname, as did one of the 2 Associate Professors in the department, and one day I joked that the Irish were taking over the department.

The Associate Prof. got back at me in a staff meeting by mumbling about "nasty Jewish-German names".

Things then went from bad to worse.

The HOD that appointed me retired at the end of 1980, and after I'd been there only 6 months, and a new HOD with a maths PhD from Cambridge was appointed.

Over the long end of year/new year academic break I condensed the 2nd, almost doubled in size 2nd edition of my FEM 'tome' to about 60% of its size, having been knocked back by CUP's syndicate (the editor Simon Mitton OK'ed it).

The almost doubling occurred after I sent the first circa 300 pp effort to Mitton. The first reviewer OK'ed it, but the second did not, his 5 page rave review complaining on several minor/irrelevant points and finally concluding that I should do a "treatise" of "perhaps two volumes".

I am sure this raving bully was the same person who had been the external examiner for the "viva" for my PhD, a Cambridge PhD bod at a campus of U Wales,

At the viva he picked me up on a minor point and I corrected it and resubmitted, at the same time proving that he and an Indian PhD student slave had 'fiddled' their 'too good to be true' results in a paper on FEM.

Indeed, my PhD supervisor turned up at my Churchill College flat one day to take away my calculations that proved this 'fiddling' of results, i.e. a cover up!

Anyhow, after so much hassle already over this book, shortening it in my early months in Auckland was a miserable job, but I felt so disillusioned already in the 'really a Maths department' TAM department that I felt I could not be bothered photocopying a longer book to send to other publishers.

Having shortened and updated this FEM 'tome' I paid myself to make a couple of photocopies of it. Then I packaged one of these copies to post to Bruce Irons, who I regarded as one of the leading researchers in FEM at the time.

Another colleague, who'd done a PhD on biomechanics at Oxford and thus had an interest in FEM (and we had shared the lectures in a postgraduate FEM subject run in my first 6 months in Auckland) then stole the large envelope containing the book copy from the department secretary's office while she was watching.

The culprit colleague, however, then proceeded to give the aging lady secretary exceedingly complicated maths equations pages to type which, in the end, resulted in her resigning.

I'm sure that he did this deliberately so that he could, I presume, complain about her to the new HOD so that he would suggest to her that she quit. This, however, was bullying in the extreme.

The other copy of the book I sent to MacMillan's and it was again rejected because of a negative review by a New Zealander who had applied unsuccessfully for the vacant HOD job a few months earlier, myself having been one of the selection committee.

In the following couple of years the new Cambridge clod HOD made my life hell, first by holding up my long overdue and 'notified in writing' promotion to Senior Lecturer for a year, then for another, and then for a third, in the meantime bullying me with, for example:

(a) Saying one day: "Civil Engineers are stupid" – his job was to lecture maths to Engineers of all sub-disciplines, and I should have 'dobbed him in' for this remark.

(b) On hearing of my jointing my FEM book with my ex-HOD back in Melbourne, saying in the corridor: "Another lousy lecturer" (he was a far worse lecturer, in fact, and his research work was virtually useless).

The excuse (in writing) for holding up my long overdue promotion was that "all" (an obvious lie) the students had "difficulty in getting their questions answered." He believed that one should only have to "write a few equations" on the board, whereas, doing as I had become accustomed to as a UG and PG student, I wrote circa three pages of lecture notes on the board, leaving relatively little time to ask for and answer questions, but I hardly ever had a single question in any case because, of course, I had given students all they needed in my notes, but I do remember one joke question during a lecture.

In hindsight it is clear that the BS about my not answering questions came from the "What did you come to New Zealand for - - ?" staff member mentioned at the start of this section. Upset by that episode (one in which I did not, of course, answer his insulting question), I complained to the new HOD about it, a complaint that no doubt just made my position worse.

One or two other colleagues may also have contributed to the BS about my not answering questions, one barging into my office one day with a stupid question on a subject I knew nothing about, and leaving in bad temper when I did not answer it. One day the HOD told me he was going to leave, and he was very surprised when I told him of this, but in the end he did leave not long after I left, no doubt also 'pushed' etc.

I also well recall, that I was looking forward to the day that I had a published book on FEM that I could base my lectures on, and that students would buy it so that we could all avoid the tedium of transcription. Having already written short 2-3 day or 'few evenings' courses on FEM in 1978 and 1981 for professional engineers I should, perhaps, have used those for UG and PG lectures.

As it happened, however, after doing half of one PG subject on FEM in my first 6 months, there were no 'takers' when I was scheduled to do the whole course myself in 1981, and I only gave about 10 – 20 undergraduate lectures on FEM thereafter in Auckland.

Instead, I ended up lecturing and doing tutorials in incredibly boring second year Maths, a largely useless first year subject run by the Mech. Eng. Dept, and other odds and ends, all an incredibly boring and largely useless exercise of little relevance to my main areas of expertise at the time, that is, Structural Mechanics and FEM (I have since learnt a lot about other subjects such as optimization techniques and Systems Analysis, and Fluid Mechanics, in conjunction with my extensive FEM research, writing dozens of papers about them).

Having held up my promotion for one year (i.e. from mid-1981 to 82), the new fat, boozing Cambridge clod HOD continued holding it up.

In the end, in late 1984 he quite illegally suggested he'd pay me a few months in advance to cover my expenses in quitting and moving back to Melbourne and, quite worn down by the bullying etc. by then, I agreed and, with nobody to talk to, put in my letter of resignation to the Dean and VC.

Returning to Melbourne at the end of 1984 with wife and 2 sons in tow (then 5 and 11), I never got another job, largely because the new Cambridge clod HOD in Auckland wrote backstabbing 'confidential' references about me, as I realized with hindsight several years later when I reflected on comment at the first job interview I had in mid-1985, and in a couple of other interviews thereafter.

More detail on this 'academic crucifixion' is given in Appendix B.

8. THE WORKPLACE

An example of a workplace bully

In early April 2019 Australia's ABC2 TV channel's '7.30' current affairs program reported on a "shock jock" on Sydney's Radio 2GB who was reported as:

> ➤ "Off air he is really a ferocious human being".
> ➤ "Scary".
> ➤ "His on-air style is really bullying – he is demonstrating power".
> ➤ Calling people a "wanker" etc. on air.
> ➤ Having fits of rage.
> ➤ Making violent threats.
> ➤ Having negative effects on people, but few of them came forward to tell about them.

A former radio colleague who had known him since childhood reported that:

> ➤ "He's a bully – thrives on intimidation – has done since he was a kid".
> ➤ Visiting his house one day he lost his temper and "ripped the machine [a tape recorder or other 'media device'] out and smashed it into the wall".
> ➤ The "shock jock's" behavior had affected his mental health.
> ➤ One night his wife had told him not to talk about the bullying he was enduring and to go to bed.

During the ABC interview he cried, saying that a psychologist had told him that he was suffering from anxiety.

He said that this was a symptom of 4.5 years of bullying, and that he was "still stressed" and his (psychological) condition was having an effect on his "wife and kids".

He said that he blamed "2GB management for not acting" and that:

> ➤ "I just think there are so many people who have been bullied by him".
> ➤ He is a "deeply flawed human being".

Another person interviewed told of a panel operator at the radio station who the 'shock jock' had called off-air a "f---head" and "f---wit" during a program. When the operator complained at the end of the program the shock jock said (about 'winding up' the program etc.): "Just do it or find another job".

When told of complaints about him, the 'shock jock' said the complainant was a "f---ing idiot" etc.

The operator told the ABC interviewer that he thought the shock jock was "an alcoholic" who was "self-medicating".

Another person interviewed said that he "felt like vomiting" after dealing with the shock jock.

It was reported that 2GB "paid out" an employee when he had given management recordings of the shock jock's bullying.

I was also reported that some people believed that he had influenced politicians by using "threats" etc. when trying to have a ban on greyhound racing (because of mistreatment and drugging of greyhounds) overturned.

Surviving in the workplace

In Table 9.1 I score two bad bosses who did much to ruin my life, giving further details of my 'academic crucifixion' in Appendix B.

One key problem was, having had an important promotion unfairly and dishonestly delayed, and then been bullied into resigning.

Had I talked to another colleague about the issue, however, I would have been advised not to resign, but to get help in dealing with the new HOD who had caused me problems.

Indeed, when doing my PhD in Cambridge in 1975 – 76, I talked to my supervisor of returning to Australia to finish it in May of 1976. He advised me against this, so I stayed, submitting my thesis in December 1976, adding a couple of pages of addenda after the 'viva' about a month later.

There is, of course, an important lesson to be learnt from these two contrasting experiences.

Conclusion

Besides those conclusions already made in the foregoing discussion, the following recommendations are suggested as worthwhile by the results of Figures 8.1 – 8.5:

[1] There should be effective communication of productivity goals.

[2] There should be thorough assessment of productivity results.

[3] Groups and tasks with low productivity should be identified.

[4] Group loyalty should be encouraged and groups should be motivated to accept new staff and 'loners' in a group.

[5] Leadership audits should be used.

[6] Supervisors should exhibit favourable attitude and communicate frequently and regularly with their staff.

[7] Group loyalty toward company goals should be sought.

[8] Supervisors should make themselves freely available to staff with complaints and other feedback and make themselves easy to communicate with.

Generally, therefore, good leadership involving sufficient efficient communication of goals and team attitudes is likely to result in very considerable improvements in productivity.

It is also important that measurements are made, however, of productivity, group loyalty and management efficiency. The results will then be useful in identifying problems requiring correction and productivity results when favourable, for example, can be used as motivational information for supervisors and their groups (Mohr, 2014b, 2018d).

Such measurements should, of course, include assessment of bad behaviours in the workplace, including harassment, bullying, and sexual harassment and abuse, the latter being found to be a widespread problem thanks to the emergence of the ME TOO movement.

☺ ☺ ☹ ☺ ☺ ☺ ☹ ☺ ☺ ☹ ☺ ☺ ☹ ☺ ☺ ☹

Chapter 9

HIERARCHICAL ORGANIZATIONS

> *I'm the boss. I'm allowed to yell.*
> Ivan Boesky, q. in *Den of* Thieves, James B Stewart, 1991.
>
> *In every one of those little stucco boxes there's some poor bastard*
> *who's never free except when he's fast asleep*
> *and dreaming that he's got the boss down the bottom*
> *of a well and is bunging lumps of coal at him.*
> George Orwell, *Coming Up For Air,* pt 1., ch. 2 (1939).

Corporate structure

Corporate structure is the hierarchical structure and communication channels giving rise to the chain of command and response in a company or organization.

Most companies have a functional structure, larger companies having a divisional structure, with a functional structure for each division, as in the example of Figure 9.1.

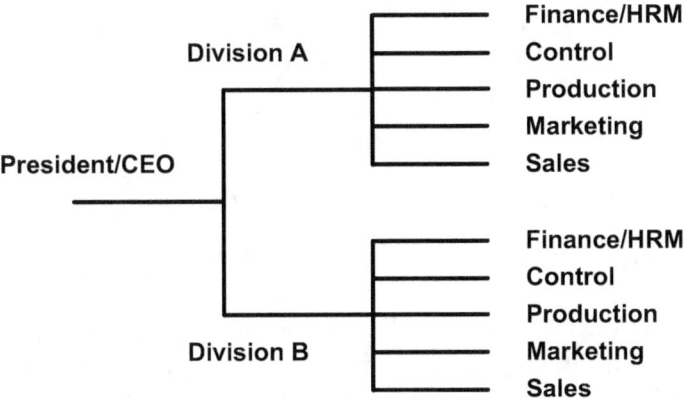

Figure 9.1. Divisional corporate structure.

109

The Peter Principle

Dr Laurence Peter drew on his experiences in the education sector to try and explain why we always seem to have lousy leaders (Peter & Hull, 1969). The result was his celebrated *Peter Principle:*

In a hierarchy every employee tends to rise to his own level of incompetence.

In other words, *the sour cream rises.*

A corollary is: *In time every post tends to be occupied by an employee who is incompetent to carry out his duties.*

In his often tongue-in-cheek book Peter gives a few excellent historical examples of his celebrated principle, including:

(a) Socrates was a brilliant philosopher but a lousy defence attorney.

(b) Hitler was a brilliant politician but a lousy general.

Mohr's Law of Hierarchies

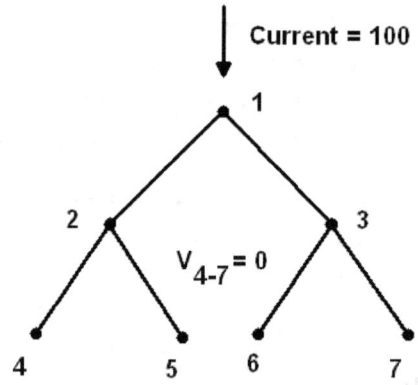

Figure 9.1. Hierarchical network.

This can illustrated by the small (hierarchical) DC network shown in Figure 9.1 which can be modeled as a DC network using a simple Finite Element Method program (Mohr, 1992, 2012a, 2018e).

At node 1 we have the pyramid building and lunatic 'boss' and a current 'load' of 100 is input. This is done by specifying the voltage at node 1 as 100, this being equivalent to adding a 'load' to the network.

Then zero datum voltage is specified at nodes 4-7 and unit resistance is given to all 6 elements so that the results from the program are:

Voltage 75 at node 1.
Voltage 25 at nodes 2 and 3.
Zero voltage at nodes 4 to 7.
Currents 50 in the top two elements and 25 in the rest.

This illustrates what the 'econobabble' of economists and politicians calls 'the trickledown effect', that is, the boss of this very small hierarchy has 3 times the voltage (or power, money and status) of his subordinates (the front line managers) one rung below. The workers at the bottom have no status at all.

If we add a further bottom row of 8 nodes in Figure 9.1 then now the 'voltage hierarchy' is 87.5, 37.5, 12.5, 0 so that the boss now does 7 times as well as the 'front line managers' on the row above the bottom row.

Then if we add a further fifth row of 16 nodes the voltage hierarchy is 93.75, 43.75, 18.75, 6.25, 0 and the boss does 15 times as well as the front line managers and infinitely better than the workers at the bottom!

The latter 'voltage hierarchy' is the fundamental principle of modern management, leading to Mohr's Law of Hierarchies:

In hierarchical organizations the amount of real material-producing work people do is inversely proportional to their rank or level in the organization.
The amount of compensation they receive, however, is proportional to their level, sometimes to an exponential degree.

For such people their earnings might be expressed as an exponential function: $\$ = C \exp(kR)$

where $\$$ = salary, R = rank, and C and k are constants.

This, of course, is not fair at all.

In ancient times philosophers felt that nobody should be paid more than about 10 or 20 times as much as anybody else, and even that is a great difference, of course, but it might be justified in the case of an elected national leader who must be able to present a strong, powerful image and might have only a relatively short term in office.

In the case of big business, however, things have got out of hand and remuneration of CEOs is often tens of millions, on top of which they get huge share issues as annual bonuses, huge 'golden handshakes' when they retire, and gigantic 'golden parachutes' then the company collapses.

To add insult to the injury of poverty, the worker-slaves endure 'top-down one-way' (TDOW) communication as they did all through their long years at school, in other words, they are treated like shit.

This is grossly unjust as the poor peasants who work on farms, in factories or on building sites produce what is essential to human life, that is, food, clothing, housing etc.

So those posters often seen in the USSR decades ago which pictured the workers as heroic perhaps made some sense. Then, of course, the hammer and sickle on their flag was also symbolic of the importance of the workers.

So the bottom line is that we have to create fairer societies which have real or *direct democracy* and leaders who 'check their ego at the door'. In these greed, hunger, famine, war and other evils will not be tolerated by the people.

Power corrupts

As figure 9.1 illustrates, the higher up you are in a hierarchy the more 'power' you have, which might be stated symbolically as:

$$P = C R^n$$

where P = power, R = rank, and C and n are constants.

Assuming the value of n is 2 then when one is twice as high in the hierarchy one has four times as much power.

Then, as we all know, power corrupts, one of the major factors in mankind's endless history of conflict.

As noted in the previous section, salaries may increase exponentially in hierarchical organizations and this result can be related to Mohr's Law of Capitalism which is the exponential growth law of money ($) with time (T):

$d(\$)/d(T) = c_1(\text{activity})$ where activity = $c_2\$$

Here the rate at which money is made is proportional to the rate of business activity, this in turn proportional to the amount of money available to fund this activity.

Combining the two constants above as $k = c_1 c_2$ we have

$d(\$)/d(T) = k\$$ where k is the *growth factor*.

where $\$$ = money made.

This last equation is *separable* which means that it can be integrated in the form

Integral [$d(\$)/\$$] = Integral [$k\,d(T)$]

giving, with the inclusion of the initial values, the exponential growth law $\$/\$_0 = \exp[k(T - T_0]$

If, for example, the growth factor is 10% per year, that is $k = 0.1$, then over 10 years we obtain the growth ratio $\$/\$_0 = 2.7$, so that we have nearly *tripled* our money.

The only real beneficiaries, however, are those higher in the hierarchy. The workers at the bottom who do all the *real work* (sitting and raving at sometimes boozy board meetings is not hard work) can't usually save any money and thus are slaves to all intents and purposes.

This is an intolerable situation and the CEOs who earn 'megabucks' are, of course, corrupt, and such corruption has always sown the seeds of discontent that have always, sooner or later, ended up as revolutions.

Thus socialism tends to be ruled by a single dictator, but capitalism by a multiplicity of petty dictators:

> *Capitalism tends to produce a multiplicity of petty dictators*
> *each in command of his own little business kingdom. State*
> *Socialism tends to produce a single, centralized totalitarian*
> *dictatorship, wielding absolute authority . . . through a hierarchy*
> *of bureaucratic agents.*
> Aldous Huxley, *Ends and Means* (1937).

Politicians too are often corrupt, of course, often being found to take bribes from big business.

Monarchs and dictators, of course, have nearly always been the greediest of all. Not only do they help themselves to plenty of money and live in grand palaces, but throughout history their hunger for power and thence territorial gain has led to one war after another.

How hierarchies operate

Hierarchies operate through a chain of command, leaders meeting with a chosen few top-level executives responsible for overseeing the various operations of the organization. In the case of government, for example, there are ministers for defence, treasury, education, health, and so forth.

In each of these areas there is a permanent and hierarchical bureaucratic department with several levels of seniority ranging from head of the organization and department heads to front-line managers who manage teams of workers.

Through the whole chain of command there is an implicit level of intimidation and fear that usually makes sure that everybody does as they are told. At the front line, however, things often get ridiculous, for example the traditional screaming of army sergeants at their miserable subordinates.

It is through such bullying and intimidation, of course, that soldiers are brainwashed into following orders without question or delay, essentially becoming expendable slaves to satisfy the whims of their leaders. Don't worry about 'executive stress,' therefore, worry about 'slave-stress.'

114

Indeed, our many sports with a relationship to conflict, for example absurd rugby with its 'charge at the enemy' no matter what the risk of injury, or archery and rifle shooting, all relate to our historical predilection for conflict.

Throughout hierarchies there is, of course, ambition to rise, often leading to a good deal of competitive behaviour, much of it often downright dishonest and unfair. In politics, for example, plenty of 'backstabbing' goes on day in and day out.

This corresponds quite closely, perhaps, with the alpha-male behaviour seen in several animal species, notably our close relatives, gorillas. The result is, of course, that those who end up as leaders may well be the most rotten people in the organization and, indeed, historically in both government and business this has always proved to be the case to some extent at least. That is, leaders are always greedy and bossy to some extent at least, but often they are exceptionally so.

Within hierarchical organizations there is also conflict, particularly over the 'rat race' involved in rising in the hierarchy.

Indeed, often ambitious, driven people are psychopathic, the pathology of their condition involving lying, cheating, aggressiveness, and bullying to get to the top.

Given power, it seems, they become psychotic with dreams of greater wealth and power and thus superiority. Alexander the Great, for example, began to think that he must be divine.

The problem is that, being people who have proved themselves good at the 'rat race', they tend to be the worst leaders, exactly in accordance with the Peter Principle.

Not only that, power not only corrupts, it makes people vain, self-centred, neurotic, obsessive, and, basically, mad. Here I must hasten to note Mohr's 10th Law, that is, that things such as madness must be judged on a scale of 1 to 10, not merely as a true-or-false judgment.

Furthermore, I like to make the important distinction between *bad mad* (depression etc.) and *sad mad* (Mohr, 2012b, 2018c; Mohr et al., 2018), and all too often political leaders have been bad mad, for example Nero and Hitler.

115

Diagnosing psychopaths

Table 9.1. The Hare checklist for psychopaths.

	TRAIT	SCORE
	Facet 1: Interpersonal	
1	Glibness or superficial charm	1
2	Grandiose sense of self-worth	1
3	Pathological lying	2
4	Cunning or manipulative	1
	Facet 2: Affective	
5	Lack of remorse or guilt	1
6	Emotionally shallow	1
7	Callous or lack of empathy	1
8	Failure to accept responsibility for their own actions	1
	Facet 3: Lifestyle	
9	Need for stimulation (easily bored)	1
10	Parasitic lifestyle	1
11	Lack of realistic, long-term goals	0
12	Impulsivity	1
13	Irresponsibility	0
	Facet 4: Antisocial	
14	Poor behavioural controls	0
15	Early behavioural problems	0
16	Juvenile delinquency	0
17	History of conditional prison release being revoked	0
18	Criminal versatility	0
	Other traits:	
19	Many short-term marital relationships	0
20	Promiscuous sexual behaviour	0
TOTAL SCORE		**12**

In 1980, Canadian clinical psychologist Dr Robert Hare, who worked in prisons, released the first version of the Hare checklist for identifying psychopaths, and several further versions followed.

As shown in Table 9.1, it divides 20 personality traits into four groups: interpersonal, affective, lifestyle, and antisocial, these measuring traits including charm, propensity to lie, lack of remorse, and need for stimulation.

After an interview each trait is scored as 0 (not present), 1 (present but not dominant), or 2 (dominant), so that the maximum possible score is 40.

Average people score from 3 to 6, non-psychopathic criminals score from 16 to 22, whilst in the UK and US respectively, scores of >25 and >30 are taken as a positive diagnosis of psychopathy (Gillespie, 2017).

In Table 9.1 I have scored a couple of bad bosses I once had, both of whom were too young and inexperienced for being HOD, and who played a major role in destroying my promising University career when I was less than 40 (some details of this are given in Appendix B).

Their total score of 12 seemed too low, as both seemed at least somewhat psychopathic, suggesting that Table 9.1 might apply more to hardened criminals for which item 17 relates to a form of 'treatment', namely continued imprisonment, presumably because of little or no sign of rehabilitation or remorse. Similarly, items 16 and 19 relate to past history.

Thus criteria for judging a bad boss should include:

➢ Bossiness.

➢ Assertiveness.

➢ Dishonesty and lying.

➢ Selfishness and greed.

➢ Vanity.

➢ Bullying.

Appendix B discusses the alternative Mohr Checklist for Psychopaths (MCLP), this working better for the two bad boss example cases scored in Table 9.1, details of how these two bad bosses ruined my life and career also being given in Chapter 8 and Appendix B.

Politics

In politics, of course, hierarchies are of great importance and in the Westminster system, for example, the Prime Minister tops the hierarchy, below that being Cabinet Ministers, then the remaining ministers of relatively minor areas of governance, and then remaining ordinary members of parliament in the governing party.

Then, of course, there is the opposition party, headed by its leader, and then with 'shadow ministers' and ordinary MPs.

Below the opposition in both numbers and influence are the minor parties, for example the 'Greens', One Nations and a couple of others in Australia.

Finally there are a usually a handful of independent MPs who sometimes vote as a bloc in order to have more influence.

In socialist governments, on the other hand, there is often a 'central committee' government and no parties etc., and this elects the national/government leader, China being the outstanding example of this at present.

Unfortunately, there have all too often in history been national leaders who have started wars, usually to gain territory, the Roman Empire being an outstanding example.

Then, of course, conflict with the peoples of areas that have been overtaken continues for long periods until, usually, they regain possession/control over the disputed territory.

Adolf Hitler was, of course, an outstanding example of a psychopathic leader, his Nazi Party's extermination of circa 6 million Jews during WW2 being the greatest act of genocide in human history.

The Hitler was a bully etc. is in little doubt, and his raving speeches were some evidence of this.

In the antiquated, farcical, and somewhat 'tribal' Westminster system of government, however, the ravings of the government and opposition members from opposite sides of the parliament often takes the form of verbal abuse and bullying.

Religion

Religious leaders have throughout history often had considerable political influence, and they often use threats of people who don't obey them or follow their directives that they will be punished by God, suffer eternal damnation, go to Hell etc.

As has become increasingly evident in recent decades, religious leaders and priests have for many centuries indulged in sexual abuse, usually of young children, to a horrendous extent, and much of this would have been associated with threats of some kind and/or bullying.

A classical example of sexual abuse was the finding of hundreds of skeletons of babies buried beneath monasteries in Europe, women cooks, cleaners etc. having been raped etc. by Monks and the resulting babies having been buried to hide the evidence of their crimes.

The military

A great deal of what can be deemed bullying occurs, of course, during military training, for example the traditional yelling and screaming of drill sergeants as soldiers practice marching mindlessly in lockstep.

This is, indeed, a good example of conditioning of people on a grand scale, and they are conditioned/brainwashed so that in combat they will obey any order with question or hesitation, for example charging mindlessly from their trenches to be mowed down by machine gun fire en masse during the many protracted trench warfare incidents of WW1.

Terrorist organizations

Leaders of terrorist organizations usually use a raving in a 'bullying type' fashion, their political or religious propaganda threatening dire consequences unless they are taken notice of.

Islamic terrorist organizations encourage Islamic Jihad which, of course, the Koran strongly advises several times in order to eliminate "unbelievers" (Mohr, 2014a; Mohr & Fear, 2016; Mohr et al., 2015b, 2018c, 2018e).

119

In line with the Koran, these Islamic terrorist leaders promise their followers that God will reward them with eternal life in heaven surrounded by countless virgins etc. if they carryout Islamic Jihad in order to establish Islamic caliphates and eliminate unbelievers (Mohr & Fear, 2015; Mohr et al., 2018d).

Dealing with psychopaths

Gillespie (2017) suggests that organizations which are run using 'Management by Objectives' (MBO) are less conducive to psychopathic bosses:

"The only way for a psychopath to succeed in a structure based on MBO would be to fall in with the objectives of his team and his superiors. Anything else would mark him out for removal from the organization."

Alternatively, Gillespie suggests that persons deemed to be psychopaths can be got rid of by getting them 'fired', but this, of course, is very difficult to bring about when the only person in the part of the organization in question able to do firing is a psychopathic boss, as is often the case.

When you do go above his or her head seeking to get them fired they counterattack, usually resulting in the person or persons complaining being disciplined or fired.

Most workers, therefore, simply have to endure bad and mad bosses and a 2016 study of Australian workplaces with "toxic leaders" concluded that the following strategies were unwise (Gillespie, 2017):

- ➤ Confronting the leader.
- ➤ Avoiding, ignoring or bypassing the boss.
- ➤ Whistleblowing.
- ➤ Worrying to excess about the boss.
- ➤ Continued anger and frustration.
- ➤ Focusing on work to try and forget about the boss.
- ➤ Taking sick leave (giving only short-term relief).

Instead, Gillespie says one should behave as a polite and compliant employee and do whatever one is told, no matter how much one dislikes it.

Then to survive in this way one should also:

➢ Think about a future, better job.

➢ Make sure your fellow workers don't 'tell' on each other.

➢ Check the accuracy of what the boss says.

➢ Don't show any anger and frustration.

➢ Build a support network.

➢ Document every bad thing the boss does, noting the time, date and names of any witnesses.

In this way one can survive for the medium term, at least, and perhaps build a case against the bad boss that might result in he or she being disciplined, demoted or shifted sideways, or even fired.

The bottom line, of course, is that there is a lesson to be learnt by any reader from this, that is, if having problems with a bad boss, give plenty of thought and get as much help as needed to deal with the problem and, hopefully, resolve it somehow, whether that help is simply support from one or two other staff members, or help from people above the bad boss in the hierarchy, and, if need be, lawyers.

Conclusion

Hierarchies are difficult to deal with over the long term.

When one is young, and not long out of the education system, they are simply a learning experience at first. Over time, however, grudges over being treated badly, and impatience over lack of promotion, grow and grow to the point at which getting another job may seem the only hope of improving one's life and career prospects.

If one has a psychopathic 'bastard boss', however, it may be impossible to get a halfway supportive reference from them, without which getting a decent job, or any job at all in line with your abilities, qualifications and experience, may prove difficult.

Some of the concepts and suggestions made in the foregoing chapter may be of some help, however, to workers with bad bass problems.

Primarily, of course, one needs at least one or two helpers within the organization in question. A problem here is that the workers at the same level in the hierarchy are also competing for the same promotion that you are. Thus, if you are in a group of, say, 10 seeking promotion to 'Senior xyz', then one might establish a mutually supportive relationship with just one of them, hoping that you will both be the next two workers promoted.

With the recent rise of the ME TO movement, bullying in the workplace has, like sexual abuse in the Catholic Church, become a prominent issue.

In dealing with a bad boss it helps to:

➢ Identify any psychopathic behaviours of the boss.
➢ Try to speak carefully to the boss about the problems, perhaps with a friend or colleague to back you up.
➢ Get as much as possible from the bad boss in writing.
➢ Consider recording bad behavior somehow.
➢ Ask advice from friends and family about any problems.
➢ Go above the bad boss in the hierarchy about problems.
➢ Speak to counselors and perhaps lawyers about problems.
➢ Consider using a simple 'person scaling' survey of fellow workers to get a 'rating' of the bad boss which might then be given to people higher in the hierarchy.

The bottom line, however, is that when one suffers bullying, threats etc. from bad bosses, one should make careful records of such behavior and seek help in dealing with the issue, being careful to behave at a professional and courteous manner at all times, hoping not to exacerbate the situation, but to resolve it as well as possible, and to the benefit of all parties.

☺☹☺☺☺☹☺☺☹☺☺☹☺☺☹

Chapter 10

SOCIAL LIFE

> *Compare society to a boat. Her progress through the water*
> *will not depend upon the exertion of her crew,*
> *but upon the exertion devoted to propelling her.*
> *This will be lessened by any expenditure of force in fighting*
> *among themselves, or in pulling in different directions.*
> Henry George, *Progress and Poverty*, bk. 10, ch. 3 (1879).

Social norms

Social norms are standards or expectations that govern people's actions in various social situations. Generally, we learn about social norms by observing what other people in our culture say and do. In almost every culture there is a norm holding that to be selfish is wrong, and to be helpful is right.

Two norms that encourage us to be helpful are (Grivas & Carter, 2005):

1. The *reciprocity norm*, which is based on the notion that we should be prepared to give to others what we receive, or expect to receive. We should, therefore, help others that help us, but many people, such as children and the elderly may not have the resources or capability to give as much help as they receive.

2. The *social responsibility norm* prescribes that we should help those that need help. Whether we do, in fact, help people in need depends on many factors, including the urgency of their need, and how much 'implicit' social pressure we feel to help them.

Social support

Social life is generally considered important, solitude being associated with loneliness, depression etc.

More important, perhaps, is that when things go wrong it is helpful to have supportive people, whether they be relatives, friends, or counselors, to turn to for advice and moral support.

Such people can provide help and encouragement that may provide hope in the most difficult of circumstances, and hope alone in most cases will help one cope in the short term.

Then, in the longer term, one can begin to fix the problem(s) in question, or 'move on' from them to work towards new goals.

Successful businesswoman Lillian Vernon recalls: *My father told me I had talent and a good idea for starting a business and I should never let anything get in the way of fulfilling my dream, or I would regret it for the rest of my life,* concluding: *So don't let challenges, setbacks, or detractors defeat or discourage you. If you believe in yourself and think positively, you will succeed* (Trump, 2004).

There are many activities, hobbies etc. via which one can meet and socialize with people, some of these being briefly discussed in following sections.

Sporting clubs and associations

An Australia, Australian Rules Football (AFL) is very popular, membership of some Australian Football League clubs totaling circa 100,000 members (for Collingwood it is 180,00 members), attendances at many games often being circa 90,000.

In Eastern states Rugby is also very popular, having two 'codes', the Australian Rugby Union, and the Australian Rugby League. Attendances for ARU and ARL games are typically 20,000 to 30,000.

In several countries cricket is a major sport, the "Ashes" tests series between Australia and England, and the Indian Premier League being of particular note, and having large attendances of up to 100,000.

Tennis remains a very popular sport globally, as evidenced by large attendances at the four "Grand Slam" tournaments in England, France, the USA, and Australia, and there are tennis venues and clubs in almost every suburb and town of substantial size in Australia.

Lawn bowls is also popular in many countries, Australia having lawn bowls clubs in most major suburbs of large cities with substantial memberships, mostly retired and elderly people.

Golf remains popular in many Western countries, the many suburban golf courses in Australia having substantial memberships and large clubhouses for social activities.

Horse racing is also a major sport in several countries, also providing an opportunity for plenty of socializing between races, as well as afterwards.

Several other sports also provide opportunities for socializing, including trotting (horses), greyhound racing, surfing, shooting, gyms, basketball, and netball.

Social clubs

There are many clubs formed for purely social purposes, examples in Melbourne, Australia, including the somewhat exclusive Melbourne Club, and the Atheneum Club.

Clubs and pubs

Pubs have a long history of providing social contacts between 'regulars', and an opportunity to meet people and make new friends.

In Australia there are now there are many "clubs" with dozens of poker machines which provide most of their revenue, with old-fashioned pubs with only a bar now regularly closing down.

These clubs also have bars and restaurants, and often have organized social groups which meet regularly.

Nightclubs and dances

In the central suburbs of major cities nightclubs provide late night booze and an opportunity socialize, and in particular meet and dance with members of the opposite sex.

There are also regular weekend dances organized at council-owned premises, most of these attended by young people with, or looking for, a girl or boy friend.

Writers groups

In many major cities many major cities there are several writers groups where people who have writing as a hobby meet once a month, some groups publishing a book of collected works by members every year.

Some members of such groups do write a book or two, sometimes using the growing 'self-publishing' industry to publish their books, and occasionally succeeding in find 'traditional' publisher to print and market their books.

These writers groups, however, are largely a social exercise providing an opportunity to meet like-minded people.

Art clubs

Few in number, there are a few arts clubs in which both amateur and professional artists meets and socialize and share ideas.

Religious activities

Religious services, of course, provide a regular opportunity to meet people afterwards, some churches, for example having a community lunch after their weekly Sunday service.

Many churches, synagogues etc. also hold occasional social evenings for members of the congregation.

The use of 'confessionals' by the Catholic Church is worth note, but the author believes it would be more helpful if churches provided a 'complaints service' instead in which people could air their problems. Not far from where the first author lives, however, the Anglican Church runs a community consultation service where people can discuss life problems.

Political meetings

Politics, of course, is very much about meetings, ranging from local branch meetings to the farcical 'raving clown show' of the antiquated and Westminster Parliamentary system of two major opposing parties yelling at each other from opposite sides of the "chamber".

Membership of the local branch of a political party, however, does provide a good deal of social contact with plenty of opportunity for discussion and sharing of views and opinions.

Helping in election campaigns, for example by 'door knocking', or handing out flyers at shopping centres and on election day, also provides opportunities to meet people and perhaps make a few new friends.

Regular local government council meetings can also be attended, perhaps providing an opportunity to meet people and make new and useful contacts.

Conflict and bullying in social life

As noted above, the tribalism of the Westminster system results in farcical scenes of raving and bullying from both sides of the 'house' almost daily.

Similarly, abuse and conflict arises in many social activities, for example both on the field in team sports, and often amongst spectators who support opposing teams. Usually this conflict involves bullying-type abuse and denigration.

Overcrowded housing, both in slum areas, and in high-rise government housing estates, often results in 'social violence', and some neuropsychologists believe that "sensory pleasure and violence are reciprocally related (Wagner, 1978).

Violent incidents frequently occur at and outside clubs, pubs and nightclubs, of course, where booze abounds, often late in the evening or in the early hours of the morning when there has been more time to perhaps 'overdose' on alcohol.

Such incidents usually initially involve verbal abuse, often with bullying-type statements and threats, which then 'escalates' until violence and injuries result.

Personal examples

Soon after I'd resigned from Auckland University and returned jobless to Melbourne I met a boozy British Army veteran Shaun at a nearby pub. I heard that, on his way by ship to Australia, Shaun beat up and hospitalized two ship's officers when they tried to deal with his drunken behavior at a bar.

Soon after I met him the woman he was living with left him, so he moved into a share house with three other 'down and out' men. Visiting this one day I saw that he had broken down the door of one man's room trying to get more booze after returning from a nearby pub one night, and had hit and injured the man in the process. Shaun heard of my visit and came to my house, damaged my front door to get in, and then tried to re-break a kneecap I'd broken a few months earlier falling down airport stairs returning from a job interview.

On another occasion I put Shaun in a headlock to prevent him attacking another man in a pub one night.

I conclude that Shaun was a dangerous bully, especially, and not only when he had had a few drinks.

A couple of years after my almost simultaneous career collapse and marriage breakup, I met an Englishwoman at a 30+ singles dance one night and, after I'd stayed at her flat for a couple of (separate) nights, I invited her to share the family-owned house I lived in which was divided into 2 flats.

One day she was upset at my breaking one of her wine glasses and attacked me, trying to strangle me, and fell onto a leg in which I'd broken the kneecap falling down airport stairs returning from a job interview. A major vein was broken and the leg swelled to twice normal size. I told my GP that I'd had an accident playing with an English Sheep Dog I'd got her to buy. The accident greatly exacerbated varicose veins in that leg that I already had after a childhood accident.

One day the husband she had left visited. Noticing that only one kitchen (of 2) was in use, he realized she was sharing more than a kitchen with me and attacked me and had me on the floor punching me. Fortunately, the lady managed to stop him, but I concluded that they were both violent.

A similar event occurred in 1990 when I was staying one Saturday night at a Serbian single mother's Housing Commission unit in the Melbourne suburb of Highett. I was playing a tape of King's College Choir (Cambridge) and she piped up: "Turn off that crap" or some such. Unthinkingly, I replied: "You'd fuck donkeys wouldn't you".

She 'lost it' and started hitting me repeatedly.

I ended up covered in blood and trying to catch a taxi home, none too easy late on a Saturday evening, and a few empty taxis passed me by before I was eventually picked up.

Like the Englishwoman, she was, indeed, a quite bossy woman, why I cite these last two incidents as bullying.

Conclusion

There are many activities, clubs, and other organizations that provide an opportunity for social contact.

Many of these organizations have regular meetings, sometimes purely for social purposes.

Branch meetings of political parties are, however, are usually relatively formal but usually have an informal chat session over drinks and snacks afterwards, as do meetings of many other social, sporting etc. organizations.

Unfortunately, some social activities sometimes provide opportunities for argument and conflict. For example, spectators/supporters at team sporting events, and customers at clubs, pubs and nightclubs, often indulge in heated abuse and threatening and bullying statements that result in conflict, sometimes resulting in serious injuries and sometimes death.

The bottom line on Part II of this book, therefore, is that bullying behaviours occur in all walks and aspects of life, just as alpha male behavior still endures and is prevalent amongst humans, though we 'inherited' it from our 'evolutionary ancestors' the apes.

☺☺☹☺☺☹☺☺☹☺☺☹☺☺☹

10. SOCIAL LIFE

PART III
ATTITUDE FORMATION & MEASUREMENT

Chapter 11

THE PSYCHOLOGY OF ATTITUDES

The body of science described in this book could only have been developed in democratic societies, where attitudinal influence is the form of control that is most often relied upon.
Alice Eagly & Shelly Chaiken, *The Psychology of Attitudes*, 1993.

Introduction

Chapter Four discussed conditioning which has important application in education where forcing pupils to sit out each day conditions them for productive life. Some aspects of conditioning are also involved, of course, in advertising and other forms of persuasion.

In the present chapter a brief introduction to the mechanics of attitude and belief formation is given. Of particular importance in advertising, *mere exposure research* and attitude measurement are also discussed.

Forbes' *contact hypothesis* regarding interactions between ethnic communities is briefly considered, this being of considerable importance in relation to religious persuasion, and, therefore, also having some relevance to advertising.

The formative years

The period from age 12 to 30 has been termed the *critical period* for formation of attitudes and it can be divided into two parts (Morgan et al., 1979):

(a) <u>Adolescence</u>, during which parental, educational, peer group, advertising and sociological influences are largely responsible for development of most of the attitudes a person will develop through life.

(b) <u>Young adulthood</u>, a time when commitments such as choosing a vocation and marriage occur, and one in which attitudes tend to *crystallize* or 'freeze' for life.

In part this crystallization may involve attempts at *cognitive consistency* in which we tend to make our attitudes relatively consistent with one another and thus avoid *cognitive dissonance* or conflicting attitudes.

An example of this might be that a person who goes to considerable effort to maintain good health, for example by exercising regularly and maintaining a healthy diet, is less likely to smoke or condone doing so.

Heider's *balance theory* is of the cognitive consistency type and assumes that we try to maintain consistent and balanced or harmonious relationships with other people and our environment. According to this theory we would not marry a person with whom we disagreed on major issues about which we felt strongly, such as abortion (Morgan et al., 1979).

That attitudes do indeed crystallize or 'firm up' in young adulthood was confirmed by a US survey of women college students in the 1930s which, when followed-up 20 years later, found that for most issues on the 'conservative-liberal' dimension the women's attitudes, except for a slight "conservative drift" typical of older people, remained the same as they had been in their twenties (Newcomb, 1963).

That attitudes tend to firm up in adolescence and young adulthood has, of course, important implication for marketing along the lines of 'get-em young and get-em for life,' an aim exemplified very well by the quotation that opens Chapter 13.

Expectancy-value models of attitude and belief formation

The most popular models of attitude formation towards an object, action, or event, are the expectancy-value models of attitude formation which are expressed as a summation of evaluations of each of several attributes of the object of the form:

Attitude, $A = {}_{i=1}\Sigma^n e_i v_i$ $\qquad$ (11.1)

where e_i is the *expectancy* about the object for attribute i, that is its score on a simple scale as to the subjective probability or extent to which the object has this attribute, v_i is the *value* or 'evaluation' of the attribute on a similar scale, and n is the number of attributes considered (Eagly & Chaiken, 1993).

For example, a person is reasonably sure that a new soft drink Choke a Dope has nice taste and is trendy but considers that it is too expensive. Using scales of 0 to 10 for e_i and -10 to 10 for v_i he might thus rate the soft drink as follows:

Attribute 1 (taste): $e_1 = 5/10$, $v_1 = 7/10$

Attribute 2 (trendy): $e_2 = 6/10$, $v_2 = 5/10$

Attribute 3 (price): $e_3 = 10/10$, $v_3 = -5/10$

giving an attitude score

$A = (5 \times 7 + 6 \times 5 + 10 \times -5)/100 = 15/100 = 0.15$

whereas a 'moderately good' score in which 5/10 is given for each expectancy and value would yield $A = 0.75$, whilst a 'middling' score of zero for each rating v_i would, of course, yield $A = 0$.

In practice there might, of course, be many more attributes and, perhaps, we might average the score as $A = {}_{i=1}\Sigma^n e_i v_i /n$, giving 0.05 in the foregoing example, and such scores have been found to correlate well with attitudes assessed by evaluative semantic differential items (Eagly & Chaiken, 1993).

Information integration models of attitude formation

The information integration theory of attitude formation calculates the response to a series of stimuli *i* as

$$R = w_0 \, s_0 + {}_{i=1}\Sigma^n \, w_i \, s_i \qquad (11.2)$$

where w_i and s_i are respectively the weight and scale of a person's attitude to a set of *n* items of information, and w_0 and s_0 are the weight and scale value of the person's initial attitude (Eagly & Chaiken, 1993).

Here the scale value of information is its location on the evaluative dimension and the weight is its *importance* or psychological impact in relation to the individual's judgment.

Simple summation models such as that of Equation 11.2 emphasize the importance of using multiple 'selling points' in advertising.

If the sum of the weights is required to be one then the model becomes an averaging model, but averaging models are more generally expressed as:

$$R = (w_0 \, s_0 + {}_{i=1}\Sigma^n \, w_i \, s_i)/(w_0 + {}_{i=1}\Sigma^n \, w_i) \qquad (11.3)$$

The initial attitude parameters w_0 and s_0 may in some instances, that of religion being perhaps the best example, represent 'intergenerational' attitudes acquired from a very early age from family and society at large.

Such initial attitudes, of course, may involve *prejudice*, for example ethnocentricity or racism, and, as history shows, such prejudices are often firmly rooted and perhaps could only be modeled by assigning them an exceptionally large weight.

More important in the modern consumer society, however, is social or imitative learning and in this context w_0 and s_0 represent initial attitude acquired by social learning from a peer or social group.

For example, a person believes that Christianity provides good moral codes (attribute 1) and that Christ did exist and provide a good exemplar of how we should live (attribute 2), but doubts that God really exists (attribute 3).

Even if God did exist, however, in view of man's disastrous history he has a low evaluation of this last attribute, so that, using scales 0 to 10 for both w_i and s_i, he might thus rate Christianity as follows:

Attribute 0 (initial attitude): $w_0 = 5$, $s_0 = 5/10$ (i.e. 'halfway' values)

Attribute 1 (morality): $w_1 = 8/10$, $s_1 = 8/10$

Attribute 2 (good life model): $w_2 = 8/10$, $s_2 = 8/10$

Attribute 3 (God): $w_3 = 2/10$, $s_3 = 1/10$

giving a response score

$$R = [(5 \times 5 + 8 \times 8 + 8 \times 8 + 2 \times 1)/100]/[(5 + 8 + 8 + 2)/10]$$

$$= [155/100]/[25/10] = 1.55/2.3 = 0.674$$

whereas a 'middling evaluation score' with 5/10 for both the weights and scale values for attributes 0-3 would give $1/2 = 0.5$.

In contrast to simple summation models such as Equation 11.2, averaging models emphasize the need to have a limited number of effective selling points in advertising.

Set size effect can be demonstrated by assuming all weights $= 1$ and an initial attitude score of 50 on a scale of 0 to 100. Then if all further pieces of information have a score of 100 the resulting weighted average score for k additional attributes is

$$R = (50 + 100k)/(1 + k) \tag{11.4}$$

giving the values 50, 75, 83.3, 87.5, . . . for 0, 1, 2, 3, . . . pieces of information, resulting in the hyperbola converging towards the asymptote $R = 100$ shown in Figure 11.1.

As might be expected, this hyperbolic result takes the same general shape as a learning curve, emphasizing that there is a diminishing return for each additional piece of information about a given subject, albeit with the unrealistic assumption that every piece of information has the same weight (w_i).

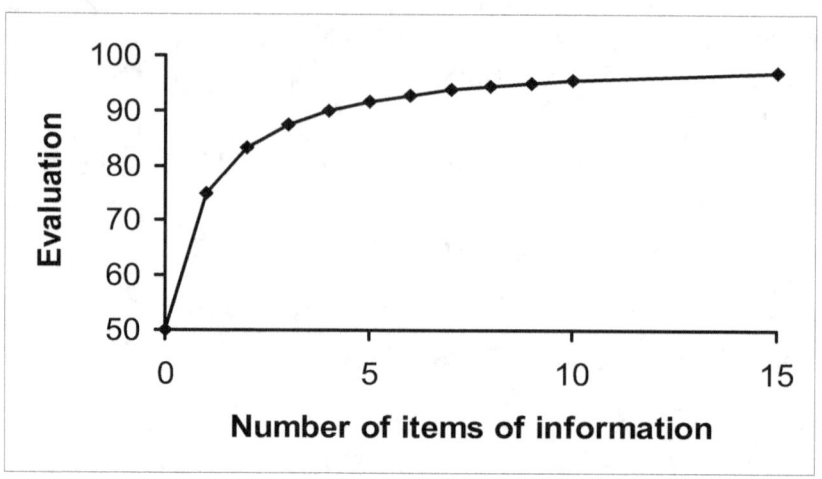

Figure 11.1. Theoretical set-size effect.

The *three hit theory* of advertising that three ads are needed to make people aware of a product, its relevance, and its benefits) would give (with $k = 3$) $R = 87.5$ (on a scale 0 to 100) in Equation 11.4, or $R = 75$ if there is no initial attitude, i.e. $s_0 = 0$ so that the number 50 in the numerator is omitted.

This is a reasonably good result and, indeed, of some relevance, the present author often finds that it takes three goes to remember items of information, presumably because they were not retained in the short term memory register (see Figure 2.2) long enough in the first instance.

Three-value model

A more general 'three-value' model is obtained by combining the expectancy-value and information integration models to obtain:

$$R = b_0\, w_0\, s_0 + {}_{i=1}\Sigma^n\, b_i\, w_i\, s_i \qquad (11.5)$$

so that three ratings are associated with each attribute (Mohr, 2009):

(1) A *belief* b_i or subjective probability or extent to which the object has the attribute ($=e_i$ in Equation 11.1).

(2) A *weight* or importance rating w_i ($=w_i$ in Equation 11.2).

(3) An evaluation or *scale value* s_i (=v_i in Equation 11.1 and s_i in Equation 11.2).

For example, a woman considers a dress that she has tried on in a ladies fashion shop is 'trendy' and her scores for this attribute might be:

(1) b_i = 7/10 (she is fairly sure that it possesses this attribute).
(2) w_i = 8/10 (trendiness is quite important for a new dress).
(3) s_i = 9/10 (she rates it as very trendy).

Whilst a good deal more difficult to use in practice, this model does emphasize that it is sometimes desirable to consider both *belief* and *importance* considerations in assessing attitudes.

Logical formation of attitudes

McGuire (1960) proposed that people maintain beliefs that are connected by the rules of formal logic. Whilst most of our early attitude formation is via parents, education, peer groups, advertising, etc., it is at least sometimes true that we take 'time out' to think about things and may reassess an attitude, trying to do so in a logical way.

As a simple example consider a confectionery product with the three attributes T = tastes OK, N = looks nice, and P = price is OK, and a positive attitude to the product is denoted as A.

Using a little symbolic logic in which $\rightarrow$ mean 'implies', $\wedge$ means 'and', $\sim$ means 'not', and denoting A = attitude to the product is OK, we can write $\sim P \rightarrow \sim A$
i.e. if the price is not OK then nor is attitude to it.

If $\vee$ means 'or' we might also write:

$(T \wedge P) \vee (N \wedge P) \rightarrow A$

i.e. if taste and price are OK, or if the product looks nice and the price is OK, then attitude is OK.

The example is a little trivial, however, but no doubt we do indeed sometimes reevaluate an attitude and use a little logic in doing so, but, generally, our attitudes are formed by the educational, imitative and information integration processes.

There is, however, scope for educators, religions, and advertisers to try and win us over with a little simple logic along the lines, for example, of: "You like to be comfortable so why not try - - -", an approach compatible with the cognitive consistency theory of attitude formation.

Mere exposure research

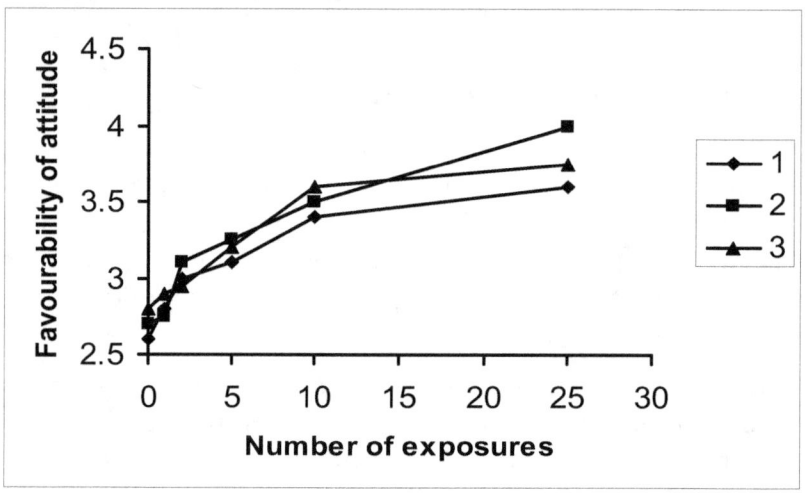

Figure 11.2. Increase in attitude favourability with increasing number of exposures to: 1. Turkish nonsense words. 2. Chinese-like characters. 3. Photographs.

Persuasion studies on message repetition usually focus on the effects of repeated exposure to *information* about attitude objects. In a classic monograph Zajonc (Zajonc, 1968) dealt merely with the objects themselves. Figure 11.2 illustrates the increase in attitude favourability with repeated exposure to three types of stimuli, showing a somewhat asymptotic behaviour similar to that of learning curves.

This result is comparable to the size effect seen in Figure 11.1 insofar as increasing response is seen with increasing amounts of information, albeit repetition of the same information in the case of mere exposure.

It should be remembered, however, that oft repeated attempts at persuasion can be irritating and result in negative attitudes, and some especially loud, haranguing radio and TV advertisements are good examples of this.

Implications of mere exposure in education are obvious, principally that students grow accustomed to new and perhaps difficult at first subjects, if not blasé about them, given time and repeated classroom exposure to them.

The latter observations might remind us that with repeated exposure we become accustomed to, if not hardened to, 'bad things' in life. For example, this is how children endure an excessive number of hours and years in classes and how adults endure jobs which may be, in reality, exceedingly tedious, arduous and boring.

It is also how, unfortunately, individuals become accustomed to essentially bad things such as cigarettes, alcohol, and drugs, perhaps in that order. This is, of course, good news for purveyors of such products.

Measurement of attitudes

One of the earliest methods of psychophysical scaling was Thurston's *method of equal-appearing intervals.* In this a panel of judges rates each of a set of attributes of an object (for example a new product) according to an ascending scale such as 0 - 10. Then the mean value of the ratings of all judges is the scale value of the attribute on the attitude dimension. For example, Table 11.1 shows the scale values that might be established for a new soft drink 'Choke a Dope'.

Then for surveys, the mean of the scale values of the attributes selected by respondents is their assessment of an object. To obtain more reliable results attributes that are rated inconsistently by the judging panel are not used for surveys.

Table 11.1.
Example scale values for new soft drink Choke a Dope.

Attribute	Value on scale 0 - 10
I don't like it.	0
It makes me feel ill.	1
It is very sweet and must have lots of sugar.	2
It has a nice colour.	3
The bottle looks nice	4
My friends like it.	5
it is trendy.	6
The price is good.	7
It tastes nice.	8

Likert's *method of summated ratings* was designed to be much easier to use than the method of equal-appearing intervals but to be at least as reliable. In this approach a large pool of items which are chosen intuitively for their relevance to the attitude object is used (Likert, 1961).

These items usually consist of statements of belief but statements about behaviours or affective reactions can also be used.

Typically each item is presented to respondents in a multiple-choice format such as:
1. Strongly disagree.
2. Disagree.
3. Undecided.
4. Agree.
5. Strongly agree.

Then, for example, a survey on attitudes towards women might contain questions like:

(a) Swearing is more objectionable from a woman.

(b) Intoxication in women is worse than in men.

With scores from 1 - 5 given to each of perhaps a dozen or so such questions the total score is then obtained for each respondent.

Desirably an initial pool of items should be pilot tested on a group of people to eliminate ambiguous and nondiscriminating items which tend to result in neutral responses.

This can be done by examining the *item-total score correlations*, each of which correlates the respondents' scores on an item with their scores summed over all the items. Then a good item will have a positive correlation and better items have higher correlations.

Likert Scaling is widely used, for example to assess the response to political advertising campaigns (Likert, 1961).

Guttman scaling

This approach gives stimulus-person scaling simultaneously and results in a matrix of data called the *Guttman scalogram*. For example, suppose we have five rods of from 5 to 7 feet in length (the exact lengths are not known) and ask each respondent to place a one in the Guttman scalogram matrix shown in Table 11.2 when they are taller than a particular rod. This raw data is then reorganized to give the result in Table 11.3.

Table 11.2. Guttman scalogram.

	Stimuli (rods)				
Persons	C	E	B	D	A
2	1	1	1	1	0
4	0	1	0	1	0
3	1	1	0	1	0
6	0	0	0	0	0
5	0	1	0	0	0
1	1	1	1	1	1
* e.g. person 2 is taller than C, E, B, D but not A					

Table 11.3 is obtained by placing the column with least ones at the left, the column with the most ones at the right, and so on. Then the row with the maximum number of ones is placed at the top (here this is for person '1' in and hence this is the tallest person) and that with the least ones is placed at the bottom.

Table 11.3. Reordered Guttman scalogram.

Persons	Stimuli (rods)					Score
	A	B	C	D	E	
1	1	1	1	1	1	5
2	0	1	1	1	1	4
3	0	0	1	1	1	3
4	0	0	0	1	1	2
5	0	0	0	0	1	1
6	0	0	0	0	0	0

The result is an upper diagonal matrix, as shown in Table 11.3, resulting in a score for each person shown on the right side in Table 11.3, this giving the ordinal ranking for each person.

The preceding example of Guttman scaling was for physical stimuli, when a perfect upper triangular matrix resulted. Generally, however, this is not the case when attitudinal stimuli are considered.

Table 11.4. Bogardus' social stimulus scale.

	Acceptance level					
	Would marry	As a friend	Would give a job	Allow as citizen	OK as visitor	No contact
Armenians						
Bulgarians						
Canadians						
etc.						

An example is Bogardus' social stimulus scale, illustrated in Table 11.4, in which respondents are asked to judge how closely they would relate to people of various nationalities or races.

Such attitudinal stimuli do not yield a perfect upper triangular matrix but it has been suggested that when about 90% of the non-zero entries do appear on or above the diagonal that this *coefficient of reproducibility* value is acceptable.

The Guttman scalogram has the advantage that the degree to which the reordered response matrix is 'triangularized' gives an immediate indication of the reliability of a survey. More complex to use, it is generally only usable for relatively small surveys, such as in-house surveys of consumer groups in advertising offices where it is an ideal tool.

Conclusion

Effective persuasion is all about changing attitude (where this, indeed, is necessary) so that some understanding of theories of attitude formation as cumulative or integrative processes is most important.

The later chapter on advertising (Chapter 13) discusses the important trio of cognitive, attitudinal, and behavioural responses and also McGuire's Reception-Yielding model of attitude formation, one that is particularly applicable in such contexts as advertising and religion.

The results of mere exposure research compellingly indicate how attitudes to new stimuli tend to improve given repeated exposure to them, the bottom line being that it is by such means that we are reduced to consumer zombies from cradle to grave.

Finally, measurement of attitudes is, of course, especially important in many areas such as consumer and political campaign surveys. Though perhaps only applicable to relatively small surveys, the Guttman scalogram is useful because the degree of triangularization of the reordered response matrix gives an immediate indication of the accuracy of a survey.

☺☺☹☺☺☹☺☺☹☺☺☹☺☺☹

11. THE PSYCHOLOGY OF ATTITUDES

Chapter 12

THE MASS MEDIA

> *The idea that the media is there to educate us, or to inform us,*
> *is ridiculous because that's about tenth or eleventh on their list.*
> *The first purpose of the media is to sell us shit.*
> Abbie Hoffman, speech at U South Carolina, Sept. 16, 1987.

The print media

The *Acta Diurna* of the Romans contained daily official reports, and the Chinese claim to have had a similar journal of much greater antiquity (Egerton Eastwick, 1896).

The earliest regular newspaper is thought to have been the *Notizie Scritte* published in Venice around the middle of the 16th century. The paper could be seen at various places in the city for the price of a small coin, the *gazeta,* from which came the term Gazette.

Around the end of the 16th century casual publications of various professions, parties and other special interest groups had limited circulation in England. In 1622 the one-page *Certaine News of the Present Week* was first printed and followed by many other one-page weeklies.

Later, two-page newspapers circulated twice a week appeared, eventually being printed daily. In 1785 a newspaper renamed *The Times* three years later was established and by 1829 it was eight pages. During the Crimean war the first war-correspondent letters appeared and the circulation rose to over 50,000. The era of the modern newspaper had begun.

Today's major newspapers are larger than ever and many have large weekend supplements devoted to such things as additional news commentary and the arts.

Articles in major newspapers tend to become a routine mix of such topics as major local and international events, local and international politics and crime, traffic other accidents, business news and sporting news

In most of these areas outcomes or results will be reported, along with editorial comment and discussion of coming events.

The many local and regional newspapers naturally focus more on events in their area so that, for example, plans for alterations to a local park might be a main article.

There are also many magazines which focus on news in special interest areas such as business, cars and computers.

For all newspapers and magazines advertisements are a major source of revenue. There are also a few newspapers and magazines devoted to advertising second hand goods for sale or to advertising products such as cars and computers.

As ever, editorial comment in the major newspapers is usually very guarded so that a rare hint of dissent with government policy is barely noticeable.

Ways in which editorial policy can influence politics, however, include:

➤ By simply giving less coverage to one party than another.

➤ By giving heavy coverage to a mistake or embarrassing incident involving a member of one party.

Over time, therefore, newspapers can have a considerable political effect and always have, so much so that they have often been subjected to government censorship.

Newspapers also play a cultural role, most obviously in discussing local arts and sporting events. The quotation that commences the next chapter is an excellent example of this role and the way in which advertisers can use newspapers to brainwash the young into becoming lifelong consumers of their products.

12. The Mass Media

Radio

Radio has been one of the great advances in human life. It allows international communication of news, embraces the people of most cities and towns, and plays an important role in ambulance, police and other essential services.

Radio has evolved from a novelty in its early days to a habit of modern life. The first author recalls the first 24 hour broadcasting by a radio station in Melbourne taking place in the early 1960s. Since then radio has evolved in major cities to provide a wide variety of 24 hour AM and FM stations such as:

➢ 24 hour news.
➢ Classical music.
➢ Popular music.
➢ 'Old time' music.
➢ Talk-back.
➢ Sports.
➢ 'Traditional' radio: a mix of news, sport, music etc.

Most of these are supported by a good deal of advertising and it is often claimed that many people spend more time listening to radio than they do watching TV and that, therefore, radio ads are more effective.

Radio stations have much smaller audiences than prime time TV, however, though in Australia the government owned ABC radio sometimes has a good sized audience. No doubt, therefore, it will eventually be privatized!

Some of the talk-back stations cater for the sick, deranged, drunk and lonely in the later evening and throughout the early hours of the morning.

Whether radio has much effect politically is doubtful, TV playing a much greater role in this area.

Culturally, however, radio has great influence. The latest styles of pop music are played to the young and this has always had an effect on their behaviour.

Before the 1950s popular recording artists sang in a semi-classical style or were 'crooners' like Bing Crosby who only older people could identify with.

12. The Mass Media

In the mid 1950s the young Elvis Presley was viewed as a potentially bad influence on the young. He was endorsed by such well-known TV personalities as Ed Sullivan, however, and that seemed to overcome early prejudice from the older generation, or at least guarantee the approval of the younger generation.

There is no doubt, however, that rock and roll music has had a bad effect on the young as its performers were often doubtful characters afflicted with all the vices. Inevitably a whole generation was influenced by such behaviour and began themselves to behave less politely and become a little more immoral. If the lyrics of a popular song talked about 'having it off' in the back seat of a car, then young people of that generation would do just that.

Currently we still have stylized singers who 'croon' a song and dress according to some current fashion. We also have bee-bop and other pop music styles that have become more and more 'in your face'. These sorts of songs are accompanied by music clips with scenes of dark alleys in the poor parts of major cities that project an image of loutish behaviour and crime that seems to rub off on young males in particular.

Popular music has occasionally had positive effects, for example through songs protesting war, and there are those that claim that the 'hippie' and 'flower power' movement in the USA of the late 1960s and early 1970s had through a few large pop concerts played an important role in galvanizing public opinion against the Vietnam war and bringing it to an end.

Evidence of the power of pop music is seen in the emergence of radio stations run by religious organizations that play 'nice' pop music for the young with only occasional interviews or ads concerning religious opinions and events.

Finally, some evidence of the power of radio is exemplified by Radio Vatican in Rome which can be heard globally on the Internet. This, no doubt, plays an integral part in the Vatican's ongoing task of propagating Catholic propaganda.

The 'brainwashing' role of radio, however, became relatively limited with the advent of TV because this became a far more potent medium for political and other propaganda.

12. The Mass Media

Television

TV has an enormous impact on modern life and people typically watch TV for at least 3 or 4 hours on most days.

The wide variety of shows on TV includes news, current affairs, interviews, panel discussions, documentaries, movies, sitcoms, children's programs, live sport, sporting panels, quizzes, cooking, home renovation and reality shows.

Most of these types of shows play a cultural role and in Australia they are a mixture of US, British and local products, exactly in line with our traditional alliances.

Many documentary shows, particularly those about past wars and other events in history, tend to reinforce those alliances. A notable example are the almost weekly documentary shows concerning Adolph Hitler which seem designed to keep us 'conditioned' for the concept of justified war and the next 'villain' around the corner that our allies the US or UK want to denigrate as a lead-up to yet another war.

As with newspapers, TV news has editorial controls rarely allowing much criticism of the status quo. The many interviews on current affairs shows allow politicians and others to express a view, but only in short 'grabs' which have little impact.

Occasional panel discussion shows allow groups to express their views but again only in short grabs, a sequence of views contradicting each other having little influence on an audience.

As with any media, however, by judicious choice of material shown the public can be brainwashed most effectively.

In Australia, for example, recent Prime Ministers seem to have had a media team that even Hitler might have envied, one that has them seen on TV almost every day saying a few mindless words on some topic or engaged in some public event to identify themselves with the public. As a result, a typically unlikely politician becomes highly successful.

Children's shows on TV play a positive role. Early morning and afternoon shows help keep very young children occupied and entertained and also have some educational content. In the later afternoon shows which sometimes include quizzes help entertain older children and sometimes have significant educational content.

Brainwashing

The term 'brainwashing' derives from a Chinese word and BW was first used by the Chinese military on Americans captured in the Korean War in trying to convert them to communist ideology using 'The Three D's' method:

[1] **Debilitation**: 'Softening up' by sleep and food deprivation.

[2] **Dread**: Rough treatment and threats of torture or death.

[3] **Dependency**: The subject realizes that they are dependent upon the brainwashers for survival and is treated as converted and allowed to mix with other converts who complete the persuasion process.

The American Heritage Dictionary of English defines brainwashing as:

1. *Intensive, forcible indoctrination, usually political or religious,*
aimed at destroying a person's basic convictions and attitudes and replacing them with an alternative set of fixed beliefs.

2. *The application of a concentrated means of persuasion, such as an advertising campaign or repeated suggestion, in order to develop a specific belief or motivation.*

In line with the second definition, most people now believe that a great deal of brainwashing is done via the mass media. In the present work, therefore, the term *brainwashing* is generalized to include implanting ideas where none existed before, not just changing a person's ideas. This is important in view of the predilection of advertisers to target children of all ages when they are open-minded, if not naive, and thus willing to try new things.

In this context advertising needs only to succeed in a small percentage of the target age group and *social learning*, a form of imitative learning, will occur and ensure that other members of the target group follow the lead of those first persuaded by the advertising.

The results are nothing short of spectacular, of course, as young children are persuaded en masse what to wear, how to act, and to smoke, drink Coke, buy mobile phones, etc.

This, indeed, is *conditioning* on a grand scale.

As well as in the mass media and advertising, conditioning techniques are used in the many stages and areas of life, particularly in educating and training young children.

An example of TV brainwashing of the public

A fine example of TV brainwashing of the public in Western nations occurred before the 2003 invasion of Iraq when for months pictures of Sadam Hussein holding a rifle were shown almost daily, accompanied by misguided speculation on whether he possessed Weapons of Mass Destruction (WMDs).

This charade was so persistent as to make many viewers want to scream the next time they heard the term WMD. The purpose of this orchestrated litany of lies and deceit was clearly to 'condition' people into acceptance of the forthcoming military invasion of Iraq by the US and the few of its allies willing to assist it.

In fact, Iraq had been so severely weakened by the 1991 invasion and subsequent sanctions and continuous bombing in the broad 'no-fly' zone placed through it that is was incapable of anything but minimal resistance.

The whole shabby and gutless affair was possibly at the behest of the Saudis, with whom the Bush family had strong connections, perhaps still regarding Sadam as a long-term irritation in the region.

Just as Osama Bin Laden wanted, however, the Iraq invasion has damaged an already sick American economy even further and removed Sadam from power, opening the way for eventual fundamentalist Islamic control of the country.

Indeed, another possibility is that al Qa'ida themselves may have fed the long-incompetent CIA misinformation about Iraq possessing WMDs to suck them into invasion.

Religion and morality on TV

Religious shows on TV mainly appear in the early hours of Sunday morning. These are bible bashing US shows which cannot be watched and taken seriously by many.

In Australia there is an interview show that concerns itself with religion around midnight during the middle of the week and the government run ABC runs a program on Sunday evenings which shows documentaries on religious topics.

These few shows with a religious basis have little influence.

Many of the banal sitcoms and movies now involve high levels of foul language, violence and sex which should not be seen by anyone, let alone children.

Panel shows also involve plenty of poor language, somewhat stupid and loutish behaviour and too much joking about sexual matters.

Some of the ridiculous and voyeuristic reality shows are also completely tasteless. *Big Brother* was filled with bad language, silly behaviour and obscene talk on such absurd topics as farts.

To top it all off there are those ads shortly after midnight for sex shops and 'sex' chat lines for 'straight' and homosexual people which are a sad reflection on a sick society.

Worse still is the increasing level of violence on TV and at the movies. Inevitably the result is 'copy cat' behaviour in the society made audience to these movies (Cipolla, 1974):

It is disturbing to see that still today, even in the most advanced countries, in large sections of human society, aggressiveness is praised as a virtue - or at least as a valuable asset - and it is constantly advertised in the motion pictures and on television. We need - more than anything else - to educate people to tolerance and gentility.

About two years ago there was considerable public angst when a young woman was raped and killed in Melbourne one evening as she was walking home from working as stand-up comedienne. Melbourne used to be considered a quiet, if not dull city, and now it is developing a history of crime reminiscent of Chicago.

The mass media, particularly the many movies that glorify crime and violence play a large role in desensitizing people to violence to the point at which is comes almost naturally to them.

The final insult is not only the violence, but city half covered in graffiti painted by mindless louts who enjoy other irresponsible and dangerous practices such as throwing rocks and bottles at the windows of cars, trams and trains.

We need to draw a firm line quickly regarding mass media that encourages this sort of behaviour before life in this society becomes intolerable for decent people.

TV advertising

TV advertising has moved from the simple situation of a presenter reading a script while holding the product in question up in front of the camera to ads that have various styles such as:

➢ 'Basic' ads that mention the product and concentrate on telling you its name and where to get it. Sometimes these have no presenter and only text messages.

➢ Sophisticated ads that show the product in 'classy' surroundings.

➢ "Laid back' ads were the presenter extols the virtue of the product.

➢ Semi-humorous ads which sometimes use cartoon characters to present their message.

➢ Ads where the reader just about screams at you not to miss some bargain sale or to go to some cheap store.

➢ Ads targeting children which involve cuddly characters and fantasy scenes and the like.

More than other forms of advertising, TV advertising is sometimes very psychological. Many ads aimed at children, for example, are tested on young children who are asked whether they feel persuaded by them to pester their parents into buying the product.

Most important, however, is that ads only have to persuade a few children to try a product and they will spread the idea to their friends by the powerful pyramid effect of social learning which, unfortunately, is the main way in which children pick up bad habits like smoking and drugs.

Movies

An example of the Christian church using movies for brainwashing is a set of 5 movies of about 40 minutes duration and involving the following leading characters and languages:

1. Dini – Indonesian.
2. Khalil – Arabic.
3. Ali – Turkish.
4. Khosrow – Tarsi.
5. Mohammad – Hausa.

#3 is about a bossy, bad-tempered, alcoholic Muslim husband who beats his wife. He has a vision that leads him to Saudi Arabia and en route he has a vision of Jesus. Telling others about it, his wife is doubtful, whilst his friends deride him. He hears the voice of Jesus again, however, and converts to Christianity, his wife doing the same, feeling it has saved them.

#5 is about a young African boy who while herding has a vision of Jesus, moving him to go to Saudi Arabia where he stays 18 months and learns Arabic. Returning home, his father pesters him about beginning to acquire wives but he has another vision, this of Jesus saving a man from attack by black-hooded men. He tells his father who sends him to a medicine man where he is given a potion without result. Another medicine man is tried before the boy has visions on six successive nights of Jesus defending him from the devil. A 7th dream promotes the Bible and the boy converts to Christianity. This upsets his father who calls him an "infidel" and the boy leaves home. Two years later, hearing his father to be ill, he returns to visit him, when his father forgives him, dying 3 hours later.

The Internet

The Internet has provided a new form of mass media which combines all the other mass media. Thus the now ubiquitous PC is linked by modem to the Internet and thence to web sites that link to newspapers, radio and TV, as well as to countless other information and advertising sites.

Through e-mail the Internet also provides an important new means of communication for both social and business purposes.

For business it also provides an alternative medium for both marketing and sales, as well as for other transactions such as bank account transactions and bill payments.

For children seeking information for school projects, for example, the Internet is often useful.

The widespread use of the Internet to present University courses, on the other hand, is deplorable and debases these greatly. Such a practice also tends to encourage lightweight courses like the absurd postgraduate courses in Sexology and Puppetry introduced at two Australian 'latter-day' Universities.

In recent years increasing numbers of people are becoming addicted to various 'social sites' such as Facebook and spend up to hours a day sharing mindless and useless gossip on them.

Undoubtedly the worst result of the Internet is the many sites devoted to sexual matters. Some of these involve the sex chat lines and dating services advertised in newspapers and on TV. Others involve pornography, including illegal child pornography, yet another indication of an increasingly sick society perhaps.

Conclusion

The mass media play a great part in our lives. They 'condition' us to accept our culture and the attitudes of our government and society.

TV is perhaps the most potent of the mass media as it is the centrepiece of the modern home and often some of its bedrooms as well.

The Internet provides social, educational and business access via telephone links and also links to the other mass media.

TV programs and advertising, however, provide the most powerful means of brainwashing people politically and behaviourally, and advertising is the subject of the next chapter.

The major newspapers, however, have considerable political influence by way of frequent poll results and editorial comment, particularly in the weeks leading up to an election.

Unfortunately, the media and advertising often encourage tribalism in relation to political, sporting etc. organizations, and bad behaviours sometimes result.

So far as bullying in society is concerned, however, it is perhaps fortunate that in recent years this issue has gained more attention in the media, and only in the last few years the ME TOO movement has further increased community awareness and concern about bullying and verbal and sexual harassment in society.

☺ ☺ ☹ ☺ ☺ ☹ ☺ ☺ ☹ ☺ ☺ ☹ ☺ ☺ ☹

Chapter 13

ADVERTISING

> *The chief customers of the public house today are the elderly and middle-aged men. Unless you can attract the younger generation to take the place of the older men, there is no doubt that we shall have to face a steadily falling consumption.*
> *If we begin advertising in the press we shall see that the continuance of our advertising is contingent upon the fact that we get educational support as well in the same papers. In that way it is wonderful how you can educate public opinion, generally, without making it too obvious that there is a public campaign behind it all.*
> Sir Edgar Saunders, Director of the Brewers' Society, Birmingham, 1930 (Sargent, 1979).

The purpose of advertising

Nowadays, of course, there are massive media and advertising industries devoted to turning us into *consumer zombies*.

The main objectives of advertisements, in approximate order of priority, are to:
1. Make the brand name familiar.
2. To give the brand a distinct image.
3. Attribute at least one key attribute to that brand name.
4. Associate the product with certain usages.
5. To convince us that this brand is the best (for us).
6. To persuade us that we should buy the product.

To meet these objectives advertisements will involve:
slogans, demonstrations, comparisons, testimonials, and repetition.

Comparisons, of course, are usually of price, but sometimes also some sort of semi-official rating, for example safety ratings for cars.

By way of style advertisement types include basic facts, 'mood', feel-good, social setting, slice-of-life, humour, fantasy, hard-sell, and anxiety/danger/risk or 'fear' ads.

An example of fear type advertisements are those for household insect sprays, and the TV program *More Hidden Killers Of The Victorian Home* reminds us that fear ads have been around for a long time, ads in the Victorian era selling such products as poisonous Borax (sodium borate) as a household cleanser, the "new science of germs and microbes" helping promote a fear of myriad household 'bugs'.

To make advertisements more appealing attractive female models, smooth talkers, or sports and movie stars are often used to promote products.

To give advertisements more authority statements by 'experts' may be used to convince us of the merits of a product.

To make purchase more imperative advertisements will scream of huge price reductions for a limited time, huge bargains for as little as two days only, and buy on the never-never deals with no interest for a year or two.

Thus advertisements range from boring to extremely irritating, from dull and routine to the heights of excess and absurdity, from mere suggestion to downright pleading, and from slight desperation to screaming at us to buy the product.

More subtle are 'advertorials' of bought space in newspapers, conspicuous 'product placement' in movies, or internet sites. For maximum tedium there are half-hour 'infomercials' on afternoon or late night TV which sometimes repeat night after night, week after week, and year after year. In these and most other types of advertisement there are often trial offers, bonus products for quick purchase etc.

The psychology of attitudes

Attitude can be defined as 'psychological *tendency* expressed by *evaluating* a particular entity with some degree of favour or disfavour.'

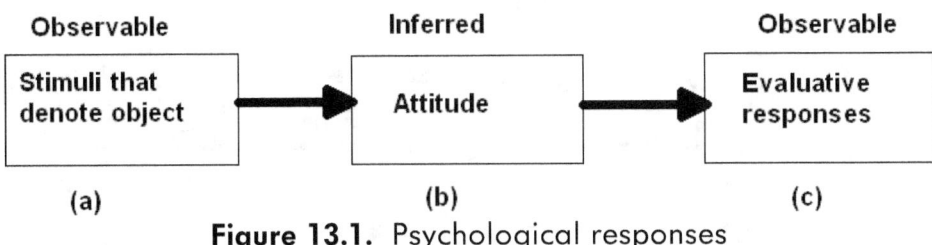

Figure 13.1. Psychological responses

Figure 13.1 illustrates the three types of response involved in attitudinal psychology. These are:

1. *Cognitive response.* This response is that of recognition of, for example, a name, a picture or other stimulus.

2. *Affective response.* This is a hypothetical construct and a latent variable. Here the sympathetic nervous system responds to (1) with feelings or emotions.

3. *Behavioural response.* This is the outward expression of (2) and may be a positive, neutral or negative response of some degree or intensity involving some observable action.

In this context conservatism, environmentalism or racism are objects. Then when we label a person a conservative, environmentalist or racist we infer an attitudinal position. Such attitudes are evidenced and also developed by the 'CAB' mechanism illustrated in Figure 13.1. Schemas are cognitive structures that represent a person's past experience in a stimulus domain by a higher order or abstract cognitive structure. Then attitude is a subset of such a schema.

Schemas have a selective effect on the remembering of information so that people have a better remembrance of stimuli that 'fit' their schemas and also for those that 'oppose.' This same selectivity applies to the 'output' of information as well as its input.

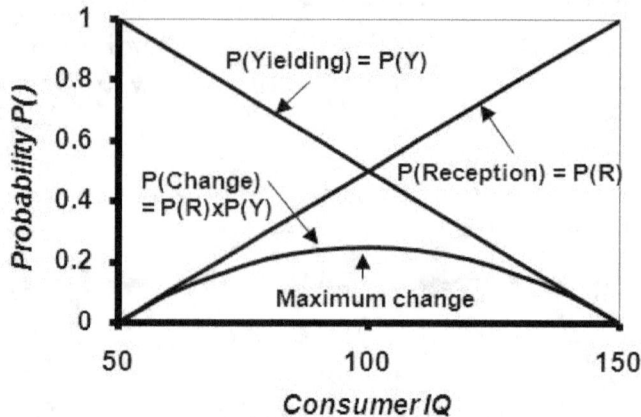

Figure 13.2.
Probability of reception, yielding and attitude change.

Figure 13.2 illustrates the reception-yielding model of attitude formation (Eagly & Chaiken, 1993). Here 'reception' refers to comprehending a 'message', for example an advertisement. This model postulates that the probability of attitude change is given by:

$$P(C) = P(R) \times P(Y)$$

so that a maximum change is obtained where the reception and yielding curves intersect, as shown in Figure 13.2.

One application of this idea is to 'get them young' so that advertising companies target the young and naive before they have the maturity or 'consumer intelligence' to develop resistance. Indeed, this is why the present author believes that the horizontal axis in Figure 13.2 should be labeled 'Consumer Intelligence' or 'Consumer IQ'.

The quotation that opens this chapter is an excellent example. Once an idea like 'beer is for men' is buried in a boy's brain he may become a beer drinker for life, the habit occasionally reinforced by ads that make the habit look completely appropriate.

The basic mechanism of persuasion, therefore, is to 'get them young' (and naive or 'less intelligent consumers') as Figure 13.2 suggests. To do this ads need only persuade/brainwash some of the target audience and then imitative or 'social' learning ensures that many of the rest follow them.

Advertisements having achieved this, regular advertising reminds the audience of a product. Then in Figure 13.1 the 'C' response will be one of recognition of your brand, the 'A' response will be one of approval of it, and the 'B' response will be to make a mental note to buy it.

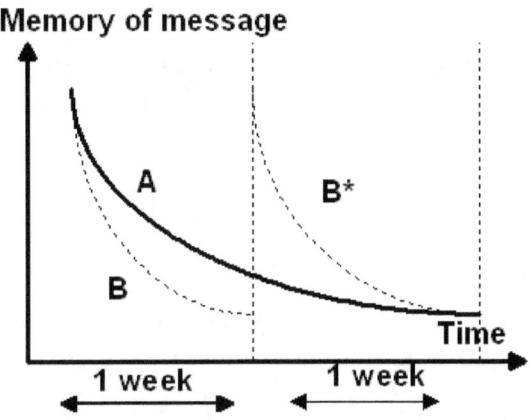

Figure 13.3. Forgetting curves.

Learning curves were discussed in Chapter 3 and in advertising it is important to have sufficient repetitions of an ad to ensure adequate average learning by the audience. The forgetting curves of Figure 13.3 also have important application in developing long-term marketing plans. Here curves A and B are for two messages and curve B* is the result after the second message is repeated.

Then, when time has elapsed after an advertisement its 'residual' effect depends upon both the *primacy* (strength) of the ad compared to others and its *recency*.

In Figure 13.3, after two weeks ad B* has greater recency than ad A, but less primacy so that they have nearly equal effect.

Such repetition of ads will ensure long-term potentiation of the remembered message, an important objective (Vander et al., 1994). Correlation between retention and persuasion, however, is by no means guaranteed and ads can be tailored to these two ends.

Targeting advertising

Maslow defined two kinds of needs (Lindzey at al., 1978):

(a) *Basic needs* such as hunger, thirst, sex and security.

(b) *Metaneeds* such as achievement, beauty, goodness, justice, order and unity.

Maslow defines achievement as a basic need but the present author prefers to classify it as a 'higher' or more human metaneed.

First, we must meet our basic or 'animal' needs. That done we can turn our attention to the higher 'human' metaneeds and thence Maslow's 'meaning of life' goal of 'self-actualization' as a human being.

These needs provide *primary goals* that may motivate us towards *secondary goals* such as money in order to achieve them.

Most of our basic needs are *intrinsic motivations* whereas most of our metaneeds are *learned goals.*

Advertising usually targets the metaneeds of your *ego.*

A Coke ad, for example, is not designed to remind you that you may be thirsty. If so, you might rush to the fridge and grab whatever drink you can find to satisfy that thirst. No, a Coke ad makes it look 'cool' to drink Coke with your friends and being 'cool' is a metaneed! So next day a young boy will want to be 'cool' when hanging out with his friends so they will all drink Coke and act foolishly, just like the actors in the Coke ads

Here again we see the down side of advertising, namely that increasingly ambitious executives will stop at nothing to sell their product, even if it has to brainwash the young into acquiring both bad behaviour and bad teeth.

In marketing to children, of course, familiar cuddly looking cartoon figures are often displayed on packaging and used to speak the lines of TV ads. Here, however, ads usually target the *Id*, the basic 'animal' personality that has basic needs like hunger. Young children tend to eat in smaller doses and often so that almost any time they are awake is a good one to put a picture of confectionery in front of them.

One of the best examples of brainwashing, however, is the use of *consumer panels* of children in marketing research. The children are often asked what they will say and do to persuade parents to buy them the product.

Finally, the extent to which children are exposed to advertising is incredible:

- - "*it is estimated that children between two and 11 years old may see over 20,000 advertisements in a year,*"
(O'Guinn et al., 2006).

Advertising, therefore, will brainwash someone in your family, even if it doesn't brainwash you!

In marketing to adults well known sporting identities are often used to market such things as golf clubs, household appliances and cars and houses. Indeed, this was the basis of Mark McCormack's very successful IMG (McCormack, 1986), and one of his earliest clients was Greg Norman who, marketed as 'The Shark', was made out to be a much better golfer than he was and he made an awful lot of money from TV ads.

Addiction

There is no doubt that advertising has the effect of conditioning people. Just as Pavlov's dogs were conditioned to associate a bell with the appearance of food so that they then salivated when only given the stimulus of the bell, so too will a psychological 'trigger' be thrown in our minds when the 'CAB' responses to an ad are invoked.

13. ADVERTISING

In the same way advertising seeks to develop *habits*. Habits can be quickly formed and very hard to break. It only takes as little as one or two first exposures to learn something. Then only a few repetitions are needed for the memory to become *long-term potentiated* (Vander et al, 1994) and more easily recalled than most other memories in your brain.

In young children the result of confectionery advertising is often a virtual addiction to sugar. In teenagers this continues but junk food and Coke are added to their habits, soon followed by bourbon and Coke and then beer for the boys and perhaps some of the new vodka based mixed drinks for the girls.

Booze ads often *associate* booze with celebration so that at 'rave' parties for young people primeval music seems to go hand in hand with drugs and booze.

The psychology of this sort of behaviour is doubtless based on imitative learning from adults. In other words, as long as adults are stupid enough to drink booze children will too.

Since cigarettes are now discouraged in the media teenagers will smoke marijuana, arguing that it is not as harmful. This is not only an intoxicating drug but a hallucinogenic one as well. So, why not harder drugs like a little cocaine after that?

Then addiction quickly becomes likely. From booze to most other drugs, poisons have two problems:

(a) They don't really taste nice unless diluted enough by other things such as water and sugar in the case of booze.

(b) They alter the metabolic rate, resulting in changes in pulse rate and blood pressure, and contraction or dilation of blood vessels in the brain and elsewhere. Thus every fair sized dose of most drugs gives you withdrawal symptoms, whether you realize it or not.

If you have a booze overdose, for example, you might want some 'hair of the dog' (that bit you) as alcoholics call a dose of booze early in the day to help overcome a hangover.

Celebration is not the only excuse for booze. Wine goes well with food, it is said, so that is another.

164

The reality is that, because alcohol is a poison, wine will tend to eat at your stomach so it is best to line your stomach with a little food to ease the discomfort that you should be able to feel after a few glasses of wine.

This somewhat corrosive property of alcohol is the reason why it causes stomach ulcers and cancer of the oesophagus and stomach. It is also the reason why it was used to dissolve the connective tissue in the frontal lobes of the brain in the first lobotomy operations.

One way or the other, booze is inculcated as a daily habit, whether that be granny's tot of fortified wine, a bottle or two of wine with dinner or while watching TV afterwards, or a six pack of beer at a party or a sporting event.

In other words *advertising* does reduce us to brainwashed zombies who will enjoy drinking poison if told to. We will leap about to primitive music like savages if told to. Many of us still smoke because ads used to tell us to.

All too many of us take drugs like marijuana, heroin and cocaine. All these addictions are practices that supposedly more civilized European explorers learnt from primitive societies and took back to Europe with them.

Push and pull marketing

Some marketing campaigns use *push strategies* which concentrate on the availability of products. In this case the ads are 'basic' and concentrate on telling you the product name and where to get it.

Examples of such ads on TV are:

➢ A presenter reads a script while holding the product in question up in front of the camera.

➢ Ads with only text messages and a voice-over.

➢ Semi-humorous ads which sometimes use cartoon characters to present their message.

➢ Ads targeting children which involve cuddly characters and fantasy scenes and the like.

➤ Ads for junk food which play on having a high 'reward/effort' ratio (Govoni et al., 1988). That 50 million people a day eat McDonald's stuff is testament enough to the success of their advertising.

➤ Ads where the reader just about screams at you not to miss some bargain sale or to go to some cheap store.

Advertisements for 'basic' food, junk food, confectionery, clothing and home appliances are usually of the 'push' type.

Marketing campaigns often use *pull strategies* which promote the product in order to attract buyers. In this case the ads concentrate on 'image' to attract the audience to the product and the product name is secondary and *associated* with the imagery. Examples of this sort of ad on TV are:

➤ Sophisticated ads that show the product in 'classy' surroundings with actors dressed stylishly.

➤ "Laid back' ads were the presenter extols the virtue of the product with, for example, an island resort as a backdrop.

➤ Ads that use glamorous people such as movie stars as actors.

This type of advertising is usually used for higher priced or more 'up market' products, including fashion clothing, cosmetics, expensive furniture, luxury cars and overseas holidays.

One of the most important 'levers' in advertising, undoubtedly, is *keeping up with the Jones's*. This is exploited heavily in marketing cars and new gadgets of which the mobile phone is the supreme example at present.

Another powerful inducement is selling on the 'never-never', for example with no repayments for a year.

13. Advertising

Ubiquitous advertising

Today advertising is literally everywhere.

On TV in Australia there used to be regulations limiting the amount of advertisements per hour to something bearable. Now there seem like 20 minutes or more of ads per hour at times. Worse still, owing to the increasing cost of TV advertising time a truly bewildering string of ads appears in each ad break, sometimes up to about a dozen.

It is almost as bad on radio where there are sometimes as many as half a dozen ads at once on the higher rating commercial stations.

Junk mail from supermarkets and other retail chains has reached epidemic proportions. Other 'direct marketing' is done by phone and is increasingly irritating, often involving requests to complete lengthy market research surveys over the phone.

In addition, free local papers almost totally full of advertisements are also stuffed into millions of letterboxes in major cities.

Trams, trains and buses carry plenty of ads, as do train stations and tram and bus stops.

Taxis and trucks all carry signage, as do many vehicles belonging to small businesses.

Shopping strips are becoming more and more cluttered with advertising signs above the shops, and sandwich boards and often products on the footpath.

More and more restaurants, coffee shops and juice bars have also spilled out onto footpaths, sometimes making little room for the pedestrians for which they were originally intended.

Shopping malls are filled with advertising and more and more stalls with spruikers have appeared in them.

Sporting grounds carry more and more advertising and sporting teams now carry prominent advertising on their clothing.

Casual clothing often comes complete with the brand name writ large upon it.

The Internet is full of advertising, of course, some of it of a lurid nature.

167

Then there is the despicable practice of placing confectionery and soft drinks near the checkouts at supermarkets, resulting in many a tantrum as young children taken shopping throw a tantrum to get another dose of perhaps the first 'drug' of addiction, sugar.

Perhaps the most predatory advertiser of all, Coca Cola, has its vending machines just about everywhere, including pubs and clubs, office buildings, stations and heaven knows where else (they are probably there too!).

Using religion

In the West Christianity has been heavily exploited in marketing for example by:

➤ The use of religious symbols such as stylized crosses in the jewelry business.

➤ The confectionery industry makes heavy use of Easter to sell chocolate. Bakeries join in by selling Easter buns and industries such as the entertainment and travel industries rely heavily on the Easter holiday period.

➤ Christmas, of course, is a bonanza for business and has become almost completely devoid of its original meaning. For example, the image of Santa is actually from a 19th century cartoon of a rich robber baron with some of *his* toys which he certainly isn't going to give away (Solomon, 1992).

➤ Not too distantly related to this are Mother's Day and Father's Day which are also exploited by, and were probably created by, big business.

Religion also makes increasing use of TV and radio programs for promotion and in the US some religious sects have also spent large sums of money to employ advertising companies to run PR campaigns to promote themselves.

13. Advertising

New trends in marketing

Some of the many new trends of late include:
1. Healthy foods, for example low fat products.
2. Recycling.
3. Pollution free and environmentally friendly products.
4. Diets and weight watching.
5. Alternative therapies. Of these the list grows daily:
   a. Aromatherapy.
   b. Herbal remedies.
   c. Acupuncture and Chinese medicine.
   d. Group therapy.
   e. Exercise therapy, for example Yoga and Pilates.
   f. Transcendental meditation.
   g. Reflexology - and so on.

In many large cities where house prices have tended to become unaffordable to new entrants to the market there is a growing 'live for today' approach to consumer spending and this is seen in:
1. The growing fast food industry, including take-away food and packaged 'heat only' meals sold in grocery stores.
2. Increasing diversity in consumption of alcohol.
3. Increasing use of drugs which may perhaps be encouraged by the legalization of marijuana.
4. Increasing use of leisure industries such as gambling.
5. Increasing use of restaurants by young childless workers (who may remain childless).
6. Greater spending by young and independent working women on cosmetics, clothes, jewelry and other beauty and fashion products including hair dressing and magazines.
7. Greater spending on magazines, videos, books, computer games, music and other home entertainment products.
8. Greater spending on cars, holidays and other major items by young childless couples or unattached persons.

In these and many other areas there seems to be a growing market which advertisers are busy exploiting. In some communities, however, one or two of the foregoing examples may be on the wane.

The disastrous sociological results

The extent to which advertising has reduced us to zombies strolling around in uncomfortable jeans and carrying a mobile phone in one hand and a bottle of drink in the other is mind boggling.

An article in *The Australian* newspaper on 23 May 2005 reported that psychologists had found that regular use of text messaging on mobile phones could reduce IQ by as much as 10 points, a staggering outcome.

More important, advertising corrupts young minds by showing young people behaving irresponsibly, for example a recent Pepsi Cola ad showing a few youths riding a large wheeled garbage container down a steep street and into a harbour.

In the early 1960s a US Department of Justice official expressed alarm at the "startling" pace at which youthful lawlessness was increasing and concluded that by 1962 a million American teenagers would be arrested each year.

The same official remarked (Packard, 1963):

We seem to have misplaced the sense of values which made this a great nation. Self-indulgence and the principle of pleasure before duty on a vast and growing scale have become a phenomenon of the adult world. These are warning symptoms of the decadence disease which has contributed to the decay of so many civilizations throughout history.

The role that advertising has played in promoting decadent movies, music and behaviour has resulted in a more violent, lawless, indebted, miserable and brainwashed society.

Propaganda has always painted socialism as communism which permits little freedom. How free are we when we are all brainwashed to dress and behave in the same, often stupid way?

Advertising contributes heavily to the increasing debt levels carried by families in the West. Many people have half a dozen credit cards and get way above their heads in debt, often leading to family disunity and breakups.

The disastrous environmental results

Closely related to advertising is the slick packaging of many products, an example being the easy to use 'heat in the tray' packaging of frozen pizza and lasagna. The economic cost of such packaging is enormous and the environmental consequences drastic.

Another example of this are the thin plastic supermarket bags used in Australian supermarkets. Unbelievable numbers of these are used each year and many of them end up littering streets and parks and clogging creeks and storm water drainage systems, and only now (mid-2018) is some action being taken on this issue.

Atmospheric pollution has reached serious levels in many large industrialized cities and global warming has already been significant not long after the term was first coined.

Parkinson's well known law: *work expands so as to fill the time available for its completion* is generalized to obtain Mohr's Universal Law:

Junk fills the time and space available.

This covers a wide range of the problems of mankind including:

➤ Bureaucratic inefficiency, as in Parkinson's Law that work expands to fill the time available, when people are the junk.

➤ The Peter Principle problem of the most incompetent people being those that rise in hierarchies. Here those rising are the junk.

➤ The problems of pollution.

➤ The problems of resource depletion as a result of excessive consumption of 'junk products' which are unnecessary, extravagant and wasteful, and have planned obsolescence built into them.

Four wheel drives and other cars with massive engines are a good example of the latter issue.

13. ADVERTISING

The Club or Rome Report (Meadows et al., 1974) pointed out that we were then running out of chromium, once so heavily used by ostentatious American cars. That we are now running out of oil promises to be a major catastrophe because we have built our major cities around the car.

All this has occurred because we have long been brainwashed into becoming mindless zombies consuming not for our own benefit, but for the benefit of insanely greedy and highly overpaid executives whose motivation is an even bigger multimillion dollar bonus.

Though the world was already becoming overpopulated by then, "adman-columnist" E.B. Weiss commented in the 1950s (Packard, 1963):

> *Ever since I've been regaled with the current multitude*
> *of wonderful forecasts of a population future sparked by a*
> *remarkable growth of our population I have wondered about*
> *the magical powers of a large population automatically to*
> *assure eternal prosperity at successively higher peaks.*
> *The most populous regions of this mortal coil*
> *tend to be the most poverty-stricken.*

In other words, capitalist industry has been happy to brainwash us into mindless consumption and has even been happy to count on excessive population growth to help boost profits even further, all the while ignoring the finite nature of the world's resources and its finite capacity to absorb the waste products and pollution arising from extravagant consumption.

Unfortunately, the media and advertising often encourage tribalism in relation to political, sporting etc. organizations, and bad behaviours sometimes result. Fortunately, bullying in society has gained more attention in the media recently, in part thanks to the ME TOO movement.

Chapter 14

THE PSYCHOLOGY OF HABITS

> *Television has spread the habit of instant reaction*
> *and has stimulated the hope of instant results.*
> Arthur Schlesinger Jr, In *Newsweek,* 6 July 1970.
>
> *A habit cannot be tossed out the window,*
> *it must be coaxed down the stairs one step at a time.*
> Mark Twain, attributed.

Accommodation

Piaget used the term 'accommodation' to describe how infants come to terms with their environment of a cot, etcetera, and also become familiar with the small group of faces that they regularly see often smiling at them so that, of course, ere long the infant copies this behaviour and smiles back. Thus WordWeb 6 dictionary defines accommodation as:

In the theories of Jean Piaget: the modification of internal representations in order to accommodate a changing knowledge of reality.

This early adaptation to a small group of 'familiar faces', and the copying behaviour associated with it, is an early form of social and imitative learning, a process by which we develop many of the habits we adopt throughout our lives.

Then, of course, the many years most of us spend in the all too long and drawn out education system inculcate many other habits, whilst throughout our lives we are literally bombarded with advertising and religious and political propaganda, from which many lifelong habits are acquired.

Early learning

A great deal of what a child learns, of course, is taught by parents, other relatives, and teachers in a relatively formal didactic manner. Indeed, modern societies rely almost totally upon teaching at schools, colleges and Universities to train children and young adults for a vocation that in many cases will occupy them for most of their life.

Indeed, for many people learning becomes a habit, and they continue to learn throughout life by reading and studying subjects related to their jobs, or subjects that simply interest them, such interests often having been 'adopted' from parents and other life role models.

Imitative learning

Young children learn many behaviours by imitating or 'modeling' those of their parents, siblings, teachers and friends etcetera. Such imitation ranges from manner of speech to eating and recreational habits. Thus many children take up the same sports as their parents, whilst others may learn swear words and such bad habits as smoking from friends at school.

Social learning

Social learning is simply imitative learning that takes place in the larger context of society, rather than the confines of home or the classroom. It includes social groups such as friends, religious groups, and sporting and other clubs that a person might belong to.

It is by a combination of imitation of parents and social learning from a small group of friends that children may acquire an interest in beer and/or wine, for example, or worse still and far more dangerous to their health in the long run, illegal drug habits usually begin with social learning, for example at teen dances and parties etcetera.

Studies have also found that children with only one parent are more likely to smoke or drink by the age of 11.

Religion

Throughout history religion has played a major role in instructing adherents in how to behave according to guidelines established by each religion. An example of this, a Pope in the 1960s said something along the lines of: *Give me a child before the age of five and I will make him a Catholic for life.*

The current plague of Islamic conflict and terrorism that afflicts much of the world at present is, of course, in part a result of Islamic teachings based on the Koran's frequent advocacy of jihad against "unbelievers" in order to establish caliphates for a particular Muslim leader.

An example of the satanic Muslim religion, in one "barbaric" episode in Mosul 'Islamic State' captured a group of fleeing women and children and burned them alive.

Political propaganda

In like fashion to that of religion, political propaganda has played a major role in human history, usually with disastrous results as often clearly insane and greedy leaders seek power over more and more people and territory, often using religion as a pretext for their aims at greater self-glorification.

Hitler was perhaps one of the best examples, the Nazis doing an excellent job of 'brainwashing' the German people with a constant hail of propaganda to support them. The Nazis also provided their troops with massive amounts of amphetamines to 'energize' their military efforts, whilst Hitler became addicted to a cocktail of drugs including cocaine during WW2, perhaps contributing to increasing depression as the war turned bad for his forces, and ultimately contributing to his suicide.

Two factors in his hate of the Jews were:

(a) The centuries old European prejudice against them because, when they had trouble being employed by Christians, they would go into such businesses as running pawn shops and banking, thereby getting rich.

(b) Rumour had it, and I tend to believe it, that he had contracted syphilis from a Jewish prostitute during WW1. Syphilis not being curable then, because antibiotics had not been discovered, the later stages of it no doubt added to his madness gradually as the years rolled by.

A globally widespread example of propaganda of sorts is the use of the terms 'right' and 'left' to compare capitalist sympathetic political parties and parties with more socialist policies, the term 'right', of course, being intended to sound 'right' in the sense of 'correct' or the 'right thing to do'. Here then is a major example of how the mass media in the West promulgates its bias towards the capitalist system that runs it.

The mass media and advertising

As discussed at modest length in Chapters 12 and 13, the mass media and advertising are the main means by which modern society is fed information, whether to 'sell' a particular religion or political party, or a household or other product.

The persuasiveness and effectiveness of advertising is, of course, sometimes remarkable, the Reception-Yielding Model of Figure 13.2 illustrating quite well why advertising is so successful in appealing to more 'gullible' or less intelligent consumers.

Recognition and *approval* are important factors in how 'consumer zombies' are brainwashed into lifelong habits of consumption, as emphasized by the 'CAB' model of Figure 13.1 in which cognitive, attitudinal and behavioural responses follow exposure to a stimulus such as that of an advertisement. Then, positive attitude or 'approval' is likely to lead to consumption of a product, and perhaps habitual consumption of it.

Indeed we are creatures of habit, much of our lives being spent in the company of just a few friends or family, consuming certain products we have come to like, and spending our spare time in certain adopted pursuits, for example going to the same pub or restaurant, and following a particular sporting team regularly.

Psychopathic behaviours

This is the largest category of abnormal psychological types, the pathology of which may involve such traits as:

[1] Assertiveness, aggression and bullying.
[2] Dishonesty and lying.
[3] Alcohol and drug addiction.
[4] Excessive sexual behaviours.

Psychopaths usually have two or more of the above traits, but are not normally classified as mentally ill, in part perhaps because such behaviours are so common.

Bullying may be learnt by an eldest brother or sister, and the first author knew examples of both cases both within his own 'nuclear family', his extended (by his own marriage) family, and people with whom he was friendly for a while.

Evidently the eldest is able to boss younger siblings around from an early age, and often stays bossy with both these siblings, and perhaps other people throughout most of the rest of their life until too old and feeble to be bossy anymore.

Bullying usually involves a 'superior' or boss, or somebody with psychopathic aggressive tendencies based on feelings of superiority, 'bad mouthing' the victim to their face with brief but hurtful and disturbing insults. These insults are repeated regularly to both the victim, often a 'loner' in an isolated situation, and to the bully's small group of friends and supporters who then repeat the same insults to the victim, increasing his or her feelings of isolation and helplessness.

In the schoolyard, for example, the bully is often bigger and stronger than the victim, who may be of the 'nerd' type. Indeed, the bully is often better at sport, but jealous of the victim getting better marks in class and perhaps occasional praise from teachers and others.

In the workplace the reasons for bullying by bosses or 'superiors' in the workplace hierarchy are often less clear, but often, for example, involve male bosses abusing women with 'sexual insults' that they are ugly, or that women in general are in some way inferior.

Addiction

Addiction to legal substances such as nicotine, a brain stimulant, or alcohol, a vasodilator and thus subtle tranquilizer, is, of course, very common.

Alcohol abuse can lead to problems in the workplace, home or social venues. Heavy drinkers suffer unusual brain shrinkage of both white and grey matter, reduction of the latter giving rise to the widespread belief that alcohol kills neurons (Sweeney, 2009).

Western governments have taken several measures to limit smoking, particularly limitation if not prohibition of advertising of cigarettes, in part to reduce the huge impact that the long-term health effects of smoking have upon public health system budgets.

Similarly, measures such as tougher drink-driving laws, earlier closing of some late night clubs and bars, and tougher penalties for family violence, have been put on place to limit some of the harmful consequences of drinking to excess.

Drugs, including alcohol and nicotine, have two problems:

(a) They don't really taste nice unless diluted enough by other things such as water and sugar in the case of booze.

(b) They alter the metabolic rate, resulting in changes in pulse rate and blood pressure, and contraction or dilation of blood vessels in the brain and elsewhere. Thus every sizable dose of most drugs gives you withdrawal symptoms, whether you realize it or not. If you have an overdose you will realize it and you might want some 'hair of the dog' (that bit you) as alcoholics call a dose of booze early in the day to help overcome a hangover.

As for quitting smoking and moderating booze consumption, the first author devoted a chapter to this subject in several books (Mohr, 2012c; 2013a; 2015; 2018a; 2018b).

Increasingly, addiction to pharmaceutical drugs such as Valium prescribed for anxiety, or the raft of drugs prescribed for relatively newly 'invented' conditions such as ADHD and OCD, is commonplace and, indeed, something of a modern medical scandal comparable to that of the practice of lobotomy and leucotomy 50+ years ago.

The global illegal drug industry is now, unfortunately, along with the global arms industry, one of the world's largest. Some of the most widely used illegal drugs include:

[1] Cocaine and its derivates, including morphine, are highly addictive and have been widely used for more than a century. High quality cocaine, however, is very expensive, so that users often turn to crime to 'feed' their habit.

[2] Heroin, a narcotic that is considered a 'hard drug', is a highly addictive morphine derivative, intravenous injection providing the fastest and most intense 'rush'.

[3] LSD became quite popular in the 1960s but is rarely used now. It binds to serotonin receptors, only very small amounts having profound effects, including altered states of consciousness and hallucinations. In some cases LSD has been associated with psychosis, particularly when taken by a person with an existing mental disorder (Sweeney, 2009).

[5] Marijuana grew greatly in popularity from the 1970s, and is still widely in use, being easily able to be grown on country farms, and in suburban backyard and sheds.

Marijuana's active ingredient delta-9-tetrahydrocanniabinal (THC) inhibits release of the glutamate and GABA neurotransmitters, reducing cognitive function. Caffeine has the opposite effect of increasing neuronal release of glutamate and GABA, thereby slightly increasing cognition.

As noted in Chapter 15, marijuana use has been found to correlate with the incidence of schizophrenia.

[5] Methamphetamines, particularly crystal meth or 'ice', have become widely used in the last two decade, and are easily able to be manufactured with quite small and simple chemistry apparatuses in suburban houses and garages.

Gambling

Gambling is now a massive global industry, ranging from gambling on various sports to the growing casino industry. Gambling on horse racing has ruined the lives of many people, but it is gambling on poker machines that has ruined many more.

Many millions of people around the Western world are addicted to poker machines which might be likened to Skinner boxes in which rats quickly learn to press a lever to obtain a food reward, soon increasing their rate of lever pressing to hundreds of times per minute.

The video screens are part of the addiction no doubt, just as they prove to be in laboratory experiments with pigs and, of course, TV and PC screens have proved to be highly addictive with many humans.

Habits and hope

Many of the most common habits involve some degree of addiction, smoking, alcohol and gambling being some of the best examples. Most habits, however, such as the foods we like, the sports we play or follow, and the types of movies we like, are generally seen as relatively harmless.

A substantial proportion of the most common habits can be seen to involve hope, particularly gambling, when we hope to win, and in supporting a favourite sporting team, when we hope that it wins.

Regrettably, however, most habits are unproductive pastimes at best, often expensive, and all too often downright harmful.

For a better quality of life, therefore, we should seek to develop habits that are likely to have positive outcomes, for example a good work ethic which we could hope would ultimately be rewarded with better job satisfaction, better pay, and perhaps a better job and life (*The Psychology of Hope*, Mohr et al., 2018).

Conclusions

Behaviours and habits, including bullying, are learnt from the outset by accommodation, modeling and imitative and social learning, as well, of course, by formal learning whether this be in the home or at school.

Such often lifelong habits as interests in and perhaps participation in music, reading, movies, and certain sports are acquired by both imitative and social learning, as well as teaching in many cases.

The mass media and advertising, of course, play a key role in modern society, informing us of current events, and also persuading us to adopt a particular religion, support a particular political party, or buy an advertised product.

Indeed, the extent to which we in today's consumer society are 'brainwashed' has all too many negative consequences and led the first author to coin the term *consumer zombie* (Mohr, 2013b; Mohr & Fear, 2016; Mohr et al., 2018e).

For a better quality of life, therefore, we should make a habit of focusing on productive and positive goals that, if achieved, will improve our lives.

Such goals might include, for example, a better job, making more money, and a better, happier, and healthier lifestyle as free as possible from bad habits.

☺ ☻ ☹ ☺ ☻ ☹ ☺ ☻ ☹ ☺ ☻ ☹ ☺ ☻ ☹

14. The Psychology of Habits

PART IV
PSYCHOLOGY AND PSYCHIATRY

Chapter 15

PSYCHOLOGY AND PSYCHIATRY

*Starting in the late 1950s and early '60s, the psychoanalysts set out
to convince the public that we were 'all' walking wounded,
normal neurotics, functioning psychotics ...
and that Freud's teachings contained the secrets
to eradicating inner strife and reaching our full potential.*
Jeffrey A. Lieberman, *Shrinks, The Untold Story of Psychiatry*,
Little, Brown & Co., NY (2015).

Introduction

Psychology is defined as the 'science' of the mind, and psychological as 'mental' or 'emotional' as distinct from physical in nature. Psychiatry is defined as the branch of medicine dealing with the 'diagnosis' and 'treatment' of 'mental disorders'. In the last couple of decades psychologists have far outnumbered psychiatrists and they consult with patients about 'mental health' issues, whilst psychiatrists mainly deal with more serious 'mental illnesses', though the line between the two practices is now somewhat blurred.

The present chapter discusses some of the early history of psychiatry, then discussing a range of common mental illnesses.

Chapter 18 then briefly discusses some of the main methods by which psychological problems are diagnosed.

15. PSYCHOLOGY AND PSYCHIATRY

Psychiatry

Sigmund Freud (1865 - 1939) believed human beings to be wholly driven by their unconscious minds, and developed what he called "the talking cure" or psychoanalysis which some regard as the first method of examining the human mind. He also proposed the division of the psyche into ego (our outer self), super-ego (our conscience) and id (our inner self).

Alfred Alder, on the other hand, saw us as social beings who create a style of life in response to the environment and what we feel we lack (Alder, 1927).

Modern psychiatry now assesses a wide range of mental disorders, several of which are discussed in following sections.

The field of psychiatry, however, has a disgraceful history. As late as 1815 the Bethlehem madhouse in England exhibited lunatics every Sunday and made a considerable amount of money in the process (Youngson & Schott, 1996).[1]

At the Bicêtre hospital in France attendants used whips to make the mad perform dances to provide traditional entertainment. At the Charenton asylum the infamous Marquis de Sade presided over theatrical performances by the inmates.

In the USSR dissidents were often confided to asylums for the insane, a policy no doubt practiced elsewhere.

The practice of lobotomy was particularly scandalous.

It can be traced back to Dr Gottlieb Burckhardt, the superintendent of a psychiatric hospital in Switzerland, who in 1890 drilled holes in the head of six severely agitated patients, thereby altering their behaviour.

Then in 1935 John Fulton at Yale University removed the frontal lobes from two chimpanzees, changing their behaviour greatly. Dr Walter Freeman, an American neurologist, was recovering from a nervous breakdown when in July 1935 he attended a seminar given by Fulton.

---

[1] The word Bedlam is a corruption of "Bethlehem."

184

Egas Moniz, a celebrated Portuguese neurosurgeon also attended the seminar and two months later in Portugal he performed the first *leucotomy* by drilling a small hole in the skull and injecting alcohol into it to destroy the fibres in the frontal lobes of the patient.

The operation succeeded in making the patient less agitated and overtly paranoid but made her more apathetic and dull than Moniz had hoped. Nevertheless, further operations were performed and the procedure was refined by drilling six holes in the skull.

When he published he gave no hint of the downside of his procedure and Walter Freeman was bursting with enthusiasm to try it and he enlisted the aid of neurosurgeon James Watts to carry out his first leucotomy on 14 September 1936.

A week later the patient became incoherent and could not even recite the days of the week and when asked to write could only scribble nonsense. Her speech improved in following days and they operated on another five patients.

In November 1936 Freeman and Watts published a report in which they wrote: *In all our patients there was a ... common denominator of worry, apprehension, anxiety, insomnia and nervous tension, and in all of them these symptoms have been relieved to a greater or lesser extent.*

Freeman and Watts renamed the procedure *lobotomy* and made it more drastic by drilling only two holes in the side of the head and using a canula, the tubing from a six inch heavy-gauge hypodermic needle, to pave the way for a cutting tool to destroy targeted brain tissue.

Watts became so proficient that he could thread the canula through the brain from the small hole on one side of the head to that on the other. Though not qualified to do so, Freeman began to perform lobotomies on his own and became a celebrity in the process. He also simplified the procedure by using electroshock to subdue the patient and then plunging an ice pick into their head, usually producing a zombie-like person.

Often the procedure was repeated a second and third time and Freeman, a neurotic with severe depressive symptoms who needed 3 Nembutal to sleep at night, enthusiastically continued his crude procedure years after it had been discredited.

Such surgery had been performed on more than 40,000 people in the USA alone by 1955. Fortunately, lobotomy has fallen out of favour though it is probably still practiced occasionally.

The misinformation that allowed this brutal procedure to be performed for some 30 years, however, is all too typical of a world in which we are fed misinformation and brainwashed into accepting any new procedure or product no matter how dangerous.

Little better, however, is widely used electroconvulsive shock therapy (ECT) in which electrodes are placed on either side of the head and short bursts of high-frequency and high intensity electrical current passed through the brain. ECT can produce a strong amnesic effect, but it is not clear by what means this occurs (Atrens & Curthoys, 1982).

Psychopaths

This is the largest category of abnormal psychological types, involving the following behaviours such as (Davies, 1971):

[1] Assertiveness, aggression and bullying.
[2] Dishonesty and lying.
[3] Alcohol and drug addiction.
[4] Excessive sexual behaviours.

Psychopaths usually have two or more of the above traits, but are not normally classified as mentally ill, in part perhaps because they are so common.

Through their assertiveness, dishonesty etc. psychopaths often rise high in the hierarchies of business. Gillespie (2017), having had "many good managers" in his "various careers", cites a personal example of a psychopathic boss:

He was constantly meddling - - micromanaging the workplace - -. He trusted nobody and his impact on the workplace was devastating.

This boss made a habit of giving select people subtle but excruciating public punishment. - - The longer I knew him the more convinced I became that everything he said was a lie.

He cites a few examples of famous people from the past and present who might be described as psychopaths, including Caligula, Lance Armstrong, and Donald Trump, quoting Tony Schwartz, the co-author of Trump's autobiography, as telling the *New Yorker* that if he were writing *The Art of the Deal* today, he'd call it 'The Sociopath'.

Another factor relating to psychopathy is that males with the genetic XYY syndrome "may be much more likely to commit antisocial acts than normal males", and 1 in 80 tall males in the general population is XYY, but 1 in 11 in institutions for the criminally insane are XYY (Weiss & Mann, 1978).

Mania

Typical manic behaviour involves a period in which an expansive, elevated, or irritable mood, along with enhanced activity and reactivity persists abnormally. During this episode symptoms such as increased talkativeness and grandiosity, distractibility, decreased need for sleep, inflated self-esteem, and excessive involvement in pleasurable yet risky activities may be present.

Such symptoms occur during normal mood changes, but it is their magnitude and frequent recurrence that may indicate a psychiatric problem. The frenetic and driven behaviour of mania results in a non-functional individual who cannot work effectively (Atrens & Curthoys, 1982).

The neurochemical alterations in mania are less clearly understood, but it is well established that drugs effective in the treatment of mania are those that antagonize dopamine and serotonin. The mechanism responsible for the therapeutic efficacy of lithium for the treatment of mania is not yet clear. Although mood disorders tend to have a familial background, the evidence for a genetic component is not convincing.

Depression

Depression is very common, and it is normal to feel depressed from time to time. Severe depression, however, is characterized by despondency, diminished interest in most or all activities, weight fluctuation not due to dieting, disruption in sleep patterns, psychomotor agitation or retardation, feelings of worthlessness, being excessively quiet, and recurrent thoughts of death or suicide.

A professional diagnosis of depression is made, however, when a person suffers frequent and/or prolonged bouts of depression of more than usual severity, perhaps associated with thoughts of self-harm or suicide.

Major depression is associated with decreased brain levels of the neurotransmitters norepinephrine and serotonin, and the most effective therapy consists of drugs that inhibit the breakdown of these compounds.

Much less common, manic depression, or bipolar disorder, involves both manic 'highs' of greater energy and activity, alternating with bouts of depression or 'lows'. Manic depression is often treated with lithium salts.

Writers and artists, many of whom work in relative solitude, have often been associated with depression (Thomas & Hughes, 2006), Vincent van Gogh being a notable example (Sweeney, 2009).

Anxiety

It is normal to feel anxious about things ranging from minor issues such as getting behind with one's work or household chores, to worrying when a child is late coming home from a party. Many people have abnormal levels of anxiety, including phobias and fears, and tranquillizers such as Valium, which enhances the inhibitory actions of the neurotransmitter GABA, are used to relieve anxiety and relax muscles.

Hypochondria

Hypochondria is an anxiety disorder in which people worry excessively about their health, for example just hearing someone mention a certain illness triggering fears that they might have that illness.

Obsessive Compulsive Disorder

Obsessive Compulsive Disorder (OCD) is a form of anxiety which makes people worry about certain things and 'overreact' to their concerns, the two most common behaviours being washing and checking, for example some people wearing away skin on their hands by frequently washing them, others repeatedly checking such things as whether the door is locked when they leave home.

One OCD sufferer, for example, feels compelled to do many things four times, another to count to seven between each mouthful of food (Carter, 2000).

Panic disorder

Panic disorder involves recurring, unexpected attack of anxiety called *panic attacks* in situations that would not concern most people. Attacks may occur without obvious cause and last from a few minutes up to an hour or more, with the person feeling sick, dizzy, breathless, tight in the chest and disoriented.

Panic disorder is often accompanied by *agoraphobia*, a morbid fear of being alone in public places.

In severe cases agoraphobics are not prepared to leave their home for fear of a panic attack, often being unable to keep a job or have a social life.

Anti-anxiety medications such as depressants are sometimes prescribed for panic disorder, but don't treat the cause of the anxiety. Cognitive Behaviour Therapy (CBT), which is discussed in Chapter 19, is often used to help treat agoraphobia.

Teaching patients how to relax with *relaxation training*, and how to use *slow breathing technique* (SBT), may also help in reducing hyperventilation which often accompanies panic attacks.

Phobias

Phobias are irrational and excessive fears of a particular object or event that disrupt normal functioning, and can be reduced by avoiding the object and thoughts about it.

Feared objects may be potentially dangerous, such as snakes, spiders, or being in high places. They may have little or no associated danger, such as flowers (anthophobia), computers (cyberphobia), or daylight (phengophobia).

Social phobia is an irrational fear of social or performance situations in which embarrassment may occur.

People are not normally classified as having a specific phobia unless symptoms of it have lasted for at least six months.

Specific phobias can be treated using CBT or *systematic desensitization,* in which patients are taught to gradually replace their fear response with a relaxed response.

Tourette's syndrome

Tourette's syndrome is also an anxiety disorder, and certainly sufferers do appear anxious and disturbed when they have a bout of Tourette's and stressfully utter a nonsensical word while some part of their body, usually the face, has a 'tic' or twitches.

Asperger's syndrome

This is a psychiatric disorder usually noted during early school years and characterized by impaired social relations and by repetitive patterns of behaviour.

Autism

This an abnormal absorption with the self marked by communication disorders, short attention span, and inability to deal with other people.

In 2016 a Finish study of 258 people found that religious people could be compared with those with autism because they didn't view the world realistically, many believing in such supernatural phenomena as demons, gods and inanimate objects being alive in some way.

ADHD

Attention Deficit Hyperactivity Disorder (ADHD) is normally associated with school children who have difficulty sitting through classes without feeling distracted and wishing to be elsewhere doing something else. They thus have trouble concentrating and their learning is affected adversely.

There is much current controversy about this condition, many feeling that it is diagnosed too freely with children needlessly being put on long-term medication that may do more harm than good.

Dyslexia

This is an impaired ability to comprehend written words usually associated with a neurological disorder. The cause of dyslexia is believed to involve both genetic environmental factors and it often occurs in people with ADHD and is associated with similar difficulties with numbers. It may begin in adulthood as the result of a traumatic brain injury, stoke or dementia. The underlying mechanisms of dyslexia are problems within the brain's language processing.

Dyslexia is diagnosed through a series of tests of memory, spelling, vision, and reading skills and should not be confused with reading difficulties caused by hearing or vision problems, or insufficient teaching.

Treatment involves adjusting teaching methods to meet the person's needs which, while not curing the underlying problem, may decrease the symptoms. Treatments targeting vision are ineffective.

Dyslexia is the most common learning disability and occurs all around the world. It affects 3–7% of the population but up to 20% may have some degree of symptoms. While dyslexia is more often diagnosed in men, it has been suggested that it affects men and women equally.

Dyslexia should not be confused with 'mirror writing', for which Leonardo da Vinci was famous, some believing that he wrote in this fashion deliberately as a sort of coding.

Schizophrenia

Schizophrenia is a chronic neurological disease of distorted thoughts and perceptions which usually begins during adolescence or early adulthood (Sweeney, 2009) It has a strong genetic component, one which research shows may be largely physiological, and not a result of a "disturbed environment" (Atrens & Curthoys, 1982).

Schizoid people worry obsessively about being watched by others and being talked about, fearing that people know too much about them and have invaded their 'space'. When walking in the street, for example, they will worry that other people are watching them, in this way 'distorting' reality.

Schizophrenia is relatively common, occurring in about 1 percent of the general population worldwide. Because the incidence of schizophrenia among parents, children, and siblings of patients with the disease is increased to 15 percent, it is believed that heredity plays an important role in the genesis of the disease (Atrens & Curthoys, 1982). However, other studies suggest that non-genetic factors such as a "disturbed environment" are also influential.

In the last decade or two, for example, a correlation between excessive and prolonged marijuana use and the development of schizophrenia has been observed.

The biochemical basis of the disease may be an excess of the neurotransmitter substance dopamine, as high levels of dopamine and its metabolites, as well as increased dopamine receptors, are found in the brains of persons with schizophrenia. Further evidence for this hypothesis is that the drugs most effective in treating the disease are those that have a high capacity to block dopamine receptors.

Psychosis

Psychosis is any severe mental disorder in which contact with reality is lost or highly distorted, including severe schizophrenia. The drug chlorpromazine was developed and widely used to treat psychosis, by 1964 ten thousand peer-reviewed articles having been published on it. According to Lieberman (2015),

Like a bolt from the blue, here was a medication that could relieve the madness that disabled tens of millions of men and women - - the widespread adoption of chlorpromazine marked the beginning of the end for the asylums.

The commercial success of this drug encouraged pharmaceutical companies to search for new antipsychotic drugs, leading to the massive pharmaceutical industry of today.

Hysteria

This is a neurotic disorder characterized by violent emotional outbreaks and disturbances of sensory and motor functions. The term hysteria comes from the Greek word *hustericos* meaning 'of the womb' because ancient Greeks associated such highly emotional and neurotic behaviour with childless women. This indicates that man has long had an interest in trying to understand human psychology and behaviour.

Dementia

Dementia is simply mental deterioration usually associated with old age. Senile dementia of the Alzheimer type (SDAT) is a result of advanced Alzheimer's disease, a progressive form of pre-senile dementia that is similar to senile dementia except that it usually starts in the 40s or 50s, the first symptoms being impaired memory which is followed by impaired thought and speech, and finally complete helplessness.

Homosexuality

Homosexuality is on the increase. Once a trait one had to keep secret it is now rampantly displayed at gay Mardi Gras festivals, at gay bars in major cities, and in late night TV ads for homosexual dating services.

Some claim that homosexuality is inherited and a study of 113 people in 33 families in which at least two brothers were homosexual found a genetic marker on the X-chromosome (Xq28) that had a very high correlation with sexual orientation (Galton, 2001).

Genes may play a minor 'predispositionary' role but, largely, homosexuality is a learnt behaviour. Typically, for example, the normal heterosexual male has one or two homosexual experiences in adolescence (Robertson, 1981), and no doubt the same applies to women.

Those who become homosexuals, therefore, presumably do so as a result of imitative learning at an early age. There are, no doubt, also psychological factors involved, for example a lack of confidence in approaching the opposite sex coupled with the fact that there are earlier homosexual experiences to draw upon as an alternative behaviour model.

If alcoholism is to be regarded as a psychiatric illness, as it often is (Davies, 1971), then homosexuality is even more obviously a treatable psychiatric condition as well.

That said, most of our heterosexual behaviours are also learnt ones, many of them hardly natural or healthy, an example being 'tongue kissing', a truly revolting and very unhealthy practice like many other modern sexual practices.

Post-traumatic Stress Disorder (PTSD)

PTSD is caused by events of great stress and trauma in a person's life, perhaps the best-known example being that of Western Vietnam war veterans, whose vulnerability to symptoms of PTSD such as depression and suicidal thoughts was no doubt increased by feelings of isolation as a result of having fought in a war which many thought to be mistake in the first place, and which the West ultimately lost.

Losing one's job, or the death of a spouse or young child are also common causes of PTSD.

According to Cozolino (2002):

Someone suffering from PTSD is, in essence, in a continual loop of unconscious self-traumatization, coping and exhaustion. When these symptoms are experienced on a chronic basis, they can devastate every aspect of the victim's life, from physical well-being to the quality of relationships to the victim's experience of the world.

Symptoms of PTSD may be *intrusive* and include:
➤ Distressing memories or dreams of the event.
➤ Mentally reliving the event.
➤ Distress when reminded of it.
➤ Physiological reactions including sweating and high pulse rate when reminded of it.

Avoidance and *numbing* symptoms to block unpleasant memories and feelings associated with the trauma include:
➤ Avoiding thinking and talking about the event.
➤ Avoiding things and places that remind one of the event.
➤ Feelings of detachment from reality.
➤ Restriction of emotions such as kindness and love.

Hyperarousal symptoms may include:
➤ Difficulty in sleeping.
➤ Difficulty in concentrating.
➤ Irritability and anger outbursts.
➤ Hypervigilance or always looking out for signs of danger.

Typically, people with PTSD have one or more symptoms from each category.

PTSD is often accompanied by other physical and psychological problems, including feelings of panic, depression, and abuse of alcohol and other drugs.

PTSD can be treated using Cognitive Behavioural Therapy (see Chapter 19) and stress management techniques, for example mindfulness meditation slow breathing, and anti-depressant and anti-anxiety medications may also be used.

Conclusion

Freud has often been accused of an obsession with sexual feelings (Gillespie, 2017), whilst both he and Jung seem to have been overly obsessed with the importance of dreams, leading many people to distrust formal "talk therapy". Chapter 19, therefore, discusses a range of treatments for psychological problems.

Bullying behaviours are, of course, common amongst psychopaths, and how hierarchies tend to produce and/or encourage psychopaths was discussed in Chapter 9, where the Hare Checklist for Psychopaths was given in Table 9.1, whilst the Mohr Checklist for Psychopaths is given and discussed in Appendix B.

☺☺☹☺☺☹☺☺☹☺☺☹☺☺☹

Chapter 16

PERSONALITY

> *Man's main task in life is to give birth to himself,*
> *to become what he potentially is.*
> *The most important product of his effort is his own personality.*
> Erich Fromm, *Man For Himself*, ch. 4 (1947).

Freud's components of personality

Freud believed that a person's basic personality is fully formed by about five or six years of age, and that it only undergoes slight refinement thereafter.

He proposed that personality had three basic parts:

1. The *id*, or inner self, representing the innate, biological needs we are born with such as hunger, thirst, sleep and sex.

Conceptually the id is the 'force' of the demanding, impulsive, illogical, irrational and selfish part of our personality, and it seeks satisfaction regardless of the feelings of others.

Freud believed that a newborn child's behavior is dominated by the id, the child crying immediately some need is experienced, whilst most young children's behavior is mostly driven by the id, resulting in them often being demanding.

2. The *ego*, or outer self, develops as infants move into childhood and begin to acquire some understanding that needs can't always be met immediately, if at all.

The ego is realistic, logical and orderly, and considers the 'real-life' restrictions that must be considered in dealing with the demands of the id.

3. The **superego** is our 'conscience' or personal understanding of what is right or wrong.

The superego develops by learning from parents and others what are acceptable forms of behaviour.

Freud believed that the id, ego, and superego forces are at a state of constant interaction within us, and that all our behaviour is governed by this interaction.

The most frequent interaction is between the self-satisfying urges of the id and the moral views of the superego, "the ego often playing the role of mediator trying to find a way to satisfy the id without upsetting the moral of the superego, within the limitations of the real world" (Grivas & Carter, 2005).

According to Freud, in a 'balanced' personality the id, ego, and superego play relatively equal roles.

When the id is somewhat dominant, one's personality may be self-centred, demanding, sulky, and childish.

When the ego is stronger than the id or the superego, one may be logical and practical, and perhaps somewhat introverted.

When the superego dominates the id and ego, a person may be moralistic and strict, often feel self-guilt, and be antisocial.

Defence mechanisms

According to Freud, the ego uses 'defence mechanisms' which take a slightly distorted, more optimistic view of reality to reduce anxiety. Some of the most common defence mechanisms are:

➢ Denial: denying painful thoughts.
➢ Repression: preventing bad thoughts from becoming conscious.
➢ Rationalization: finding an explanation for one's thoughts and actions that justifies them.
➢ Intellectualization: using reasoning to block out emotional stress and conflict
➢ Compensation: ignoring bad outcomes by thinking about one's successful activities.

> ➢ Sublimation: modifying the natural expression of an impulse or instinct (especially a sexual one) to one that is socially acceptable.
> ➢ Projection: attributing your own shortcomings and emotions to someone else.
> ➢ Regression: fleeing from reality by assuming a more infantile state.

In summary, defence mechanisms are unconscious processes that tend to reduce the anxiety associated with instinctive desires, bad memories, bad outcomes etc.

Behavioural psychology

The ancient Greeks classified people as having four temperament types: sanguine, choleric, phlegmatic, and melancholy.

Hans Eysenck classified people according to three the 'supertraits' or dimensions of psychoticism, extraversion/introversion, and neuroticism (Gillespie, 2017).

This came to be known as the PEN model, it's characteristics including:

Extraverts are is less 'internally' excitable than introverts so they seek contact with others for stimulation. They tend to be optimistic and lively, and are sometimes unreliable risk takers who care little about how they are perceived.

Introverts are more 'internally' excitable and moody and this 'internal preoccupation' is mentally taxing so that they minimize social interaction. They worry more about life and tend to be pessimistic, and have low self-esteem.

Neurotic people are anxious and stressed, they over-react to stimuli and tend to be emotionally unstable. Neurotic introverts are worriers susceptible to phobias and panic attacks, whereas neurotic extraverts tend to repress their fears and concerns.

Psychotic people tend to be reckless and mentally unstable, in the extreme being an antisocial psychotic or sociopath/psychopath.

Type A and B personalities

US Cardiologists Friedman and Rosenman (1959) proposed that there were two basic personality types, Type A and Type B.

People with type A personalities are ambitious, competitive, industrious, goal-oriented, time conscious, impatient, highly motivated, energetic, easily annoyed, suspicious, verbally aggressive, and get angry when their efforts are frustrated.

Such people are often successful, but rarely satisfied, and keep trying to make more money etc., often being impatient, easily irritated, and indulging in bullying in the process.

People with Type B personalities tend to be the opposite of Type A, and are generally easy going, patient, calm, not overly ambitious, not highly competitive, in less of a hurry, and satisfied with their lives.

Friedman and Rosenman's research team interviewed each participant in their survey about their work and eating habits. During the 8.5 year study 7% of the participants had heart attacks, all of these with Type A personality, leading to the conclusion that Type A males were twice as likely to have a heart attack as Type B males.

Other studies on this issue gave mixed results, and other researchers suggested that only the higher levels of anger and hostility of Type A personality were significant risk factors for heart disease, and that hard-working people who enjoy their work are at no greater risk of heart disease than others.

Type C personality

Research has also indentified a Type C personality associated with an increased risk of cancer.

People with Type C personality tend to have a strong need to conform, be introverted, and be more submissive to the demands of others. They also tend to be pessimistic, avoid facing problems, and to be prone to depression.

In one research study, participants with Type C personality were found to be 16 times more likely to have developed cancer, whereas only 1% of those not of Type C personality developed cancer (Shaffer et al., 1987).

One explanation for this finding is that suppression of negative emotions such as anger and sadness is associated with suppression of immune system function (Eysenck, 1994).

Studies have shown that periods of intense or prolonged stress or depression do indeed impair functioning of the immune system, but other studies have failed to find a link between Type C personality and cancer.

The three A, B and C personality types do, however, provide a useful classification of human behaviours, as illustrated in Table 16.1 (Mamonov, 2001).

Table 16.1. Characteristics of personality types A, B and C.

Type A	Type B	Type C
Very competitive	Non-competitive	Passive
Quick to anger, easily irritated	Consciously controls anger	Suppresses anger
Copes via hostility and competitiveness	Expresses emotions appropriately	Tries to please others, doesn't show negative feelings
Focused on own needs	Capable of meeting own needs and of responding to others	Self-sacrificing, denies own needs
Always rushed	Never feels rushed, even under pressure	Lethargic
Wants a good job and to recognition	Prefers to satisfy self, no matter what others think	Tries to please others, avoids conflict
Impatient	Patient	Obedient, even when manipulated by others
Fast (eating, walking, speaking)	Normal speed	Slow in doing things
Hard-driving	Easygoing	Neutral
Struggling	Confident and content	Gives up easily
Few interests outside work	Many interests	Put interests of others above own
In control	Self-supportive	Sense of helplessness
Emphatic in speech (may pound desk)	Slow, deliberate speaker	Does not speak about own needs
Pursues opportunities the world offers	Moderately ambitious	Sense of hopelessness
Rejecting	Offering	Accepting

Conclusions

Freud's *id, ego,* and *superego* where, of course, an important early milestone in the early development of the science of psychology, and its competing components of basic needs, logical thought, and 'conscience' provide a still useful model of how the mind works.

Eysencks's four classifications of extraverts, introverts, neurotic and psychotic, on the other hand, combine aspects of personality (the first pair), and also mental health disorders (the second pair) such as depression and anxiety, and psychopathy.

Type A, B and C personality types do provide a simple classification of personalities and associated behaviours.

Comparable to these types, but somewhat simpler, 'Mohr's Morphology,' postulates three personality types based on a scale of aggressiveness (Mohr & Fear, 2015; Mohr et al., 2018d):

(a) Aggressive/assertive (the bossy-bully types).

(b) Neutral (the OK guys).

(c) Placid (the meek).

The meek do not inherit the earth, as The Bible has it, for the bossy 'little Hitler types' usually end up as boss. These bossy bullies typically have 'type A' behaviour associated with stress. Research has found that, contrary to popular belief enshrined in such terms as "executive stress," being boss involves less work stress and it is the slaves, of course, that really are stressed, and perhaps never more so than in today's consumer society.

Human history might not have been so catastrophic, in fact, had quieter, less aggressive, more intelligent, more honest, and harder working people been leading us.

Finally, whilst clearly much of our personality develops early in life by modeling, imitative and social learning, it is also important to note that there is some evidence that up to 50% of personality may be genetic (Galton, 2001).

☺☺☹☺☺☺☹☺☺☹☺☺☹☺☺☹

Chapter 17

THE PSYCHOLOGY OF CONFLICT

> There is no contradiction between saying (a) that contact tends to
> reduce the cultural differences among ethnic groups and
> (b) that contact also tends to stimulate efforts to preserve
> or increase these differences.
> H. D. Forbes *Ethnic Conflict,*
> *Commerce, Culture, and the Contact Hypothesis* (1997).

Contact hypothesis

Forbes (1977) proposed that ethnocentricity of different ethnic groups tended to be increased by cultural differences and (presumed negative) contact between them, expressing the ethnocentrism within two groups *A* and *B* as:

$$E_a = a_1 \, C_T \, D_T \tag{17.1a}$$

$$E_b = b_1 \, C_T \, D_T \tag{17.1b}$$

where a_1 and b_1 are assumed to be positive, and are measures of the latent tendency of each group to respond ethnocentrically to each other, C_T is the amount of contact between the two groups at time T and D_T is the magnitude of the cultural differences between the two groups at time T.

He further proposed that the amount of contact and the cultural differences between the groups depended upon their proximity, incentives for contact such as trade, and upon the ethnocentrism of the groups, expressing this as:

$$C_{T+1} = C_T \, (1 + g)/(1 + a_2 E_a + b_2 E_b) \tag{17.2}$$

$$D_{T+1} = D_T \, (1 + a_3 E_a + b_3 E_b)/(1 + h C_T) \tag{17.3}$$

where g is a factor that represents the factors that determine growth or decline in contact other than the repulsive ethnocentrism and cultural differences of the two groups.

In equations 17.2 and 17.3 ethnocentricity decreases contact and increases cultural differences, as might be expected.

The denominator of the last equation ensures that cultural differences are reduced by contact so long as h is positive (the normal situation).

Contact theory has obvious application in marketing, PR and other activities involving persuasion, for example:

[1] It emphasizes that attitude changes with contact or, in general, information transfer.

If contact is 'positive', however, rather than negative as has generally been the case throughout man's sorry history, then equations 20.1 could be modified to reflect this by writing them in the form

$$E_{a,T+1} = E_{a,T} - a_1 C_T + a_4 D_T$$

where a_1 and a_4 are positive. Indeed, it might be hoped that the latter situation might be more likely in today's age of electronic communication and high speed travel. Moreover, it is in this situation that such equations might be applicable to advertising with E = 'resistance.'

[2] It reminds us that ethnic or 'local' considerations are important in international marketing of a product.

[3] It reminds us of the importance of targeting advertising towards an appropriate demographic for a product, and that cultural differences exist between teenagers and their parents and, more so, their grandparents.

An attitudinal model of conflict

Mohr proposed a simple 'first approximation' formula for assessing the potential for conflict between persons or groups. The basic formula is (Mohr, 2014a; Mohr et al. 2018c):

$$A^* = A + xB + yC + zD \qquad (17.4)$$

where A^* = current 'overall' attitude,
A = initial or 'basic' attitude (based on 'known history'),
B = attitudes towards behaviours of the second party,
C = contact history between the two parties,
D = degree of difference between the parties considered,
and x, y, z are scaling factors that indicate the relative importance of the terms and here these will be assumed unity for simplicity.

Equation 17.4 can, of course, be used to assess the attitude of both parties involved in the assessment.

Here attitude is assessed in the same way as attitude is measured by the information integration model of Equation 11.2 but for simplicity only scale values (but not weights) will be given to a small set of items in measuring A.

Similarly, only scale values are used in assessing B, C and D. These extra terms add a great deal to the 'basic' A assessment to give a 'picture' of the 'overall' attitude.

Example application

As an example of application of the simple model of Equation 17.4 the attitude of a typical individual towards a hypothetical terrorist organization 'HTO' is considered.

To assess this only five items are assessed by simple questions for the initial attitude, behavioural, contact and difference terms in Equation 17.4. Assessment is similar to that used for the 'five-factor' model of personality (Larsen & Buss, 2002) and uses five possible scores:

+2 = strongly like/very similar etc.
+1 = like/similar etc.
0 = neutral
-1 = dislike/different etc.
-2 = strongly dislike/very different etc.

Table 17.1. Person's hypothetical attitude towards 'HTO'.

SCORE:	-2	-1	0	1	2
A, initial/basic attitude	Dislike/Like				
The people			0		
Their government(s)		-1			
How they look		-1			
What they say	-2				
What they do	-2				
B, group behaviour	Dislike/Like				
Sectarian conflict		-1			
Negative rhetoric		-1			
'Pushing' their religion	-2				
Threats	-2				
Terrorism	-2				
C, contact history	Uncomfortable/Comfortable				
See on TV			0		
See on street			0		
Close to		-1			
Talk to		-1			
Socialize	-2				
D, differences	Different/Similar				
Language		-1			
Economic				1	
Culture		-1			
Religion	-2				
History		-1			
TOTAL SCORE, A*:	-22				

Table 17.1 gives an example assessment for a hypothetical individual. Here total scores less than -30 are 'very negative', -10 to -20 'negative', -10 to +10 are moderate, +10 to +20 'positive', and more than +20 'very positive'.

Thus the results of Table 17.1 are mostly 'negative', the total of -22 indicating a considerable degree of disapproval. It is only very negative scores of less than -30 that might be a cause for concern if they were obtained for a significant percentage of a population.

Weighting factors can be assigned to items in Table 17.1 to reflect differing importance associated with them, for example the 9th and 10th items might have weights >1.

Effect of Societal views

The effect of the views of society on individuals and groups can be included in Equation 17.4 by adding an extra term to account for the affect of social norms on attitude formation:

$$A^{**} = A^* + fS = A + xB + yC + zD + fS$$

where f *is a scaling factor* here assumed = 1 for simplicity, and the factors x, y, z are also assumed =1 so that:

$$A^{**} = A + B + C + D + S \qquad (17.5)$$

and S is the person or group's assessment of the attitude or 'position' of society, society here including the media, politicians, religious leaders, the public, friends and family.

Then measurement of S is done in the same way as for A, B, C and D in Table 17.1.

Table 17.2. Person's assessment of society's attitude.

SCORE:	-2	-1	0	1	2
S, perceived society view		Negative/Positive			
TV/radio/papers		-1			
Politicians			0		
Religious leaders		-1			
The public		-1			
Friends & family		-1			
TOTAL SCORE:			-4		

For the views of a typical person regarding society's attitude towards 'HTO' the result might be that shown in Table 17.2. Adding this result to that of Table 17.1 the aggregate score is -26, a 'negative' overall result.

A 'very negative' score would be less than -30, so the combined result of Tables 17.1 and 17.2 (i.e. -26) for an individual or a group is not of concern but worth taking some notice of.

Responses to conflict

When the group, attitudes towards which are sought, is in some form of dispute or conflict, whether this be economic, concerning mistreatment of a few people, or armed conflict on any scale, the attitudes concerning what measures should be taken against the group can also be measured in like fashion to Table 17.1.

Table 17.3. Attitudes towards measures against group.

SCORE:	0	1	2	3	4
	Level of support for action				
Government condemns					4
Cut diplomatic ties				3	
Trade embargo			2		
Public demonstrations				3	
UN sanctions		1			
War	0				-
TOTAL SCORE:			13		

Table 17.3 shows an example of such an assessment for a hypothetical individual concerning his or her views towards HTO's terrorism around the world. The total score is $R = 13$ out of a possible 24, perhaps a 'fail' mark by way of assessment of the group in question, but not an extremely bad score.

Total scores of close to 20, on the other hand, would indicate very strong feelings of which, perhaps, considerable notice should be taken should they be found to apply to a significant number of people.

The results of Tables 17.1 – 17.3 can be combined as:

$$A^{***} = A + B + C + D + S - (R - 12)$$

with the last term adjusted to allow for its different scale of measurement, giving $A^{***} = -27$ for the present example case.

Other factors affecting attitudes & conflict

[1] Hierarchical influences.

These include the influence of strongly hierarchical organizations that have very great influence on society and its individual people, some of these being:

(a) Governments of any type, whether they be monarchies or dictatorships have considerable influence on the populace by way of propaganda and enforceable laws, for example those of conscription.

(b) Political parties. Even when they are not in government, supporters of political parties are often considerably influenced by their views.

(c) Religions. These, of course, have had great influence throughout history but have less influence in the West now, whilst in contrast Muslim sects still have great influence on many of the world's 1.5 billion Muslims.

(d) TV, radio and print media also tend to come from 'on high' and also have considerable influence.

[2] Social norms.

Social norms have a great influence on the thinking of individuals and groups within any society, for example the wearing of scarves, veils and burkas by Muslim women is still very widely practiced.

The structure of society has also been an important factor. Fairly soon after the Agricultural Revolution and the formation of man's first permanent towns and farms the first small armies would have been formed to defend them, at first only temporarily.

Indeed, with the diversification of occupations that the Agricultural Revolution brought, permanent armies were one eventual result, notably in Rome and its empire, for example. Then, of course, given the availability of armies, there has always been a tendency to use them sooner or later, most obviously as the 'external police force' to deal with external problems, albeit a very large force all too often in history.

[3] Economic factors.

Economic considerations have often been the cause of human conflict, for example competition for resources, a good historical example being the Spanish Empire's enthusiastic search for gold in the Americas.

Man has always been inventing new tools and weapons, particularly since the Industrial Revolution. Now the arms industries have become massive and are able to considerably influence government policy in many countries whose economies have suffered a steep decline in their manufacturing industries in recent decades (Sampson, 1977; Thomas, 2006).

An example of the absurdity of it all, the CIA knew that chemical weapons were pouring into Iraq from Chile and South Africa in the 1980s. Cardoen industries in Santiago, for example, sent its chemical weapons, and the German-made artillery 'cups' or shells to contain them, to Iraq (Ben-Menashe, 1992). Then, the US later condemned Iraq for using these weapons on the Kurds and used this as an excuse for their first invasion of Iraq early in 1991.

[4] Growing populations.

Even as far back as early man's troglodyte days it is not hard to imagine an extended family group growing to the point at which a second cave was needed.

Similarly, when man had towns and then cities these too grew in size, needing ever more space and, more importantly, resources, particularly food.

This, coupled with man's habit of exploration, which no doubt dates back to his hunter-gatherer days and thence the hunt for food, has led man to engage in conflict with neighbouring populations.

Conflicts may have arisen simply out of the suspicion that the sight of strangers aroused when they suddenly appeared. Perhaps, for example, a spear might be thrown to scare them away. Then, of course, there might be retaliation and thus conflict.

As man's population continued to increase, of course, the tendency for migration and thence conflict must have increased, for example people leaving crowded and disease-ridden cities in Europe to colonize the 'New World' from the 16th to 19th centuries.

[5] Proximity.

Proximity also affects people's attitudes as does contact which, of course, is facilitated by proximity, the more 'negative' the contact the more negative the attitude formed.

Thus for tribal man, as with his chimpanzee relatives, proximity was a key factor in regular tribal conflicts.

Indeed, until only about two thousand years ago, human conflicts were only between neighbouring cities, regions, or countries. With the building of ships capable of sailing hundreds of miles, however, came the ability to explore more widely, and human conflict began to occur over greater distances and on a greater scale.

Bullying in schools and workplaces, of course, involves proximity as a major factor in both stimulating conflict, and making bullying easier to carry out.

[6] Competitiveness.

In the Roman Empire, for example, there was a competitiveness in its governments, an obvious drive that made it wish to become 'bigger and grander' and go out and conquer other lands to achieve that end.

This obsession with competition runs all through the history and cultures of Homo sapiens, an example being our obsession with sport, or any kind of competition even if it is called a 'game.' It seems fundamentally related to the alpha-male behaviour of several other animal species.

Man, however, takes the alpha-male issue to absurd lengths, for example the original Olympic Games in Ancient Greece being conducted in the nude and, indeed, it seems to be returning slowly towards that situation now.

Equally, man has often indulged in war without good reason, usually because some loony leader and his acolytes want to 'beat' some other foe.

Conclusions

Very relevant to attitude also is the vexatious question of ethnic conflict and, indeed, the equations of Forbes' contact hypothesis do emphasize that, over time, attitudes change. Moreover, models like that of contact hypothesis could be applied to the effects of advertising.

The simple formula of Equation 17.4 combines the measurement techniques of attitudinal psychology with the concepts of the contact hypothesis to assess the attitudes of individuals and groups of people to other groups of people. The point of this exercise is that, when the attitude of one group to another is very negative, then conflict between the groups is, of course, more likely.

The attitudes of leaders are of particular importance, as it is these that may lead to conflict and war. The attitudes of leaders will, of course, be influenced by many of the same factors and stimuli that affect the public.

There are many other factors that affect modern human conflict. For example, particularly in modern times, alliances between nations have played a part in many wars, World War 1 and World War 2 being notable examples.

One difficulty is that, if two groups of 4 nations are allied, then a single nation attacking some part of another may quickly result in 8 nations being at war. In other words, the larger the parties involved, the bigger the conflict.

One fear for the future, therefore, is the increasing power of such huge nations as China and India, and also of the 1.5 billion Muslims around the world, so many of whom become involved in Islamic jihad all around the world, and to the extent that many believe that we have been in the midst of *World War 3* for some time (Mohr et al., 2015b, 2018g).

The numbers involved here are an order of magnitude greater than those involved in the two world wars of the last century and war between any of these three entities and another of perhaps similar size could well be the war to end all wars.

Mankind's disastrous history of conflict seems unlikely to end and we face other threats as a result of overpopulation, resource depletion, climate change etcetera. The authors HOPES we can solve some of these problems, however, and thus increase our chances of avoiding the extinction forecast for many animal species, including ourselves (Mohr, 2012a).

To improve our prospects we should push for *real democracy*, as outlined in *The Doomsday Calculation* (Mohr, 2012a) and *The Population Explosion* (Mohr et al., 2018b), rather than the highly oligarchical and antiquated Westminster system that still governs much of the Western world today, and only then, perhaps, might there be any real chance of avoiding increasing global catastrophes and perhaps extinction.

With the 'population explosion', and the increasing social and financial pressures that result from it, bullying behaviours are likely to become more widespread, some evidence of this being provided recently by the growing ME TOO movement.

☺☺☹☺☺☹☺☺☹☺☺☹☺☺☹

17. THE PSYCHOLOGY OF CONFLICT

Chapter 18

PSYCHOLOGICAL ASSESSMENT

> *We have lost the art of living; and in the most important science of all, the science of daily life, the science of behaviour, we are complete ignoramuses. We have psychology instead.*
> D. H. Lawrence, *Etruscan Places*, ch. 4 (1932).

Introduction

Chapter 15 discussed some of the early history of psychiatry, then discussing a range of common mental illnesses.

The present chapter briefly discusses some of the main methods by which psychological problems are diagnosed.

Mental illness

Mental health professionals use the term *mental health problem* when a person experiences difficulties that are mild, temporary, and able to be treated in a relatively short term.

The term *mental illness* is then used when a person's problems are more serious and likely to persist for a relatively long time, and thus require long-term treatment.

Mental illness can be defined as a psychological dysfunction involving distress, difficulty in coping with everyday life, and inappropriate behaviours.

Psychological dysfunction involves a breakdown of cognitive, emotional and/or behavioural functioning during which thoughts, feelings or behavior differ from those normal for the person in question, and the situation involved.

A key characteristic of mental illness is *atypical* thoughts, feelings, and behavior.

If, for example, a person usually friendly, but becomes withdrawn and uncommunicative for extended periods such behavior would be deemed atypical.

In contrast, a person whose behavior is normally eccentric, would not be deemed to be mentally ill because their eccentric behavior would not be atypical for them.

If a person's thoughts, feelings, or behavior appear abnormal, but are, in fact, 'normal' in the society or culture to which they belong, they too would not be considered mentally ill by that society. If they were members of the Islamic State terrorist group, for example, with that organization they would be considered normal, but in the world at large they would be considered criminal, and their behaviors might be deemed to involve mental illness.

Homosexuality is perhaps a good example, for in Western societies it was deemed by many to be an aberrant behavior requiring psychiatric treatment, but is now widely accepted.

Similarly, ADHD or Attention Deficit Hyperactivity Disorder, is relatively new in the annals of psychology, but now a great many young children are diagnosed with it and given prescription medications for long periods.

Mental health professionals use a variety of methods of assessing a person's mental health, including clinical interviews, behavioural observations, and various kinds of tests such as personality tests to develop a *clinical profile* of the thoughts, feelings, and behaviours of a person, and the factors and life experiences that may have contributed to their current mental health status.

In dealing with both perpetrators and victims of bullying, evidence from witnesses to the bullying being investigated should be obtained where possible. This may help in counseling bullies, for example by pointing out any negative attitudes etc. reported by witnesses. It may also console victims to be reminded that other people have seen the bullying and are supportive of the victims.

Clinical interviews

These are usually the first step in assessing a person's mental health, and involve a *mental status exam* which records the results of observations and questions about five aspects of a person (Grivas & Carter, 2005):

1. *Appearance and behavior,* including grooming and cleanliness, hunched or upright posture, smiling or sad facial expressions, slow or lethargic body movements, downcast eyes. Then, for example, downcast eyes, a sad expression, and hunched posture might be indicative of depression.

2. *Thought processes* as indicated by a how a person talks. For example, fast, disjointed speech about unrealistic experiences suggests a distorted sense of reality, perhaps indicating schizophrenia.

3. *Mood and affect. Mood* is a person's current emotional state, for example, 'down' or 'highly excitable'. *Affect* here refers to responses. For example, our affect is 'appropriate' if we laugh at something funny, but 'inappropriate' if we laugh about the death of a friend or relative. If, on the other hand, we show no feeling at all about a highly emotional situation, our affect may be recorded as 'flat'.

4. *Intellectual functioning* and aspects of intelligence, such as vocabulary, and response to questions requiring problem-solving and decision-making ability. Sometimes a formal IQ test is done.

5. *Sensorium* or general awareness of one's surroundings, for example does the person know who they are, where they are, the day, date, time, place etcetera. People with some types of brain damage, or psychological dysfunction as a result of substance abuse, may be unable to answer some such questions.

This mental status exam enables the mental health professional to initially assess which aspects of a person's thoughts, feelings, and behaviours require more detailed assessment using a psychological test designed to diagnose a specific mental illness.

Psychological testing

One of the most widely used *diagnostic tests* is the Minnesota Multiphase Personality Inventory (MMPI) which focuses on the 10 aspects of personality called *clinical scales* shown in Table 18.1 (Kassin, 2004).

Table 18.1. Clinical scales of the MMPI.

	Clinical scale	Description
1	Hypochondriasis	Chronic and abnormal anxiety about imaginary symptoms and ailments
2	Depression	Sad feelings of gloom and inadequacy, low morale, pessimistic, hopelessness, unhappy, sluggish.
3	Hysteria	Attention-seeking emotional outbreaks
4	Psychopathic deviation	Impulsive, selfish, unreliable disregard of social rules and authority
5	Masculinity-femininity	Identification with masculine and/or feminine sex roles
6	Paranoia	Feelings of persecution &/or grandeur, suspiciousness, overly sensitive
7	Psychasthenia	Fears, self-doubt, guilt, obsessions and compulsions
8	Schizophrenia	Social isolation, confusion, disorientation, bizarre perceptions
9	Mania	Hyperactivity and impulsiveness
10	Social introversion	Shyness, social withdrawal, inhibited

The 'inventory' has 567 questions presented in random order, each related to one of the 10 clinical scales, to which the respondent answers 'true', 'false' or 'cannot say'.

The scores for each clinical scale range from 0 to 120, a score of 50 being considered average, and two-thirds of the population score between 40 and 60 on each scale.

A score above 65 on a particular scale may be deemed 'clinically significant' or abnormal.

Validity and reliability of tests

Psychological tests for a specific mental illness should have (Grivas & Carter, 2005):

1. *Construct validity*, for example, a test for depression should differentiate the characteristics of depression from those of other categories of mental illness such as anxiety disorders.

2. *Concurrent validity* or results consistent with those from another test for the specific mental illness in question known to be valid for that illness.

3. *Reliability* which can be assessed by giving repeating the test on the same individuals on a later occasion, and then checking to see if the results are consistent. A problem here is that people may remember the answers they gave the first time, and simply repeat them, and to help reduce this problem another version of the same test can be used the second time.

Classification of mental illnesses

The most widely used system for identifying and classifying mental illnesses is the Diagnostic and Statistical Manual of Mental Disorders (DSM), which was first developed in by the American Psychiatric Association in 1952. The 2000 "text revision" of the fourth edition, the DSM-IV-TR, uses the following five 'axes' to classify mental disorders:

1. Clinical disorders: symptoms causing distress or impairing occupational or social functioning such as anxiety disorders.

2. Personality disorders and mental retardation: chronic disorders impairing occupational and social functioning.

3. General medical condition: physical disorders that may contribute to a psychological disorder.

4. Psychosocial and environmental problems: contributing negative life events and personal relationship problems.

5. Global assessment of functioning: overall level of functioning in occupational, social and leisure activities.

Axis 1 comprises 400 mental disorders in 16 categories, these including (Grivas & Carter, 2005):

➢ Disorders usually diagnosed in infancy, childhood, and adolescence, including autism, ADHD and separation anxiety disorder (anxiety etc. when separated from home or family).

➢ Mood disorders involving inappropriate and extreme highs and lows for extended periods, including bipolarity (manic depressive disorder).

➢ Eating disorders including anorexia nervosa and bulimia.

➢ Substance-related disorders involving substances that affect the central nervous system, including alcohol, opioid, amphetamine, cocaine and hallucinogen use disorders.

➢ Anxiety disorders, including generalized anxiety disorder, phobias, panic disorder, obsessive-compulsive disorder (OCD), acute stress disorder, and post-traumatic stress disorder (PTSD).

➢ Impulse-control disorders including pathological gambling, kleptomania, and pyromania.

➢ Sleep disorders including insomnia, hypersomnia, sleep terror disorder, and sleepwalking.

➢ Somatoform disorders involving physical symptoms mainly caused by psychological factors, including conversion disorder (mental conflict causing paralysis or anaesthesia) and hypochondriasis.

➢ Schizophrenia and other psychotic disorders involving a loss of contact with reality.

➢ Cognitive disorders such as delirium, dementia, and amnesic disorders, including Alzheimer's disease and Huntington's disease.

Axis 2 disorders, for example mental retardation, are less common but usually continue for the rest of a person's life and are thus part of a person's personality.

Axes 3 and 4 provide mental health professional with additional information that may be relevant to diagnosis and treatment, for example heart disease (axis 3) or problems with family or at work (axis 4).

Axis 5 involves assessment of how well a person copes with everyday life and this is done using the Global Assessment of Functioning (GAF) scale and extract of which is shown in Table 18.2 (Grivas & Carter, 2005):

Table 18.2. Example scores from GAF scale.

Score	
91-100	Superior functioning with no symptoms.
81-90	Good functioning with minimal symptoms such as anxiety.
51-60	Some difficulty with work, friends etc. and occasional moderate anxiety etc.
21-30	Serious impairment of function and communication, for example no job, home or friends.
11-20	Some risk of hurting self or others through self-harm, violence, or carelessness, poor hygiene etc.
1-10	Serious risk of " " " " "

One research study on the reliability of the DSM-IV-TR as an assessment tool found 70% agreement of classifications of mental disorders by mental health professionals (DiNardo et al., 1993).

Labelling and high rate of misdiagnoses

'Labelling' a person with some mental disorder can, of course, have a negative effect upon that person, also influencing how they are viewed by others.

A classic study had eight normal people present at psychiatric hospitals as 'pseudo-patients' saying they had been hearing voices. All were diagnosed as having schizophrenia and admitted. Their stays ranged from 7 to 52 days, and all were released as being "in remission", leading to the conclusion that psychologists could not recognize 'normal behaviour'.

In a follow-up study staff at one hospital were warned of pseudo-patients appearing in the next three months, and staff were asked to identify which of their patients were pseudo-patients. No pseudo-patients were actually sent, but one staff member identified 41 out of 193 patients as pseudo-patients.

Such results emphasize that accurate diagnosis of mental health issues is often difficult, for example because much reliance is placed upon patient interviews, but some patients may not provide accurate or honest answers to key question, not wanting, of course, to admit to weaknesses and faults.

Conclusions

Mental illness involves, of course, psychological dysfunction and thence difficulty in coping with life that may involve, for example, excessive anxiety.

Diagnosis of mental illness involves clinical interviews and psychological tests and relies heavily upon the patient's performance and the tester 'reading between the lines' at times to interpret this.

Testing of attitudes, which was discussed in Chapter 11, might also be helpful in diagnosing mental illnesses.

Many of the most common mental illnesses were discussed in Chapter 15, and Table 18.1 summarizes some of these.

The most common clinical disorders were summarized in a preceding section, ranging from autism and ADHS in childhood to Alzheimer's disease in the elderly.

Table 18.2 shows example scores in the Global Assessment of Functioning scale for assessment of a how well a person is coping with life in general, this being Axis 5 of the Diagnostic and Statistical Manual of Mental Disorders.

Psychopathy is the largest category of abnormal psychological behaviours and was briefly discussed in Chapter 15, whilst the Hare checklist for diagnosing psychopaths was given and briefly discussed in Chapter 9 (see Table 9.1).

☺☺☺☺☺☺☺☺☺☺☺☺☺☺☺☺

Chapter 19

TREATMENT OF MENTAL DISORDERS

> *Yet today's practitioners too easily forget their debt
> to Freud's original "talking cure" of listening to and analyzing
> the content of a patient's mind, and his insight that
> a person can simply be sabotaged by the irrational within.*
> Tom Butler-Bowdon, *50 Psychology Classics* (2017).

Introduction

Chapter 15 discussed the early history of psychiatry, a wide variety of psychological ailments, and treatment for some of these was briefly discussed.

In the following section various broad classifications of psychological traits are discussed.

According to Gillespie (2017), everyone experiences some sort of behavioural disorder at some time in their lives, and low 'scores' or assessments of psychological traits are relatively normal. High scores, especially for prolonged periods, however, may indicate a need for treatment and several types of treatment for psychological problems are discussed in the remainder of this chapter.

Behavioural psychology

According to Gillespie (2017), psychological behaviours these fall into three categories:

1. **Schizophrenic:**
   - (a) Paranoid – irrational suspicion and mistrust.
   - (b) Schizoid – detached from social relationships.
   - (c) Schizotypal – extreme discomfort with social interaction.

2. **Dramatic:**
   (a) Antisocial – disregard for others, lack of empathy and manipulative behaviour.
   (b) Borderline – unstable self-image and relationships.
   (c) Histrionic – attention-seeking behaviour.
   (d) Narcissistic – needing admiration; lack of empathy.

3. **Anxious:**
   (a) Avoidant – feeling inadequate and very sensitive.
   (b) Dependent – needing care from others.
   (c) Obsessive-compulsive – perfectionism: rigid conformity to rule and procedures.

Treatment of psychiatric disorders

Psychiatrists and psychologists use interviewing techniques and tests to diagnose mental illnesses.

Treatments for psychological problems may include:

➢ Regular appointments for 'talk therapy'.

➢ Cognitive therapies are now the most widely used procedures used by psychologists and are discussed in the following section.

➢ Hypnosis in which patients are told to relax, clear their minds, close their eyes etcetera, eventually being coaxed into a hypnotic or semi-conscious state in which their minds are supposed to be open to suggestion, for example that they don't really need to smoke and should not want to when they awake.

➢ Prescription drugs, for example, lithium salts for manic depression, Valium for anxiety disorders, and several new drugs for ADHD.

➢ Group therapy, for example monthly meetings of AA (Alcoholics Anonymous) or groups of people with OCD, the latter usually being chaired by a psychologist.

➢ Mindfulness meditation groups chaired by a practitioner in which quiet music is played and patients are told to clear their minds, relax, breathe slowly, close their eyes, and picture some beautiful scenery in their minds.

In extreme cases, of course, patients are confined to 'mental hospitals', usually for short periods in cases where patients are having bouts of severe depression accompanied with thoughts of suicide, for example, but for periods of several years or more in extreme cases of schizophrenia in which patients begin to lose all contact with reality and are unable to care for themselves.

In a few extreme cases ECT (Electroconvulsive shock therapy) is sometimes used. ECT was once regarded as causing significant permanent damage to the brain. Now, thanks to modern anaesthesia, it is much safer with a morality rate 1/10th that of childbirth. ECT is used to treat extreme depression and schizophrenia (Lillienfeld et al., 2010).

Cognitive behavior therapy (CBT)

Cognitive therapies in which patients talk about their mental issues, sometimes in groups, are now the most widely used procedures used by psychologists (Grivas & Carter, 2005).

Cognitive behavior therapy (CBT) assumes that emotional or behavioural problems are caused by unrealistic or irrational thinking about oneself, others and situations, resulting in 'mentally unhealthy' thoughts and behaviours.

A student who gets a low mark on an exam, for example, may begin to lose hope of coping with the subject satisfactorily and, to some extent at least, give up trying to do so.

According to the principles of CBT one can think more positively and optimistically and plan to work harder to obtain better results in the near future.

CBT is often used to treat anxiety and depression, with the patients being taught to identify irrational negative thoughts and replace them with more realistic, more optimistic ones. For example, a student fearful of bad marks in exams, may be encouraged to think along the lines: *Relax. If the exam is hard, it will be hard for everyone else too.*

Thus, cognitive therapy's "revolutionary idea" is that depression isn't an emotional disorder, and the bad feelings of depression stem from negative thoughts which can be replaced with positive thoughts (Burns, 1980).

19. Treatment of Mental Disorders

Issues concerning psychiatric treatment

It was Freud who pioneered hypnosis as a means of psychotherapy, later discarding it in favour of "free association" in which a patient was encouraged to reveal repressed memories responsible for hysterical symptoms that Freud thought were always of a sexual nature, a view which many other psychiatrists felt incorrect, if not obsessive (Krapp, 2005).

A modern medical scandal is the way in which such drugs as Valium are prescribed for the long term to people. Such drugs are bound to be addictive and when patients forget to take their daily dose there will inevitably be withdrawal symptoms.

Such drugs, like the brain stimulant tobacco or the depressant and tranquilizer alcohol, alter pulse rate and blood pressure. Smoking two or three strong cigarettes in an hour, for example, will increase pulse rate significantly. The discomfort we feel when the next 'dose' of the drug is missed is known as 'withdrawal', in the case of alcohol overdose the symptoms being an increase in blood pressure and pulse rate.

Unless absolutely necessary, therefore, it seems madness to addict people to pharmaceutical drugs when they might only be briefly affected by some stressful event in their lives.

In an article entitled *Medication*, the *Weekend Australian* magazine of 10/9/2016 reported that: "Children are being over diagnosed as having ADHD – and now even 'daydreaming'." They are then put on drugs for the long-term and left feeling that they will suffer this really nonexistent disease for life, when in fact the problem will usually be one of poor study habits and motivation, often exacerbated by lack of a home environment that encourages good study habits, and the much too long and drawn out education system.

All this is good for the 'pysch. professions' as they can much increase the size of their practices with the many visits children will have to make for further prescriptions.

It is also good for the pharmaceutical industry which sometimes rewards doctors financially or with holidays and other perks to encourage them to prescribe their drugs.

New treatments

Examples of new treatments for psychological problems include:

> Many people with depression, for example, suffer from social isolation, and regular social 'chat groups run at local council centres are a simple low-cost alternative to psychotherapy. AA have long had good results with comparable groups for several decades, whilst groups mediated by a counsellor are also used for people with OCD.

> "Motivational Interviewing" in which patients are motivated to think positively etc. (Arkowitz et al., 2015).

> Just a few sessions with a psychologist in which the patient writes down their bad memory/experience and reads it out aloud 'as though it happened to someone else' can help reduce PTSD. Good results have been had in conjunction with the drug propanol (Miller, 2017), but no doubt good results could also be had using such 'thought transference' without this drug.

> Comparable to the latter, patients suffering many psychological problems can be helped by being told to 'couple' their negative feelings with positive ones.

Support organizations

There are several organizations that help people with mental health problems, including:

> Lifeline – a free phone chat service to help people with mental health crises such as suicidal thoughts.

> Beyond Blue – free phone chat service to help people with mental health issues such as depression.

> Organizations such as Rainbows, "the world's largest grief support organization for children and young people" (Marta, 2004).

> Anxiety Disorders Association of Victoria.

> SANE Australia.

> Anxiety Treatment Australia.

Conclusion

It should also be noted that recent studies in which one group of depressed patients were given a healthy Mediterranean-style diet, and a second just regular 'consultations' with a counsellor, found that the healthier diet option significantly reduced levels of depression.

Notably, the 'Mediterranean diet' usually includes a couple of glasses of red wine daily for 'relaxational purposes', the procyanidins and other antioxidants in red wine being particularly helpful in reducing cardiovascular disease, and in this context it should be noted that brain function, and thence such ailments as Alzheimer's disease, are affected by poor diets that increase atherosclerosis. Thus 'natural therapies' involving healthy diet, including plenty of appropriate dietary vitamin and other supplements, and plenty of exercise, relaxation and sleep, improve both physical and mental health (Mohr, 2012c, 2013a, 2015, 2018a, 2018b).

The author therefore recommends improved diet and lifestyle, including occasional contact with supportive and helpful friends and neighbours, as a means of improving mental health, perhaps in conjunction with professional counselling if need be, though in most cases the latter should only be required for the short term, for example to help deal with a particular event such as a death in the family, divorce etcetera.

In the case of marriage problems, of course, marriage guidance counsellors have traditionally been used by many people, whilst some Christian church groups now run more general counselling services in offices run at sites not connected/adjacent to a church.

In choosing a counsellor one might, for example, be wary of those overly obsessed with sexual issues or dreams as being the root of many problems, as the author believes Sigmund Freud and Carl Jung were.

When professional 'talk therapy' is used, however, the patient should take care to choose a counsellor intelligent enough to quickly work out what memories etc. are affecting them and suggest sensible and effective ideas to deal with any 'mental problems', and using pharmaceutical drugs only when clearly necessary, and then only for the short or medium term.

In dealing with psychological problems in children, of course, teachers should also be involved as soon as possible to help children cope. As with adults, involving children with sports or other activity or 'interest' groups can provide social connections that may reduce such issues as depression, and autism, and ADHD.

In dealing with both perpetrators and victims of bullying in schools, workplaces etc. counselling is, of course, important, and this may be by parents, teachers, management staff, and psychologists and psychiatrists.

Optimism and hope, of course, can greatly improve mental health, and life outcomes, as discussed in the recent books *The Psychology of Hope* (Mohr et al, 2018), and *The Psychology of Success* (Mohr et al., 2018f).

Viktor Frankl's *logotherapy*, which encourages one to believe that each individual's life has a meaning, and is not just a product of one's environment, is perhaps also worth note in the context of optimism etc. (Frankl, 1969).

Carl Rogers' view that the main problem most of his patients had was that they approached life with "'false roles" or "masks" and were usually worried about what other people thought of them and expected them to do, and that they needed to become their "real selves" is also perhaps worth note (Rogers, 1961).

Finally, note that, in emergency situations people in psychological crisis should establish phone contact with organizations such as Lifeline and Beyond Blue.

☺☺☹☺☺☹☺☺☹☺☺☹☺☺☹

19. TREATMENT OF MENTAL DISORDERS

PART V
CONCLUSIONS

Chapter 20

IMPROVING LIFE

> *There are many paths to the top of the mountain,*
> *but the view is always the same.*
> Chinese Proverb
>
> *If A is a success in life, then A equals x plus y plus z. Work is x;*
> *y is play; and z is keeping your mouth shut.*
> Albert Einstein, quoted in: Observer, London, 15 Jan. 1950.

Introduction

When one undertakes a self-assessment of one's current situation and finds one or two aspect of one's life need improvement, it is best to begin thinking about how to improve those aspects as soon as possible, taking any advice and offers from friends etc. along the way.

Being 'less than happy' and underpaid etc. in your current job, for example, is a major issue that will probably affect most other aspects of your life, including health and wealth, happiness, quality of family life etcetera. If that is the case producing a half-way good CV and beginning the search for another job, or perhaps giving though to starting one's own business, perhaps with some financial help from extended family.

Alternatively, one might have been living in the same place for several years and want to move, perhaps to live closer to work to make life easier for yourself, and perhaps the rest of the family.

Whatever the life improvement you seek, it is best to for it as well as possible, and following sections make a few suggestions that might be helpful to some readers.

Life assessment

One can assess the quality of a particular aspect of one's life using the Expectation-Value and Information Integration methods of attitude assessment.

To assess the quality of several key aspects of one's life the simplest and most widely used method is Likert Scaling.

Table 20.1 shows an example assessment for an adult person, scoring being done simply by using a printed copy of this table and circling the scores/ratings given to each of the items listed in the first column.

An 'average' rating of 3 on all 20 items gives, of course, a total score of 60. More important, perhaps, ratings of 1/poor for such important items as the first two (job and pay) might motivate one to try and improve these important life factors.

Similarly, a low rating for some of the health items might spur one into taking action to improve one's health.

In the wide range of items in Table 20.1 some items are much more important than others. Generally recreation and social life, for example, are not as important as one's job, and some jobs, of course, involve long hours 6 or 7 days a week, allowing little time for social life in any case.

Thus an evaluation such as that of Table 20.1 could be extended to include weights for each factor, as in the Information Integration method of attitude assessment discussed earlier, and this is done for the 'work' items of Table 20.1 in the following section.

Note that in Table 20.1, for students the first 5 items become: Classwork; Marks; Relationship with teacher(s); Conditions at school/college; Relationships with classmates.

Table 20.1. Life quality questionnaire using Likert scaling.

Aspect of life: Circle the appropriate number	Very good	Good	Aver -age	Fair	Poor
Your work:					
1. Your job	5	4	3	2	1
2. Your pay	5	4	3	2	1
3. Relationship with boss	5	4	3	2	1
4. Workplace conditions	5	4	3	2	1
5. Relations with workmates	5	4	3	2	1
Your home life:					
6. Your financial situation	5	4	3	2	1
7. Your home	5	4	3	2	1
8. Your parent(s) or partner	5	4	3	2	1
9. Your siblings or children	5	4	3	2	1
10. Your health	5	4	3	2	1
Recreation and social life:					
11. Evening activities	5	4	3	2	1
12. Weekend activities	5	4	3	2	1
13. Friends	5	4	3	2	1
14. Regular outings	5	4	3	2	1
15. Social, sport etc. groups	5	4	3	2	1
Your health:					
16. General health	5	4	3	2	1
17. Fitness	5	4	3	2	1
18. Diet	5	4	3	2	1
19. Weight	5	4	3	2	1
20. Mental health	5	4	3	2	1
Add the numbers you circled:	Score/100:				

Assessing a key aspect of life

One can assess the quality of a particular aspect of one's life using the Expectation-Value and Information Integration methods of attitude assessment discussed earlier.

As an example, we shall now assess the five 'work' items of Table 20.1 for a 'typical' person using the Information Integration method, giving the following result with weights and scores 1-10.

Attribute 1 (job): $w_1 = 5$, $s_1 = 5/10$ (i.e. 'halfway' values)

Attribute 2 (pay): $w_2 = 8/10$, $s_2 = 3/10$

Attribute 3 (relationship with boss): $w_3 = 7/10$, $s_3 = 4/10$

Attribute 4 (workplace conditions): $w_4 = 5/10$, $s_4 = 5/10$

Attribute 5 (relations with workmates): $w_5 = 4/10$, $s_5 = 5/10$

giving a total score

$$= 5 \times 5 + 8 \times 3 + 7 \times 4 + 5 \times 5 + 4 \times 5$$
$$= 25 + 24 + 28 + 25 + 20 = 122$$

whereas a 'middling evaluation score' with 5/10 for both the weights and scale values for all five items would give a total score of 125, so that the situation is perhaps 'satisfactory', for the present at least, but the low score of 3/10 for 'pay' is deserving of some attention sooner rather than later.

If one is having problems with bullying at school or the workplace by workmates/schoolmates then, of course, the score for Attribute 5 might be about $s_5 = 1/10$ to indicate a bad situation. Such serious problems, however, should be given priority treatment, but if a simple assessment such as that of the foregoing example do help reveal such problems, well and good.

Dealing with problems at work

If you are having problems at work, whether these be boredom with the job, finding it too hard, or finding being too low in the hierarchy too hard, then using a simple table like that of Table 20.2 might be a good start in dealing with the issue.

Table 20.2 illustrates an action plan to improve the work situation with one or two actions suggested for each of the five work items, including an approximate timing for each action.

Perhaps the key item is 1, where the plan is the cautious and sensible one of staying for a couple of years, but beginning to look for another job immediately – sensible because it can take a long time to find a job, and even longer to find a good one.

Most important, however, is that a simple plan such as this is far wiser than, for example, impatiently barging into the boss's office and abusing him about being underpaid, not an entirely unheard of situation.

Table 20.2. Action plan re. job.

Item		Actions	Timing
1	Job	Stay Look for another job	1-2 years Now
2	Pay	Ask for a pay rise	Now
3	Boss	Talk to boss Make complaint	Next week In 3 months
4	Conditions	Talk to union Talk to boss	Next month In 3 months
5	Workmates	Meeting to raise issues	Next month

Furthermore, having a sensible plan gives one hope for the immediate and medium term, as well as time to come up with other ideas to improve one's work situation, and to obtain help and advice from others on it.

In the case of students at school, college etc., the 5 items of Table 20.2 change to: School; Marks; Teacher(s); Conditions; Classmates. The 'actions' change to: Stay/find another school; Try for better marks; Talk to teacher(s)/complain; Talk to teacher(s)/management; Talk to classmates.

When bullying at school or in the workplace is an issue then, of course, talking to teachers, managers etc. is usually the most important step one can take in trying to resolve the problem.

Job searching

When searching for a job it is, of course, important to have a good Curriculum Vitae (CV).

This might have the following sections:

➤ A short summary section of about 10 lines.

➤ A table summarizing you professional experience with column 1 = type of experience , column 2 = details of this, entries in this being, for example, management, sales etcetera.

➤ A table summarizing your work experience with column 1 = years (e.g. 2015-2019), column 2 = company you worked for, and a line or two on what work you did. This might include, for example, any voluntary work, work you did privately to help friends or relatives, or writing work you did at home.

➤ For an academic, for example, a list of courses given, and perhaps another on publications in journals etc.

➤ A list of any organizations you belong to: for example the local branch of a political party, a charitable organization etc.

➤ A list of any special achievements.

➤ A list of any awards you have received.

➤ A list or table of any good comments you have received throughout life.

➤ The contact details of 3 referees, including at least one of your last bosses, if you are young one of your school teachers or University, TAFE etc. lecturers, and perhaps a 'personal referee' to attest to your good character etc.

At least once in life, it might be well worth paying a professional CV writer such as those who advertise in the local newspapers, and some of these will often also give advice on how to get a job, interview well etcetera.

In the case of school/college students, finding another school/college will, of course, usually require help from parents, who may also be required to consider the financial implications of a change of 'venue'.

Referees and job references

In choosing who to nominate as referees one should be careful to consider several factors, including:

> ➢ Preferably they should be 'relevant' in some way to the job in question.
> ➢ They should be people you trust.
> ➢ Always ask for an 'upfront' referee statement to be given to you, and take it to the interview and quote the best lines from it.
> ➢ Often the organization offering the job will get a 'confidential' referee statement from a past boss, either over the phone or by email. Always ask at interview for a copy of (or what was said if verbal) these references. If they differ significantly from the upfront statement you got then this proves that ex boss is dishonest/a liar.
> ➢ When you have references from two past bosses, point out that the best reference should be that considered.
> ➢ Get past colleagues to give you a 'statement' about any past boss you use as referee. If this is weak or somewhat negative, that will help overcome any negativity that he might have said about you in confidence.

For personal referees, who are usually friends etc., the latter step should not be necessary.

In the case of school/college students school reports and, in particular, summary statements of marks received in recent years, and in particular the last year, are very important in seeking a job, or entry to a new school or course of study, and referees are also, of course important in this context.

When trying to resolve issues of bullying in schools or workplaces witness statements, and perhaps statements of personal support, should be helpful when teachers or managers are contacted to tell them of the bullying as it will strengthen the 'case' against the offender(s).

Improving family life

Improvements in family life might include:

➤ Moving house so that you or your wife live closer to work.

➤ Moving house so your children are closer to school.

➤ Changing school for your children, perhaps so they are close to home which has many advantages.

➤ Improving family health with improved diet, exercise, and lifestyle routines.

➤ Improving family recreation options to healthier and perhaps cheaper ones close to home.

➤ Improving the family's social life.

➤ Resolving any issues related to bullying by peers or parents.

Conclusion

There are many things one can do to improve life, and thereby perhaps make life more successful, and only a few examples have been considered in the present chapter.

Many others were given in preceding chapters, however, and a couple more are given in the following chapter.

To conclude this chapter on an optimistic note I shall quote 'the bard', William Shakespeare:

JAQUES. All the world's a stage.
And all the men and women merely players;
They have their exits and entrances;
And one man in his time plays many parts;
His acts being of seven ages.
As You Like It (1599), Act 2, Scene 7.

Those 7 "acts" could be deemed to be:

1. Infancy.
2. Childhood.
3. Schooldays.
4. Training, apprenticeship etc.

5. Working life – first stage.

6. Working life – second stage +.

7. Old age, retirement etc.

Then, for example, stage 5 above would be one's first full-time job, perhaps in the vocation for which one trained, whilst stage 6 might then be moving on to a better job, or starting one's own business etcetera, and perhaps achieving greater SUCCESS in life by doing do.

One key event, usually during stage 5, is finding a 'life partner' (in the 'old days' one got married) with whom one will (if possible) probably have 1+ children. To a considerable extent, in doing this we follow social norms and do as our parents etc. did, learning while young to **act** like a man, or woman, as the case may be and, indeed, probably doing so to some extent (i.e., /10 as per Mohr's 10th law) for the rest of our lives by, for example, dressing and perhaps behaving/acting in a 'relatively opposite' way to our opposite sex 'life partner'.

In the context of the present book, self-assessments such as that of Table 20.1 may be helpful in evaluating one's overall situation, and in dealing with any bullying that one may have been victim of. More important, some of the advice given in this chapter regarding witness statements and statements of support from friends etc. may be help in dealing with and perhaps resolving bullying problems.

As an example, recently (on 27/10/2018) an ex-colleague told me I was a "workaholic" on hearing I had done a new book, having done several in the few years previous. I wish I had 'collected' &/or 'noted' supportive comment, some of which I still remember well, to perhaps help me in dealing with the promotion delay in Auckland that led to my resignation and thence career destruction.

☺☺☹☺☺☹☺☺☹☺☺☹☺☺☹

Chapter 21

DEALING WITH BULLYING

> *He who does not hope to win has already lost.*
> José Juaquin Olmedo, (1780-1847), attrib.
>
> *True hope is swift, and flies with swallows' wings.*
> William Shakespeare, *Richard III,* act 5, sc. 2, 1.23 (1592-3).

The bullying epidemic

There has, unfortunately, been an increase in the incidence of bullying in schools, workplaces etc. in recent decades, and there have been an increasing number of reports of bulling in schools and workplaces in the media in recent years.

The ME TOO movement of recent years has also provided much further evidence of this increase in bullying etc. behaviours, including both verbal and sexual harassment and abuse.

Most disturbing perhaps, as noted in Chapters 5 and 7 victims of bullying often commit suicide, sometimes committing mass shootings in schools before doing so.

As noted in the following section, bullying is one of several types of event that can effect mental health and, therefore, victims of bullying may often require treatment for PTSD, depression etc.

As noted in Chapters 9 and 15, bullying is one of several traits that may be associated with psychopaths so that, of course, bullies should also receive psychological treatment, and in the most serious cases, of course, punishment by law.

On 10/4/2019 ABC2 TV news reported that there had been 1500 complaints by NDIS customers in Victoria and New South Wales in just 6 months, 62 being of sexual abuse, 496 being of physical abuse, and 250 being for serious injuries.

As a result of such reports a three-year Royal Commission into abuse and neglect in the disability sector is planned, and according to ABC2 TV news on 5/4/19 this is "set to be the most expensive in Australian history".

This comes on top of a Royal Commission being established to deal with abuse in the aged care sector, several TV reports having showed horrifying examples of decrepit old people in aged care homes being abused and beaten by staff, the incidence of such bullying and abuse reportedly being widespread.

Mental health

Mental illness can be caused by events that can occur in any person's life, for example:

➢ Stress-related conditions.

➢ Unemployment.

➢ Retirement.

➢ Bereavement.

➢ Child abuse, including bullying.

➢ Workplace bullying.

➢ Marriage breakdown.

➢ Alcoholism or drug addiction.

Being diagnosed with a mental illness can have negative affects upon a person both:

Externally: withdrawal of friends, relatives, neighbours and employers.

Internally: feelings of rejection, loneliness and depression.

People suffering from mental illness, therefore, should be encouraged to take an optimistic view that envisages them overcoming their problems and leading healthy, successful life.

Positivity to improve life

Table 21.1. Turning negativity into positivity

Negative self-talk	Positive self-talk
I've never done it before.	It's a chance to learn something.
It's too hard.	I'll try and make it easier.
I don't have the time.	I'll try and fit it into my plans.
I'm too tired.	I'll try and make the effort.
It won't work.	Let's try anyway.
It's too radical a change.	So much the better
Nobody talks to me.	I'll keep trying.

Taking a more positive, optimistic outlook is one of the keys to success, whereas negative-minded people tend to say: "It won't work" etcetera to most propositions and ideas (Mohr et al., 2018f).

Table 21.1 gives some examples of how to turn negative thinking into positive thinking, including examples suggested by Kemp (2014).

The bottom line here is that it is often best 'to give it a try' when it comes to things that might improves one's life at home or in the workplace.

In the case of victims of bullying, some of the measures suggested in Chapter 5 for dealing with it, for example ignoring it, may not work, but it least they are worth trying before perhaps more drastic measures are taken.

Such more drastic measures include, of course, reporting bullying to teachers and/or managers when the perpetrator(s) may punished and/or required to undergo counselling.

Optimism improves health

A team of psychologists, having done preliminary experiments with rats that showed the 'helplessness' weakened the body, studied 120 men who had had a first heart attack (Kemp, 2014).

The interviewed the men extensively to rate their optimism, counting the "because" statements they used to explain events in their lives. They found that none of the usual risk factors such as blood pressure, cholesterol levels, or how extensive the damage from the first heart attack was, predicted death, but that "only the men's level of optimism eight and a half years earlier predicted a second heart attack."

Of the 16 most pessimistic men, 15 died, whereas of the 16 most optimistic men, only 5 died.

A meta-study "Optimism and Physical Health" analyzed 83 separate studies of the relationship between optimism and physical health, 18 of which involved 2,858 patients and their cancer history. The results gave "robust" support to the notion that more optimistic people had better cancer outcomes (Kemp, 2014).

A recent German study showed that 'priming' of people to increase their confidence resulted in a 35% better chance of their succeeding (ABC2 TV news report, ^PM, 16/6/2018).

As emphasized in the recent book *The Psychology of Hope* (Mohr et al., 2018), the bottom line here is that not only will optimism improve quality of life, and the likelihood of success in life, but it also improves both mental and physical health.

Slow down, don't overstress

Cheryl Richardson suggest that often we should "slow down to succeed", allowing ourselves regular 'downtime' because we "all need a holiday from thinking too much", and try to lessen the impact of things in life that we find stressful and worrying (Richardson, 1998).

The Yerkes-Dodson law of arousal suggests that there is an optimum stress level at which we perform best, and to be *in the zone* for a purely intellectual activity such as reading a book we need only a low stress level, to be in the zone for activities that combine physical and intellectual performance a medium stress level is needed, whilst purely physical activities may involve higher stress levels, if they are very competitive *fight or flight* hormones sometimes having negative effects such as shrinking the hippocampus, reducing self-control, memory function, and emotional regulation.

In dealing with victims of bullying it will be helpful, of course, to advise them not to 'overstress', but to calmly think about the problem and how best to deal with it, perhaps getting help from friends, teachers/management to deal with it. 'Slowing down' etc., may also reduce the likelihood of such bad outcomes as suicide, which is uncommon amongst victims of bullying.

In dealing with perpetrators of bullying it may also be helpful to advise them to 'slow down' and 'think about' their actions and their worst possible consequences, both for themselves and their victims, before considering bullying someone.

Self-assessment

Table 21.2. Daily record of progress etc.

Item	Results	Action needed
Progress	What achieved?	New goals?
Affect on others	Positive?	Any regrets?
Reputation	Increase?	Anything needing fix?
Support	Who supported me?	Who else might?
Supporting others	People I helped.	Who should I help?
Time	Did I waste time?	Avoid next time
Problems solved	What fixed?	What needs fixing?
Skills, connections etc.	Increased?	What needs increase?
Personal life	OK?	New goals?

Accurate self-assessment is, of course, very important in helping pinpoint problems, and in solving them, and Tables 20.1 and 21.1 are examples of such self-assessment, whilst the expectancy-value and information integration methods of attitude evaluation may also be useful in this context.

The 2017 book *Success: The Psychology of Achievement* gives a "daily diary" which includes such items as those shown in Table 21.2 [we suggest that this need only be done monthly].

In assessing just about anything, and any aspect of life, Mohr's Metrology, which is the 10th law of Mohronism, and which is briefly outlined in the following section, is also useful (Mohr & Fear, 2015; Mohr et al., 2018d).

Mohr's Metrology

This requires a little elaboration. It asserts that all human traits can be measured. Madness, for example, is not a black and white thing, and we should be given a score, though this may vary a little according to such factors as the weather and countless others that hardly need mention.

For this law one can use the **Mohr Scale**, noting that a score of 10 is not possible as perfect madness, for example, would surely be rapidly terminal. Furthermore a score of zero is not possible as perfect sanity would surely constitute insanity.

In the case of general health, or how much alive one is, 0 would be dead (not a valid health score), whilst 10 would be too good to be true (also not a valid health score).

As an example, the first author (now 73) recently asked an ex-colleague circa 5 years older what his 'alive score' was, and he said 8, which was perhaps slightly optimistic.

Hence the Mohr Scale is 1 - 9, and the median score is the sum of the possible scores divided by the number of possible scores, that is $45/9 = 5$. This is the median score with four possible scores above and below it. With this score you don't pass or fail but are borderline.

The Mohr scale is also useful in the study of *ethics* where the questions of what is 'right' or 'good' are put, quickly followed by the question: "how good?" For this purpose the Mohr scale provides a set of ordinal numbers where, for example, 9 is the maximum 'goodness' (10 would be too good to be true).

Dealing with bullying

Several measures that can be taken to deal with bullying have been discussed in earlier chapters, particularly Chapter 5.

An example case of how a young schoolgirl dealt with bullying was reported on Melbourne's Channel 7 TV news at 6 PM on 3/4/2019.

The girl said she had been bullied for 13 years, for example being told by one bully to go and bury herself.

She said that she "was on a mission to stop other children from going through hell at school", offering the advice to victims of bullying: "Never give up if you're having a hard time, go and tell someone".

As part of her campaign to deal with bullying she read an open letter at the school assembly, also giving some "top tips" for parents, including:

➢ Talk to the child affected, and to the school.

➢ Seek professional help.

21. DEALING WITH BULLYING

Melbourne's local newspaper the Wyndham StarWeekly on 3/4/2019 reported that Westbourne Grammar School had introduced "restorative practice" which "repairs relationships rather than punishes", senior students in years 11 and 12 acting as "restorative practice facilitators".

These dealt with such issues as "year 7s and 8s squabbling over space to play" a game called 'downball'.

The Principal said she believed that restorative practice had made a "massive difference" at the school, which has students of more than 40 different nationalities.

Evidence of this, the school won an award for Schools that Excel and in 2017, and 2018 students obtained a 'median study score' of 33, well above that state median of 30.

One year 11 student said: "When someone is doing well they don't get backlash from friends. I feel that's slightly different in some places".

As a final piece of advice on dealing with people, it might pay to remember a tactic for 'getting on' with people mentioned in John Dean's book *Blind Ambition*.

Dean was President Nixon's Attorney General and the youngest ever to occupy that post. He wrote that in the White House at that time they used the term *stroking* to describe how one can 'butter up' (with perhaps artificial compliments, praise, niceness etcetera) a person who one wanted to persuade in some way.

Such 'stroking' might, of course, be helpful in dealing with nasty bosses, bullies, and people in general.

Myself, I feel that such things should be taught in school as part of a broad-ranging 'coping with life' subject, and I regret not thinking of using 'stroking' on colleagues at the same or similar level in the academic hierarchy, and thence competitors.

More important, I greatly regret not telling people, and perhaps senior management, of bullying by the two bad bosses/HODs that virtually ruined my career and life, and who were discussed in Chapters 8 and 9, and are discussed a little further in Appendix B. Note, however, that one must be careful about how one goes about making workplace complaints.

Try a little voodoo

One action a victim of a bad and bullying boss might make that can be construed as largely humourous, but which might actually achieve positive results such as gathering evidence of other people also having negative views about that boss, is to secretly post a voodoo doll type picture bearing the person's name on an office notice board.

An example of such a picture is shown above with a few needles inserted. As the picture is only of a doll, not a person, a note below it could say who the doll is meant to represent.

Alternatively, the note could ask for people to write the name they would like to associate with it.

Better still, of course, a voodoo doll could be purchased from a toy shop or the Internet, and thus hung on an office notice board.

One problem is that, perhaps sooner rather than later, the boss in question will remove the voodoo doll or picture and begin exhaustive enquiries as to who posted it, so the person who posted the doll or picture should therefore make sure nobody knew they were the person responsible.

Conclusions

There are many things one can do to improve one's life and mental health and wellbeing, including:

➤ Sound diet.

➤ Regular exercise.

➤ Getting plenty of sleep.

➤ Allowing plenty of quite time for relaxation.

➤ Spending time with friends and family.

➤ Sharing feelings with others.

➤ Discussing problems with others.

➤ Having regular and enjoyable recreational activities.

➤ Volunteering and helping others.

➤ Working hard to eliminate any bad habits.

➤ In the case of victims of bullying, seeking help from friends and/or reporting the bullying to teachers and/or managers may be advisable.

For best results one must, of course, tackle life and its occasional problems with the inter-related personal characteristics and behaviours (Butler-Bowden, 2017b):

➤ Self-esteem.
➤ Self-confidence.
➤ Self-reliance.
➤ Self-belief.
➤ Self-regulation or control.
➤ Self-assessment in similar fashion to the Expectation-Value and Information Integration models of attitude formation and assessment.
➤ Realistic goal-setting.
➤ Support from friends etc. with problems, and in achieving one's goals.

Then, if one has self-confidence, achievable goals etc., one might have a good chance of success in life, and along the way dealing with problems such as bullying, wherever they occur.

One bottom line, trivial as it may seem, is that, as Macy emphasizes (Macy, 2015):

Never quit . . . except when you should quit.

Another more important one is creativity, and according to Wallace Wattles (Wattles, 1910):

Consider that other people can't 'beat you to it' if you are creating something unique out of imagination, skills, and experience that make up your own personality.

and that to succeed you must provide people with results that are seen as greater in value than the financial etc. resources used.

In the case of victims of bullying a statement similar to the foregoing one may apply, and be helpful in coping:

Consider than bullies can't 'beat you' and that you will win out in the end, given a little help from others if need be.

In addition, some of the measures suggested in Chapter 5 should be considered, for example trying to ignore bullying or being more assertive, confident etc.

And, of course, should such 'response' measures prove unsuccessful, help and/or advice should be sought from family and friends and/or the bullying should be reported to teachers/managers etc., identifying any witnesses if possible to corroborate your side of the story.

☺☺☹☺☺☹☺☺☹☺☺☹☺☺☹

The End

21. Dealing with Bullying

Appendix A

THE MOHR PSYCHOLOGICAL INVENTORY

> *Considered in its entirety, psychoanalysis won't do.*
> *It's an end product, moreover, like a dinosaur or a zeppelin;*
> *no better theory can ever be erected on its ruins,*
> *which will remain forever one of the saddest and strangest*
> *of all landmarks in the history of twentieth-century thought.*
> Sir Peter Medawar, *The Hope of Progress*,
> "Further Comments on Psychoanalysis" (1972).

Introduction

The Science of psychology is still relatively new, in broad historical terms, and still in a relatively primitive state.

Freud's division of personality into just three basic components, the id, ego, and superego, for example, is somewhat simplistic. In addition, his obsession with sex many people find questionable, if not somewhat psychotic.

Similarly, Jung's obsession with dreams, seems somewhat psychotic, as dreams generally are somewhat random in nature and thus of little importance. Nightmares, more common in young children, may sometimes have some real meaning in terms of fears etc. that they may have, for example, of ghosts etc. that they have heard of in 'fairy tales'. Generally, however, dreams are a minor issue in relation to the totality of the human psyche.

Eysenck's classification of people as extroverts, introverts, neurotic, and psychotic is of some use, but limited in scope, as there must in reality be far more 'types' of human personality.

The type A, B and C personality classification has, however, proved popular, type A corresponding approximately to psychopath.

In contrast, Frankl's "logotherapy" is an absurdly overly simplistic idea in contrast the complexity of the human psyche (Frankl, 1969).

Herewith therefore, are the basics of the 'Mohr Psychological Inventory' (MPI), which seeks to give a modestly detailed view of the contents and workings of a person's mind.

The Mohr Psychological Inventory

The Mohr Psychological Inventory (MPI) divides the human mind and its workings into circa 20 categories, some of which can be evaluated and given a score for a particular individual, scores with negative connotations in some categories perhaps being indicative of mental health problems.

In a somewhat logical order, these categories are:

1. *Basic animal instincts.*

These include basic needs for survival such as for food, and shelter, basic hormonal 'urges' such as those for sex, and 'fight or flight', and basic 'societal' practices such as pairing for breeding purposes and thereafter, and living in groups (tribalism).

2. *Basic identity.*

One's age, sex (M or F), skin colour (B or W etc.), other key physical characteristics such as height, weight, hair colour, 'figure', baldness etc. Also, where one was born (town, country etc.), and key characteristics of one's family (size, wealth etc.).

3. *Childhood and education.*

Place in family one grew up in (e.g. youngest child), childhood hobbies etc., education and training: schools etc. attended, marks obtained in exams, qualifications obtained.

4. *Life history.*

Childhood (as in 3) + past jobs, old friends, old hobbies and pastimes, past beliefs and religions etc.

5. *Present life role.*

Job/occupation (work, unemployed, disabled, retired etc.), rank or 'status' (manager, front line worker etc.), family (wife, children etc.), home and key possessions such as car(s) etc.

6. *Memories.*

(a) Positive memories: good marks in exams, praise, prizes, winning at sports etc., good friends, good experiences such as happy holidays.

(b) Negative memories: illnesses, accidents, injuries, bad marks in exams, disputes/fights/arguments, losses (money, deaths in family etc.)

7. *Personality.*

Extraverted or introverted, happy or depressed, neurotic or psychotic etc. + self-perceived effect of past on personality [noting that up to 50% of personality may be genetic (Galton, 2001), and much of the rest from imitative and social learning].

8. *Beliefs.*

Religious, political, and 'societal' beliefs of what is 'right or wrong' etc., these beliefs constituting our 'conscience' or moral and ethical principles.

9. *Likes and dislikes* (including prejudices).

(a) Likes, e.g. dogs or cats, fast food such as pizza, certain types of music etc.

(b) Dislikes, e.g. people of a certain religion, ethnicity or sexual persuasion/inclination, certain foods (for example sausages or 'mystery bags') etc.

10. *Habits.*

Sleep, diet, and exercise routines. Hobbies and routine recreational activities, including TV, music, reading etc. Consumption of 'fast food', alcohol, prescribed drugs, and 'recreational' drugs.

11. *Social life.*
Friends and family one meets regularly, active membership of sporting clubs and other organizations (religious, political, etc.), restaurants or pubs/clubs attended regularly etc.

12. *Goals.*
Things one hopes to achieve in life, for example promotion, more money, better house, better health, lose weight etc.

13. *Worries.*
Things one is worried about, e.g. unhappy with job and pay, losing job, cost of living, paying off a mortgage, health etc.

14. *Fears.*
Real and imagined things that scare one, e.g. spiders, heights, ghosts etc.

15. *Behaviour.*
Bossy, controlling, argumentative etc., shy/retiring, sexual habits, e.g. sexual identity & preferences, or sexual promiscuity.

16. *Appearance.*
e.g. unkempt, unclean, sad looking, hunched body, fidgeting etc.

17. *Mood.*
e.g. short-tempered and impatient, excitable, easily angered, disagreeable, depressed etc.

18. *Awareness.*
Accuracy of perception of surroundings, current events etc.

19. *Communication.*
Comprehension, ability to communicate effectively etc.

20. *Thinking skills and IQ.*
Responses to ideas and suggestions, e.g. responding with good alternative ideas quickly is suggestive of intelligence (a formal IQ test can, of course, also be used).

21. *Inner thoughts.*
Inner thoughts kept private, such as dislike, hatred or envy of certain people, or thoughts of self-harm or suicide.

22. *Health.*

(a) Physical: e.g. any physical problems/ailments that may affect mental health such as chronic heart disease.

(b) Mental: neural system ailments such as Alzheimer's disease, mental retardation etc.

(c) Psychological: anxiety, high levels of psychopathy (bossiness, dishonesty etc.) etc.

Category 22 is largely of a summary nature and issues in it may be found by examination of some of the other categories.

High levels of undesirable traits in one or more of these inventory categories may be indicative of a mental health problem, for example (see also Chapter 18 & Table 18.1 etc.):

➢ Traumatic memories of bad experiences in 6(b) may be suggestive of *PTSD*.
➢ High levels of *depression* in 7 are, of course, suggestive of mental illness.
➢ High levels of concern about a wide range of issues in 13 and/or 14 are suggestive of an *anxiety* disorder.
➢ High levels of ambition in 12 and bossiness and shortness of temper in 17 are suggestive of *psychopathy*.
➢ Low levels of response and 19 and 20 are suggestive of *low intelligence*, or in extreme cases *mental retardation*.
➢ Thoughts of *suicide*, especially if relatively frequent, may be indicative of a need for supportive counselling etc.

Conclusion

The MPI can be used as a guide to examining a person's psyche, and perhaps identifying any psychological issues and problems that may be indicative of a mental health problem or illness. Then one should follow Mohr's Metrology and give the issue a score from 1 to 9 to prevent people assuming the person is a 'full blown'/hopeless case, and to reflect that some degree of anxiety, for example, is normal and required for survival.

A smaller animal crossing an empty field, for example, would need to be a little anxious and look hither and thither to see if any larger animals of prey such as lions etc. might be around and thus a potential threat.

Similarly, whilst introversion is viewed negatively, people who talk and gossip too much should be viewed more negatively, suggesting a scale for introversion/extroversion.

Note that in items 2 and 15 'sexual identity' and 'sexual behavior' could be made additional, separate categories because of the apparent growth in homosexuality etc., in part because of the LGBT 'movement', and in part a result of the 'reverse evolution' discussed in Appendix C.

As noted in the penultimate section of Chapter 18 (*Labelling and high rate of misdiagnoses*, some studies find incorrect diagnosis of mental illness is all too frequent, and the success rate in diagnosis of just 'some sort of mental illness', and not which particular mental illnesses the person has, is quite poor.

A program on Australia's SBS1 TV channel at 8.30 to 9.30 PM on the 11th and 18th of October 2018 had 3 experienced psychologists assess 10 people, 5 of whom had suffered from, and been diagnosed with, a mental illness several years earlier. The 'experts' only identified one of the 5 people with mental illness, i.e., they got only 1/10, so we should all be wary of psychological diagnoses these days, driven by the the relatively primitive state of the science of psychology and the practice of psychiatry, and the greed of 'Big Pharma' which, for example only, has resulted in far too many young children being unfairly diagnosed with ADHD and put drugs for years, if not life.

Mental health issues, however, do seem to be a growing problem. In recent decades asylums were greatly reduced in number to 'deinstitutionalise' mental health systems in the West. Now, however, "more than 600 Victorians die annually from suicide. They don't have terminal illnesses and their deaths are therefore preventable" (Patrick McGorry, *Our mental breakdown,* The Age, Thursday, October 25, 2018).

☺☺☹☺☺☹☺☺☹☺☺☹☺☺☹

Appendix B

THE MOHR CHECKLIST FOR PSYCHOPATHS

> *Psychopathic personality: Madman, the maladjusted, psychopath, psycho, psychopathic personality, sociopath, unstable personality, aggressive personality, antisocial personality, dipsomaniac, drunkard - - drug addict,* Microsoft Bookshelf dictionary, 1994.
>
> *To treat a psychopath – at any time, in any place, or under any set of conditions – is the most onerous and unrewarding job a clinician can undertake.* Robert Lindner, *The Fifty-Minute Hour,* ch. 4 (1986).

Introduction

The Hare checklist for psychopaths was discussed in Chapter 9, the checklist being shown in Table 9.1.

It was also noted that the author (GAM) had scored a couple of bad bosses he once had, both of whom were too young and inexperienced for being HOD, and played a major role in destroying his promising University career when he was less than 40. They were given seemingly too low scores of 12, because the Hare checklist was developed to apply to criminals in prisons, and thus has a few items relating to such people, for example items 17 and 18, respectively "History of conditional prison release being revoked", and "Criminal versatility".

Table B.1, therefore, shows the Mohr Checklist for Psychopaths (MCLP) in which a few items of the Hare checklist are replaced by new ones more relevant to 'bad bosses' etc., and a few items are replaced by hopefully better alternatives.

After an interview or other assessment/judgment each trait is scored as 0 (not present), 1 (present but not dominant), or 2 (dominant), so that the maximum possible score is 40, but note that the MCLP also allows scores such as 1.5, as shown.

The MCLP

Table B.1. The Mohr Checklist for Psychopaths (MCLP).

	TRAIT	SCORE
	Facet 1: Interpersonal	
1	Glibness or superficiality of a salesman	1
2	Excessive sense of self-worth	2
3	Pathological lying	2
4	Cunning or manipulative	1.5
	Facet 2: Affective	
5	Lack of remorse or guilt	2
6	Emotionally shallow	1
7	Callous or lack of empathy	2
8	Won't accept responsibility for own actions	1.5
	Facet 3: Lifestyle	
9	Excessively ambitious	1
10	Excessively greedy	1
11	Parasitic life style	1
12	Extravagant life style	0.5
13	Irresponsibility	0.5
	Facet 4: Antisocial	
14	Bullying	1.5
15	Focuses only on own problems	1.5
16	Little care about others, such as subordinates in the workplace	1.5
17	Mixes only with other managers etc.	1.5
18	Stretches rules to make more money etc.	1.25
	Other traits:	
19	Vanity	1.25
20	History of sexual promiscuity	0
TOTAL SCORE		**25.5**

With the MCLP 'OK' people score from 1 to 10, 'borderline' people circa 15+, whilst scores of 20+ indicate psychopathy, and 30+ serious psychopathy that can be classified as a serious mental illness.

I have re-scored the aforementioned two bad bosses as shown in Table B.1, the score of 25.5 giving a positive diagnosis of psychopathy, a diagnosis I wish had been made many years earlier before the two men in question ruined my career and life all too many years ago.

Further personal case histories

My late eldest brother, 'BB', was also somewhat bossy, and having lost his job, started his own business with a lot of cheap help from family and friends (including me for several years). He got rich thanks to an old spinster lady walking into the company office one day, talking of building and donating to the local council a childrens' day-care centre on just a small part of a huge block of land in inner Melbourne that had once had a huge diary behind a large house, and she had inherited.

BB got her to just about 'give away' the huge property to him and never looked back, but, as noted below, later played a key role in ruining my prospects of recovering from the 'academic crucifixion' I had suffered thanks to one of the two aforementioned bad bosses.

I also had a wife for many years who, having also been an eldest child (of 3), was a bit of a bully, and by talking behind my back and the gossip reaching my workplace, did much to undermine my career (see also the footnote below[2]).

Then, when I was at rock bottom, having been bullied into resigning a promising career at age 38.8, she had BB help get me committed (for 2 days) for refusing to see a marriage guidance counsellor.

---

[2] In mid-1981 when I was working at Auckland Uni. I was unwell one day and the new HOD told me to take time off. I took only 2 days off (the only 2 days I ever took off work in my whole career!), but on one of those the wife had the GP visit with a 'shrink' circa 2.30 PM.

She was hoping I'd be having a beer but, in fact, I was having a pot of tea, a habit of mine. This act on her part was, not for the first time, a sure indication of mental health issues involving psychopathy.

Badly upset, a few days later I swallowed a paltry couple of spoons of weed killer, and she had me committed for another few days, putting the last nail in the coffin of my reputation.

This event added to the PTSD/depression I suffered (unconsciously) as a result of my 'academic crucifixion' when the new HOD at Auckland U bullied me about being "a lousy lecturer" and "Civil Engineers are stupid" (he, a typical 'Cambridge clod', was far worse!) and into resigning and *walking the plank'* (in fact the HOD might have quit had I got help from friends, a lawyer etc.[3]).

In hindsight it is clear that my ex-HOD at Monash U, (Dillmer) was complicit in an agreement with the Auckland U HOD that he would offer me a research job when I returned to Melbourne, after being bullied into resigning.

When that offer was made I refused. I'd had enough of Dillmer, having in 1983 invited him from Auckland to help with my ever-expanding treatise on the Finite Element Method. Dillmer had me fly to Melbourne to pick my brains for 3 weeks in Dec. 1983/Jan. 1984, then flying to Auckland in August 1984 to do 2 more weeks of the same, bringing with him a few useless pages it had taken him a year to produce, having promised "two" secretaries to type the then 500 page book.

In the end I had, as usual, to do the typing!

And, when the 'tome' was belatedly published by OUP, after CUP had mucked me around for several years during which edition 1 was enlarged, edition 2 was cut from 500 pp to 330 pp, then increased again slowly to 600 pp with far wider scope, I left out Dillmer's 6 useless pages (Mohr, 1992).

As for typing, a bad bit of timing was in early 1984 buying a Spectravideo PC (at twice the price they cost in Australia) and writing (at home as usual) a short course:

A Microcomputer Introduction to the Finite Element Method.

I put in my letter of resignation in August 1984, but next month got good news that attendance was going to be good.

---

[3] Not long before I quit I recall the Dean mumbling to me one day simply: *"Lawyers are expensive"*, a clear hint that I did indeed need to take some action about my promotion having been delayed unfairly.

I ran the course alone with an RGB projector connected to my 'kid's PC' Spectravideo over 2 days, 1 in late October and 1 in late November (1984) with circa 60 people from *all over New Zealand* in attendance[4]. I then flew to Melbourne the next day, leaving my wife to sell the house, because Dillmer was supposed to have started the same course in Melbourne, my having given him a copy. The Melbourne course was cancelled because nut-case Dillmer could not get an audience, though he had contacts in the right places to get one, was HOD etc.

So back in Melbourne in December 1984, I'd had enough of Dillmer, but to do the right thing I kept his name on the Auckland 'PCs for FEM course' when I got a contract to publish it in expanded form in late 1985, even though he'd never read a or written a word of it (Mohr & M-----, 1986, 1987).

But I never used the mean Dillmer as a job referee, though I badly needed a referee about my recent work (i.e., the very successful Auckland course and finally getting a book on FEM out), whilst the Auckland bully and Cambridge Clod HOD, it is clear in the 20/20 clarity of hindsight 30+ years later, was backstabbing me in confidential referee statements, in contrast his open statement given to me being OK (but *only* just OK).

The result: interviewed for several HOD, Dean and CEO positions in Australia & New Zealand, I never got another job, in part, of course, because before very long it had 'got around' that I did not have a job, so that one interviewer remarked scathingly about my "fancy letterhead".

Thus I wrote in my limited edition memoirs that there were 4 "villains" involved in my downfall, the two bullying & psychopathic HODs, my uncommunicative (to me) & occasionally (verbally) bullying ex-wife who played Judas or backstabber once too often, and BB, whose role is noted above (Mohr, 2016).

---

[4] Indeed, the remarkable success of this course, all equipment & typing paid for by me, as always, was convincing proof of myself being a successful lecturer etc., whereas the bully-boy HOD was pathetic, for example, in a 'demo' lecture about his useless research given when he was interviewed for the HOD job he was both dishonest, and pathetic.

Conclusion

This Appendix tells part of my sad story and people mentioned in it, such as my ex-wife, for example, may not agree with some of my views.

I have not sought the views of a qualified mental health professional on these people and it is now far too late to do so, all of them now being retired etc. and thus living in far different circumstances (if still alive) than in the past when they had an effect/bearing on my life.

Indeed, I thought briefly of making this Appendix B a case study of myself, producing half a dozen pages of scribble notes for the purpose.

But then I decided instead to present the MCLP, using the '4 villains' as examples of it, and also as a part of my case history, e.g., they increased the levels of PTSD I suffered for 30+ years, symptoms being unconscious depression at my seemingly 'hopeless/helpless no friends to help' position as an unemployed Cambridge PhD (done in record time), soon to become somewhat famous (1992+), rather than memories of any particular events.

Last lines

The main point of this appendix was to present Table B.1, the MCLP, also scoring it for 2 bad bosses who were 2 of the 'four villains' in my 'academic crucifixion', and then also writing a little about the other 2, namely my ex-wife and a relative 'BB', thus involving some degree of 'case studying' for 5 people: myself and the 4 villains.

I have given the 2 bad bosses a score in Table B.1, and discussed some of the key history of my involvements with them.

I have also very briefly mentioned BB, and discussed 'the ex' at more length.

Since this book is about bullying it is, of course, relevant to mention the 'four villains' who were instrumental in ruining my life, namely, the typical 'Cambridge clod' Auckland Uni. HOD, the ex-HOD in Melbourne, 'BB', and 'the ex' as, obviously psychopathic, they used bullying, backstabbing etc.

On the MCLP I was inclined at first to give BB a score of about 20, and thinking of giving the ex-wife perhaps 15, suggesting the ex-wife as somewhat borderline psychopathic, and BB as definitely so but, of course, at least a second opinion should be had if possible.

In relation to item 20 in Table B.1 (sexual promiscuity), I suspect that in the late 1960s BB lied that he had started a branch of his new consulting business in Sydney, and he used this as an excuse for weekend trips to Sydney to visit the notorious red-light district of King's Cross a few times, no doubt visiting one or two of the many brothels that still abound there. I can deduce this, because a man I met at a pub in my early 'down and out days' in the late 1980s had done the same thing while working (also in the late 1960s) as a Real Estate Agent in the Melbourne suburb of St Kilda, which was and still is also notorious for brothels and prostitution.

I also recall that BB from circa 20+ liked Playboy magazines and when I returned from New Zealand after being bullied into resigning, his wife ordered him to get rid of a large collection of Playboy magazines, and he left them at the house I had just moved into. For fun I took out all the centerfold pictures and 'plastered' a quite large wall with them, but this would have annoyed BB, no doubt a factor in his having me briefly committed (for 2 days) when I refused to see a marriage guidance counsellor (he having done so not long previously).

For BB and my ex-wife just 3 of many subsequent examples of bullying etc. in the years that followed:

[1] A few years after ruining my career by backstabbing that reached the ears of my colleagues, and then having BB get me briefly committed back in Melbourne, my ex-wife proudly told me over the phone: *"I'm boss of twelve people"*, referring to her managing a day care centre, the 12 including staff (mostly part-time/rotational) and a cleaner.

[2] Knowing my poverty, largely thanks to her and BB, my ex-wife boasted over the phone one day in 1992: *"I've got a 486"* (PC), knowing that I had only been able to afford a cheap XT PC without a hard drive in 1987 and was still using this.

[3] Knowing that I had had to walk to various places for years to pay to get photocopying done, BB boasted one day circa 1992: *"I've got a photocopier"*.

As for myself, I rate my score for anxiety between 1 and 2/10, much of that being the habit of liking to finish work fairly quickly/promptly.

On the depression scale, my score on that varied, of course, over the years, being >1 perhaps in 1965 and 1966, in 1966 having to repeat the whole of 2nd year Engineering being no fun at all. Likewise it might have been from 1 to 2 in 1971 working in my second full-time job which I called in retrospect "the sweatshop". In my 2 Cambridge PhD years there was great financial and thence time stress, finishing in record time (< 2 years) and flying home with only about $50 in the bank.

After my 'academic crucifixion' I had PTSD, of course, largely resulting in depression varying from 3/10 to 4/10 for a couple of decades, and perhaps reducing to circa 2/10 in the last decade.

One 'hangover' from the career-destroying bullying from 2 nasty (male) bosses was that, having placed flat-share ads in the press occasionally circa 1988 to 1995, I had become somewhat wary of men. Thus I usually lied to men responding to an ad by phone that the room was "taken", and would eventually make the flat-share agreement with a woman of 'half-way similar' age, though I discovered a couple of times that this could be hazardous, women entering into such agreements having been left 'on the shelf' and looking for a marital-type relationship and thus to have children etc.

☺☻☹☺☻☹☺☻☹☺☻☹☺☻☹

Appendix C

REVERSE EVOLUTION

> *We must, however, acknowledge, as it seems to me,*
> *that man with all his noble qualities . . . still bears in his bodily*
> *frame the indelible stamp of his lowly origin.*
> Charles Darwin, *The Descent of Man* (1871), ch. 23.

Reverse evolution in mankind?

This appendix discusses a consequence of man's excessive breeding, that of *reverse evolution,* the following two sections discussing experiments with rats showing that:

(a) 'Enriched' environment improves their brain size and intelligence.

(b) Learning in rats changes their RNA.

Case (a) involves the *nurture* component of intelligence and case (b) the *nature* or genetic component of intelligence.

Findings (a) + (b) demonstrate how greater intelligence can develop and be passed on genetically in a species.

Leading biologists and anthropologists believe that we are evolving 100 times faster than our hunter gatherer ancestors were (Callaghan, 2008), but is this rapid evolution for the better or for the worse?

The thesis of this appendix is that our increasingly overpopulated, capitalist and greedy consumer societies have become unethical and are beginning to regress, resulting in lower physical and psychological standards, in turn resulting in reduced intelligence and *reverse evolution.*

There is much evidence of this reverse evolution, including the increasing prevalence of bullying in human societies.

The effect of environment

Modern man is distinguished from other creatures by having a larger cerebral cortex, the centre for our thinking and language. This larger cortex must have evolved by the adaptive processes inherent in Darwin's theory of natural selection.

Clues to just how this occurred were given by the work of social psychologist David Krech and his group at UC Berkeley (Packard, 1978).

In this they provided a group of rats with an "enriched environment" of large cages with various things rats enjoy such as slides, wheels and the like. Then a maze with a sugar reward at the end was added. This had a dark and a lighted alley and the rats soon learnt which led to the sugar.

Then the maze lighting was reversed regularly so that the rats had to relearn the 'sugar route'.

A second control group of rats lived normally and a third group was kept in a deprived dark and noiseless area.

After 90 days it was found that the 'enriched' rats had developed thicker cerebral cortexes.

This was perhaps the first evidence that the brain is modified by experience. The enrichment conditions caused the following changes (Atrens & Curthoys, 1982):

[1] The size of the cerebral cortex was increased.

[2] The size of the cortical neurons increased.

[3] The size and number of synaptic contacts increased.

[4] The quantity of acetylcholinesterase, the compound responsible for breakdown of the neurotransmitter acetylcholine, increased.

Therefore, the rats which had experienced environmental enrichment were apparently anatomically and biochemically superior to those which had endured a deprived environment.

This result provided laboratory evidence that environmental enrichment could physically and chemically alter the brain. This ability of neural tissue to change because of its activation is called *plasticity*.

It seems likely, therefore, that as early man discovered fire, began to make tools and advanced in many other ways his brain gradually evolved into that of *Homo sapiens sapiens* or modern man.

Biochemical learning and evolution

Two further research results indicative of the biochemical nature of learning processes have been obtained:

(a) The work by George Ungar's group (Ungar et al., 1972) in which peptides in rats conditioned to shun darkness were isolated. These peptides seemed able to transfer the conditioning to other rats. [Peptides are small organic molecules that link hundreds or even thousands of amino acid molecules together to form polypeptides].

(b) Changes in RNA in rats given a learning task found by Hyden's group in Sweden (Rosenfeld, 1972).

Hyden's group also found an increase in a brain-specific protein S-100 in rats trained to use their non-preferred paw. They then found that an antiserum to S-100 stopped this learning.

Subsequently much further work has been done to investigate the effects of inhibition of protein and RNA synthesis by antibiotics upon memory. One finding was that drugs that interfere with the uptake of amino acids by cells can selectively interfere with memory retrieval or formation.

Proteins are naturally occurring polypeptides.

Genes are nucleoproteins formed by combination of polypeptide and DNA (deoxyribonucleic acid) chains.

The process of cell reproduction or *mitosis* occurs when the two strands of the DNA double helix separate and manufacture protein and a new 'opposite' strand to form a new cell.

This process is assisted by RNA (ribonucleic acid).

If learning changes RNA then perhaps a process like the cell mutation that causes cancer (Weinberg, 1999) might also be responsible for human evolution, both physically (Selmes, 1974) and mentally (Darwin, 1999).

Cell mutation is the result of a DNA copying error. This may just be a statistical fluke, having a probability of one in a million or less.

A ground breaking case study of the mutation process was the *ras* oncogene found in a smoker with bladder cancer (Weinberg, 1999).

After 30 years of smoking, some of the many highly toxic carcinogens he had inhaled had not been detoxified in his liver and had passed into his urine.

The ras oncogene is 5000 DNA bases long but one base was incorrect where a sequence that should have been GCC GGC GGT was instead GCC GTC GGT with just one base incorrect, a T appearing instead of a G in the middle of this mutated 'string'.

The incorrect gene then governed the growth of this cell and its descendants, resulting in a cancer tumour years later.

It might be possible that, over time, gradual development of language 'enriched' our mental environment and produced lasting changes in human RNA and thence DNA that resulted in the evolution of our larger cerebral cortexes.

That we have a comparatively large brain size, therefore, might indeed be the evolutionary result of sometimes vicarious thinking over millennia, as often assumed.

Man's deteriorating environment

If some of Krech's rats got smarter because of an 'enriched' environment then it would appear that in the more affluent West we are now going through the opposite process as our living standards decline.

Now more and more of us live in bloated and crowded megacities where even houses in the outer suburbs are becoming unaffordable and they also involve the downside of large numbers of hours spent commuting on crowded freeways or increasingly strained and packed public transport systems.

To cut commuting times many live in high rise apartment buildings that can only be likened to filing cabinets for forgotten and soulless people that have once again reverted to being troglodytes.

At the same time big business has bought out so many farms that many rural communities and towns have shrunk to a less than viable size.

Back in the 'big smoke' big business grows still further while job conditions and security have decreased drastically, for example most retail businesses now working seven days a week, often with extended hours, and often without compensating employees for these ludicrously unnecessary 'rat race' hours.

To make matters worse, these slaves are brainwashed zombies hooked on increasingly junky, if not frivolous, products.

In other words, most have become like Krech's deprived rats and, just as our lives become duller, so too do we and our children. When we start to talk about economics, however, the picture becomes even bleaker.

Economic influences

According to Lynn and Vanhaven (2002), the world average IQ is 90, understandable bearing in mind that IQ tests originated in more advanced Europe and the USA. Only one in five countries have average IQ near the British average of 100, half have IQ < 90, and Africa rates bottom with average IQ of only 70.

They find that the GDP of nations correlates halfway well (to 0.7) with national IQ, the next most important factor being whether the country has a socialist or market economy, the third most important factor being it's natural resources.

They argue that more progressive and freer countries have greater inventiveness or IQ, in turn improving GDP, pointing to Japan's progress in the 20th century and China's current progress as examples.

In other words, some countries in Asia have undergone industrial revolution somewhat later than those in Europe and North America.

In the once most affluent countries, however, things are now doing downhill.

Thanks to wrongful marketing practices, government taxes and childishly crude economic modeling and management house prices in many countries have grown absurdly high.

At the same time governments in the more affluent countries have run up increasing national debts while their politicians electioneer with bullshit that we've never had it so good and that they have a budget surplus, that is, they have increased national debt only marginally less than their deliberately high forecast figure.

Meanwhile big biz continues to go offshore to use cheap labour so that, for example, most of our clothes and household goods now come from China or thereabouts.

Ourselves, we have increasing job insecurity and are expected to be prepared to retrain two or three times in our life, this despite being expected to study for increasingly long periods before beginning work in the first place. To add insult to injury more and more of the courses of study are ridiculous, ranging from postgraduate courses in sexology and puppetry to MBAs that are largely, if not totally, high school level.

Young students today, therefore, run up increasingly large higher education debts, study longer and thus spend less time in the work force, and yet face retraining further down the track along with ludicrous house prices. The result is that they can't afford to get married, let alone have children or buy a house, and are worse off than primitive man was!

Lower standards

Standards are falling more generally than just economically, however. Big biz is increasingly unethical with tunnel vision for the bottom line so that CEOs make absurd amounts for sitting on their backsides and coming up with lousy ideas while the increasingly insecure workers suffer increasingly and are little better off than Roman slaves were.

Correspondingly, therefore, these modern slaves live increasingly miserable lives of brainwashed consumerism to the limited extent they can afford it. The result can only be a decline in intelligence.

To make matters worse, according to the Peter Principle that 'the sour cream rises' in human hierarchies, the rich brainwashers are even more stupid in most respects except for the something akin to animal cunning and viciousness with which they accumulate money for their own frivolous amusement.

Meanwhile, we see a 'reverse Keynes δG effect' of massive injection of capital by transnational companies setting up in China and India to find cheap labour [the original 'Keynes δG effect' was the notion that increasing government spending G has a snowball effect that increases GNP].

Now, therefore, the economies of these countries are growing rapidly and their peoples, at least to some extent, now see themselves as the smart ones.

In India, for example, their education sector has been turning out engineers in droves for decades. As noted in Chapter 7, however, in the West we have dumbed the education system down to the point at which:

(1) Teachers are sometimes not allowed to fail students.

(2) Up to half of primary students in the USA are given drugs for the recently 'invented' (by nut cases in the 'psycho' professions) ADHD.

(3) Almost from infancy children are locked up in long day care instead of being given the sort of specialist attention that, as noted in Chapter 7, would increase their intelligence.

(4) Apprenticeship to be a hairdresser takes up to 6 years.

(5) School remains an excessively drawn out 12 years.

(6) A high proportion of courses at so-called Universities are quite simply ridiculous, for example courses in sexology and puppetry, whilst others like MBAs are so low-level and commonplace that they are almost worthless like the latter-day institutions that run them simply because they are popular and therefore good money spinners.

(7) Only 40% of US school students score at the level that 80% of students in some other countries achieve (Sykes, 1995). A similar decline has occurred in Australia and like countries.

Speaking of education, however, where else but the USA could it happen? That is, there are more people in jail that at University. This in the 'land of the free' and all that bullshit.

This dumbing down has extended throughout our society. Long ago noted psychologist Hans Eysenck aroused public condemnation for saying the black people were less intelligent though in Africa to this day that does prove to be the case.

Recently a (male) president of Harvard University was heavily criticized for saying that women had somewhat different abilities to men.

The bottom line now, therefore, is that we must all be equally stupid and nobody is allowed to be otherwise.

Brainwashed zombies

It is pitiful to see how many of us are brainwashed into carrying a drink bottle or cigarette in one hand and a mobile phone in the other, wearing stiff denim jeans and choking ourselves with ties that derive from the scarves that Roman soldiers carried to bind sword wounds.

We morons must also have the latest fashion in cars, houses and other possessions. Never mind that the cars are often gas guzzling 4WDs with 'aircon' and the houses 'McMansions' way beyond the needs of shrinking modern families and which consume massive amounts of energy, much of it for air conditioning that is usually unnecessary.

Then there are the lifetime habits, or should we say addictions, like smoking and booze, the quotation opening Chapter 13 being an excellent example of how the beer barons bring such public addictions about.

The startling reality is that a great many of the things we do we don't really like anyway. Few, for example, like smoking or beer at first try but like fools we persist and condition ourselves and especially our brains to bear each new and ludicrous habit.

The same goes for dry white wines such as Chardonnay which tend to eat away at the oesophagus and stomach like acid, a reminder that alcohol tends to cause cancer all the way through the digestive path.

As for food, the list of ludicrous and downright nasty things we eat and claim to enjoy is endless, including tripe, offal, frog's legs, snails and so forth.

Often, of course, we acquire such ridiculous habits by imitative learning, that so many of us must have dogs as pets being an excellent example, this simple being a comparatively modern 'fashion' that caught on and is copied by one generation after another.

Usually, however, we are encouraged a good deal, if not a lot, by the skillful brainwashing of attention demanding and repetitive advertising. Arguably, in fact, the way in which humans are affected by advertising is directly comparable to lab experiments on conditioning of animals.

No better example can be found in the mindless poker machines that seem to hypnotize countless people for hours and hours on end. Such suckers are very comparable to rats in a Skinner box except that they seem dumber than the rats because, far from being rewarded, they are punished by being 'milked' of a great deal of money.

As for mass BW, the bullshit about Saddam Hussein having 'WMDs' that the US administration used to justify their invasion of Iraq is one of the better BW examples in history. Like Vietnam, Iraq has been a disaster for the US army as is sadly highlighted by the statistic that at present 17 US war veterans commit suicide a day, this toll each year far exceeding the total toll of US soldiers in the mistaken Iraq campaign over five years.

Ever worsening diet

Nowhere is evidence of our reverse evolution greater than in our deteriorating diet. Now, more and more of the global population fill up on fast junk food, salty and fatty snacks such as potato crisps, biscuits, cake, sugary soft-drinks and, of course, the demon booze.

Indeed the medical profession in the West at large considers the modern diet problem as something of a crisis because obesity has reached epidemic proportions as a result of excessive consumption of fatty and sugary foods.

Still probably a billion or so of us smoke, which we like to consider part of the 'total diet' because we believe substituting food for cigarettes, and especially chewing gum, is helpful in quitting smoking. Indeed the first author found this approach helpful in finally quitting.

Then, of course, there is the growing problem of drugs in society. As a result we have to have regular drug testing in sport and elsewhere, we would suggest in parliament judging by the raving performances one sees there which, everybody knows, may well be fuelled by generous doses of booze with lunch and long dinners in favourite restaurants.

A couple of years ago the author (GAM) saw an elderly man on crutches who had lost the lower third of his right leg. Having done much research on atherosclerosis, I asked him what had caused his loss of much of a lower limb. He told me that the cause had been a twenty-something male drunk driver, a hoon who had had a blood alcohol reading in excess of 0.20 and was also loaded up with illicit drugs.

Having moved to one of Melbourne's much cheaper, less affluent, Western suburbs from a suburb on its Mornington Peninsula a few years ago, the author noticed that more people smoke and/or are obese. This, he believes, relates to the Reception-Yielding model of Fig. 13.2. That is, as he prefers to term it, people here have lower 'consumer IQ.'

Monkey business

Much of our so-called education of young children should be called monkey business because they are encouraged to act like monkeys on climbing frames and in often senseless ball games, some of which, like football, are positively dangerous and reduce some players to paraplegics.

Then there are the ludicrous crazes we fall for. When the first author was a child there was a mindless yo-yo craze. More recent were skateboard and roller blades crazes.

As for dangerous activities, roller blades and skate boards are bad enough but those concrete slopes built for kids to do bike tricks on are highly insane.

The list of insane human activities here is endless, including sky diving, climbing up vertical rock faces, skiing, and so on.

As for racing, it seems that we will race just about anything that can be made to move ranging from dogs to camels.

Most of these activities have become spectator sports, some of them viewed by massive audiences brainwashed by hype and heavy media publicity into taking childish games played by overpaid adults seriously.

The complete insanity of this is that worrying oneself greatly over who wins a silly ball game is supposed to be recreational, that is, entertaining and relaxing. That riots often occur both off and on the field, however, are anything but relaxing.

Worrying too are the increasingly animalistic celebrations that accompany scoring and victory in most sports.

In addition, that many people enjoy watching brutal sports such as boxing and kick boxing doesn't say much good about the human race and only suggests that it is somewhat sick.

When you think about it, in fact, most of our ridiculous sport and recreational activities make us look like Krech's 'environment enriched' rats on their running wheels and slides.

The bottom line is that, as they used to say, *small things amuse small minds*, in other words we sure as hell are not getting any smarter.

Sociological devolution

Not only is our environment in polluted and unsightly megacities unpleasant, but our societies are becoming meaner, nastier and more violent. Violence is on the increase everywhere to the point that many older people and women don't feel safe on the streets at night and, of course, there is no shortage of street crime during the day as well.

Experiments with rats show that when they are housed beyond a certain population density they begin to fight each other. Evidently humans do the same and we are now accustomed to associating crime and violence with big cities like Chicago and New York.

Increasing numbers of us are addicted to booze, illegal so-called 'party drugs,' as well as prescription drugs like valium for anxiety, Ritalin for ADHD, and lithium for bipolar disorder (formerly called manic depression).

With divorce rates around 50% we are living less safely in this respect at least than our Neanderthal ancestors did. Childhood is miserable enough at times under the best of circumstances and family breakups often make it much more so for far too many children.

Women loose tolerance of the fact that men, especially when younger, can drink far more booze than they. They also fear violence from men though they are more often than not the instigators by way of foul, hysterical, bossy, and bullying abuse. Try that on the footy field and, predictably, you can 'get an opponent in' so that they take a shot at you and risk being 'rubbed out' for a few weeks by the umpires.

In marriage, as well as in courtship, there is little or no meaningful communication. If you eavesdrop on a couple that has been married for a decade or two, you will find the dialogue at all times entirely trivial, for example "do we need milk?," in modern times this being said as often as not over a mobile phone while one partner is in the supermarket.

To complicate matters further, in the fast declining West women are taking over to some extent. Only about 100 years ago women were not to be seen in Cambridge. Now far more women than men go to University in Australia.

Women also have a lower unemployment rate, already having the advantage that, merely by lying on their backs and having children they have a job for life as motherhood was certainly construed to be in the '[good] old days.'

One billion Muslims are more old-fashioned and tolerate the man being the boss still and, indeed, with the West in decay, it may well be that they have same sort of potentially winning advantage in this regard.

The ghastly music that young and not so young listen to and gyrate all night too mindlessly boozed and/or drugged in discos is another indicator of social decay. The manic pop groups of today dress and sing atrociously and leap about like primitive loonies.

The bottom line is that you can see the writing on the walls, that is, the graffiti that covers much of our miserable megacities, a sure sign that we are regressing back to grunting cave men.

Sexual proliferation and deviance

Amongst the most disturbing indications of the corruption and decadence in our society are the all too frequent reports of sexual abuse of children by priests, teachers and others. It seems therefore that even the once most trusted people in our society can't be trusted any longer.

Sex, of course, is ubiquitous in our increasingly depraved society. Brothels were once illegal back street affairs. Now they and all manner of sexual products are widely advertised on late night TV, a pathetic attempt to shield children from it, and also in free local newspapers which children of all ages collect from the letterbox after coming home from school.

A fundamental change is that homosexuality is on the increase. Once a trait one kept secret it is now rampantly displayed at gay Mardi Gras festivals, at gay bars in major cities, and in late night TV ads for homosexual dating services.

Some claim that homosexuality is inherited and a study of 113 people in 33 families in which at least two brothers were homosexual found a genetic marker on the X-chromosome (Xq28) that had a very high correlation with sexual orientation (Galton, 2001).

Genes may play a minor 'predisposory' role but, largely, homosexuality is a learnt behaviour. Typically, for example, the normal heterosexual male has one or two homosexual experiences in adolescence (Robertson, 1981), and no doubt the same applies to women.

Those who become homosexuals, therefore, presumably do so as a result of imitative learning at an early age. There are, no doubt, also psychological factors involved, for example a lack of confidence in approaching the opposite sex coupled with the fact that there are earlier homosexual experiences to draw upon as an alternative behaviour model.

If alcoholism is to be regarded as a psychiatric illness, as it often is (Davies, 1971), then in my view homosexuality is even more obviously a treatable psychiatric condition as well.

That said, most of our heterosexual behaviours are also learnt ones, many of them hardly natural or healthy. A seemingly innocent example might be what was called 'French kissing' in my youth, that is what can be described as 'tongue kissing', a truly revolting and very unhealthy practice like many other modern sexual practices.

The bottom line on sex, though, might well be that if we were aiming to get any smarter and wiser then abstinence might be the wiser course, especially as a sound exercise regime is clearly a healthier option. Obviously, however, quite the opposite is happening, all part of our *reverse evolution.*

Decline and fall of empires

Modern civilization is based on our learning from the Greek, Roman and also Middle Eastern civilizations of 2-5 thousand years ago.

From these civilizations we learnt sophisticated art, music, architecture, mathematics and philosophy.

These civilizations became great empires but declined and fell ultimately, suggesting that, in the long run at least, the basic need of humans to live on a more 'local' basis is paramount.

That is, our priority is, and should be the wellbeing of ourselves, our family, and our immediate community, not grand visions of empire achieved by violent war, or grand visions of a global economy motivated by greed.

Thus, in the last few hundred years, the British, Dutch, French, Germans, Portuguese, Spanish and Turks have built empires and then lost them.

The British Empire dominated much of the world but finally collapsed after WWII, in part because of the massive debts, much of them to the USA, incurred by that war. As a result, in the words of Dwight Eisenhower: "This conjunction of an immense military establishment and a large arms industry is new in the American experience."

As always, the devastatingly accurate Peter Principle applies, and corruption and stupidity cause society at large to lose out, an example being that between 1978 and 1998 the US Air Force requested only 5 C-130 transport aircraft but funding for 256 was approved. An example of why came later when the four biggest arms manufacturers gave more than $11M in campaign donations for the 2000 election.

Then, in 2002, the proposed increase in the US military budget was $48B, more than the entire UK budget, bringing the US total budget to $396B, more than the combined total of the next 15 big military spenders, including Russia and China.

Long before that, however, the US had 'liberalized' its economy, cutting the top tax rate from 70% to 50%, and eventually to 28% and reducing controls on banks.

The result?

During Reagan's 8-year Presidential tenure the total deficit grew from $900B to $3,000B (note that $1B = 10^9$) and in the 1980s more than 650 Savings & Loan companies collapsed as a result of widespread fraud.

During that period the average American's leisure time per week was reduced to 16.6 hours from the 26.2 it had been in 1973 while, of course, the rich got richer than ever as a result of increasing slavery.

Since then we have seen the spectacular demise of Enron and the 2008 GFC in which major US banks collapsed and others, along with GM and Chrysler, had to be bailed out at great expense, along with increased government expenditure to prop up the economy, further drowning the US in debt.

Yet another example of economic mismanagement, banks have been getting into trouble in the USA and Europe, in particular, because statutory reserve deposit (SRD) and liquidity guarantee ratios have been reduced to ridiculously low values, as little as 2%. Traditionally the very basis of the banking system was SRD circa 10% (it was 7% in Australia in 1985).

In 2011 the US raised its debt limit yet again, after a long drawn-out battle in congress, and it looks certain that the days of the US being the "world's only superpower" are numbered.

To add insult to injury, the last century having been referred to by some as "The American Century," we are now hearing this new century being referred to as "The Asian Century."

With Europe now in economic crisis as well, a total reversal of fortunes seems to be happening on a grand scale as China, India and other countries undergo their own, belated, industrial revolutions which, given their massive populations, are bound to have still further transformative effects on the world economy at the expense of the USA and Europe.

Globally, however, the problems of overpopulation, resource depletion, global warming, and desertification are likely to limit the prospects of future prosperity for all but the richest people in the world.

If the world's population reaches 10 or even 12 billion by the middle of the century, however, it seems certain that the long-term prospects for the human race are poor, this the subject of the recent books *The Doomsday Calculation* (Mohr, 2012a) and *The Population Explosion* (Mohr et al., 2018b).

Cultural crap

Even the most intelligent of us, however, are likely to pick up a few mindless habits. Most of the intelligentsia laugh at modern pop music which certainly is crap, but many of them get dressed up as though they were going to a funeral to go to the opera, which is equally farcical. Opera singing at the best of times is somewhat ridiculous, involving both fat men and fat ladies making a ludicrous and comical racket. In the pop sphere 'rock' concerts and so-called 'musicals' are equally absurd.

Any form of dancing is animal stuff but ballet, with loonies in tights and ladies in very short skirts, is simply for closet perverts.

Even grandiose symphonies perhaps make little sense if one considers that music really should be for relaxation and thus should only require few instruments and fairly quiet scores.

The intelligentsia, however, is more concerned about snob value than intelligent culture so they still like stage plays. Whether Shakespearean or modern, plays are rather childish to say the least.

Many people regard choosing wine as an exercise in intelligence and 'wank' themselves into old age over the virtue of this or that 'red'. This too is pretty mindless stuff when, truth be told, most wines are really not as nice as some modern fruit juice mixtures and just an acquired taste.

When it comes to snob value, of course, flash cars and big houses are key items but these are expensive and not necessarily affordable to the intelligentsia, some of whom are happier to 'slum it' and, indeed, look like down and outs. This only indicates how stupid they really are, however, another symptom of our *reverse evolution*.

Falling IQ

Vernon (1960) and Lynn & Vanhaven (2002) point out that we have dysgenic fertility trends so that the least intelligent people have the most children.

Burt (1957) found that average IQ in the UK had dropped by 1.5% between the years 1920 and 1950 for this reason and he predicted a further 2.5% drop by the year 2000.

Vernon (1960) also points out that a Royal Commission on Mental Deficiency in the UK discovered a "big increase" in the numbers of defectives between the years 1907 and 1929.

It has also been suggested that IQ in the USA is in decline (Fancher, 1985), some claiming that the rate of decrease is 1 point per generation.

Remarkably, Internet search for 'declining human intelligence' yields over 3 million results, for example:

(a) Norwegian conscripts were found to have scored lower in IQ numerical subtests after the mid 1990s.

(b) Danish men assessed for military service in 2003/4 dropped in IQ by almost two points compared to those in 1998 (Teasdale & Owen, 2005, 2008).

The picture is far worse from a global point of view.

As noted earlier, average IQ in Africa is only 70 and it is in such places that population has exploded in the last century whilst in more advanced countries it has ground to a halt.

Therefore, on average, the human intelligence has decreased for demographic reasons. Considering that even the most intelligent of us in the most advanced countries, however, have been also reduced to brainwashed idiots in part, at least, the overall situation is grim to say the least.

The implications of declining average intelligence are far reaching. It has been shown, for example, that a drop of just 3 points in average IQ results in increasing numbers of:

(a) Men in jail - 13%.

(b) High school dropouts (permanent) - 15%.

(a) Women chronically dependent on welfare - 15%.

No doubt declining IQs have also produced even more 'low IQ/high cunning' people trying to brainwash the rest of us into 'believe anything/buy anything' consumer oblivion.

284

Interbreeding amongst Muslims

An article posted recently by Cairns News entitled *Muslims suffer insanity, low IQ, recessive disorders from 1400 years of inbreeding* said that "the massive inbreeding in Muslim culture may well have done virtually irreversible damage to the Muslim gene pool, including extensive damage to its intelligence, sanity, and health."

According to Danish psychologist Nikilai Sennels, close to half of all Muslims in the world are inbred, and in Pakistan the numbers approach 70%, whilst they are 67% in Saudi Arabia, 64% in Jordan and Kuwait, 63% in Sudan, 60% in Iraq, and 54% in the United Arab Emirates and Qatar. As a result British Pakistani families are 13 times more likely to have children with recessive genetic disorders.

According to Sennels, research shows that children of consanguineous marriages lose 10-16 points off their IQ and that social abilities develop much slower in inbred babies. The risk of having an IQ lower than 70, the official demarcation for being classified as "retarded", increases by an astonishing 400% among children of cousin marriages. He concluded: *There is no doubt that the wide spread tradition of first cousin marriages among Muslims has harmed the gene pool of Muslims.*

The article concluded:

Bottom line: Islam is not simply a benign and morally equivalent alternative to the Judeo-Christian tradition. As Sennels points out, the first and biggest victims are Muslims.

Simple Judeo-Christian compassion for Muslims and a common-sense desire to protect Western civilization from the ravages of Islam dictate a vigorous opposition to the spread of this dark and dangerous ideology.

These stark realities must be taken into account when we establish public policies dealing with immigration from Muslim countries and the building of Mosques.

Physically past optimum

Let's face it, take our clothes off and have a look at Homo sapiens sapiens. We look damn stupid, like an evolutionary mistake or Martians on this damned planet: like we don't belong.

We are, in fact, less evolved physically than chimpanzees.

Quite simply, we are pathetic, for example:

➤ Male baldness appears to be on the increase.

➤ In contrast, we have hair too long in places and have to cut and shave our hair off frequently, a ridiculous situation.

➤ Somewhat anachronistically we have evolved with men designed for hunter-gathering and women for child bearing.

➤ Since that time mankind got smaller, the average European male being only 165 cm tall in Shakespeare's time. Thanks to improved diet our height has returned to that of the hunter gatherers (178 cm average for men) but we have lost a good deal of muscle tissue (Callaghan, 2008), no doubt why it has been found that Negroes have a genetic factor that makes them better sprinters.

➤ The disturbing obesity epidemic sweeping more affluent countries where, of course, people are most brainwashed by advertising. The result has been that, although not a great deal taller, women weigh on average 20% more than they did in 1926 (Callaghan, 2008).

➤ Poor diet caused generations of us immense amounts of tooth decay and type II diabetes is now 5 times more prevalent.

➤ We seem increasingly susceptible to new viruses like HIV and VRE which already pose a very serious threat.

➤ The incidence of most types of cancer has increased dramatically, often as a result of defective genes (Weinberg, 1999).

➤ Even amongst children blood pressures are significantly higher.

➤ A French TV documentary *Men in Danger* (Cuthbertson, 2008) notes that pollution is causing significant changes in humans:
(a) Decreased testosterone levels in men.
(b) Greater prevalence of genital abnormalities in males at birth.
(c) Male sperm counts decreased by 50% in Copenhagen in the last 50 years and by 40% in the last 20 years only in Paris.
(d) A huge 150% increase in breast cancer in women since 1960.

➤ Our eyes evolved for far field vision but thanks to man's invention of writing and then TV and the PC we are 3 times more likely to be short-sighted, a telling example of how our evolution is unable to keep pace with our rapidly changing environment.

The inescapable conclusion, however, is that we are becoming a genetic joke physically, part of an overall *reverse evolution* process.

Deteriorating gene pool

In *The Descent of Man* Charles Darwin cited the work of his cousin Francis Galton more than ten times. Galton did much important scientific work, including proposing and defining the term *eugenics*, on which subject Darwin wrote:

We civilized men, on the other hand, do our utmost to check the process of elimination; we build asylums for the imbecile, the maimed, and the sick; we institute poor-laws; and our medical men exert their utmost skill to save the life of every one to the last moment. Thus the weak members of civilized societies propagate their kind.

Carlo Cipolla (1974) pointed out that our population growth graph went almost vertical with the coming of the industrial revolution and implored that what we needed was 'quality not quantity,' a phrase the first author recalls his fifth grade teacher Miss Bachelard repeating often.

As Lynn and Vanhaven (2002) point out, however, we have dysgenic fertility trends so that the least intelligent people have the most children.

As part of that the none-too-intelligent but overpaid greedy executives whose businesses brainwash us to buy their often shoddy products can indeed afford to have children and buy them the right qualifications to carry on the family line in a capitalist fashion.

In contrast, many of the brightest children who struggle to come top at school will end up as scientists and engineers and the like, make relatively little money and struggle to afford a house and children, avoid divorce and stay sane enslaved as underpaid back room boys.

In addition, modern medical science is able to keep alive people with serious genetic disorders and there is concern in some quarters that this will lead to a deterioration of the human gene pool:

Many people are born each year with genetic defects that in the past would have hampered their reproductive potential. Now, medical treatment enables them to survive, reproduce, and pass on the defective genes. Followers of this view, such as the Nobel Prize winning geneticist H.J. Mueller, see this tampering with selection as a black cloud hanging over our future. Someday, Mueller says, all people will be born with one major genetic problem or another: diabetes, PKU, hemophilia.

M.L. Weiss, A.E. Mann, *Human Biology and Behaviour* (1978).

The bottom line once again, therefore, is that we are into reverse evolution both mentally and physically, in part because eugenics became a dirty word because of ill-conceived attempts at reducing 'bad breeding,' for example:

(a) From 1907, 27 US states passed sterilization laws to prevent such people as epileptics, the feeble-minded, habitual criminals, and 'moral perverts' from having children. In most states these laws were not enforced but in California 10,000 people were sterilized by 1935.

(b) Other countries including Denmark, Germany, Norway, Sweden and Switzerland passed similar laws, in Sweden 60,000 young women being sterilized between 1935 and 1976.

(c) Eugenics was supposedly the justification for the massive extermination programs of the scientists and geneticists of the Third Reich, leading to the stigma attached to the word.

In the economically decaying West, having spent the best part of a century fighting socialism, we have now have gone too far in our quest for equality, insisting that regardless of sex, race or any other factor, we are all equal.

We have dumbed down our education systems, our political systems, and our 'consumer zombie' society in general in which we now breed 'willy-nilly,' perhaps with a quick copulatory act between yet another raft of mindless TV ads.

As our society regresses it is now, once again in history, more and more a fight for survival in an increasingly fierce economic rat race whilst the planet's resources and its environment gradually diminish in quantity and quality.

The first author's father, despite having had 3 children (he was the third!), believed in ZPG (zero population growth), quite correctly at that time.

Since then China has had its one-child policy which we might call NPG, and has become the world's second largest and strongest economy.

The author, told by a woman he had made pregnant that the child would be "mildly retarded", consulted some experts who inferred that 'mildly' was really quite serious. He then persuaded the woman to have an abortion though 5 months pregnant. She did, about which he has no conscience.

David Galton concludes that:

Society as a whole should embrace the new [eugenics] *technology and the opportunities if offers less timorously, or even with some measure of enthusiasm* (Galton, 2001).

Animal farm

Most, if not all, the terrorism, revolutions and wars in history have been about a "fair go" because it isn't really sane, for example, that Buckingham Palace should have 650 rooms, and that this is just one of several palaces owned by the British royal family.

No doubt that sort of anomaly, along with hard times, helped inspire the French and Russian revolutions.

Few countries, if any, are still governed by monarchies and most have so-called democracy. These are not truly democratic, however, and are in fact corrupt capitalist oligarchies in which a few rich families, powerful bureaucrats and business leaders are able to make most of the input into the important decisions at all levels of government.

All too often our leaders fit the Peter Principle well, that is, they are incompetent. This is borne out by the results as we are always lurching from one disaster to another and constantly fed a load of bullshit saying we've never had it so good.

Lynn and Vanhaven (2002) note that in the richest nations the correlation of IQ with earnings is only 0.35. This is a low figure bearing in mind that high earnings should enhance performance, and suggest that the fattest capitalist pigs have more animal cunning and greed and less intelligence.

George Orwell was a socialist, of course, and we think of capitalist pigs when we think of his *Animal Farm* and wish that we had *real democracy*, a topic discussed further in the recent book *Real Democracy* (Mohr et al., 2019b).

Rich bosses live off and cheat enslaved workers, of course, often bullying and sometimes sexually abusing them, as the ME TO movement has shown of late. Yet this is what they are paid megabucks to do, along with produce shoddy products which they hire expert brainwashers usually called advertising agencies to addict people to.

The bottom line is, therefore, that our leaders are usually greedy unethical pigs of pretty average intelligence, if that, thus being an important cog in the machinery of our *reverse evolution*.

Conclusion

A 'Cambridge man' like the author, Ian Morris, author of the book *Why the West Rules - For Now*, opines that people everywhere are essentially clever chimps.

My guess is that the human race past its peak around the 1960s. WWII was long over and there was relative peace in the world, we had TV, tape recorders and transistor radios, and the first PCs were just a few years away. Then the world's human population was perhaps already about double that for comfort if everybody was to have a good standard of living that might be sustainable for the long term. Now it has more than doubled again to a clearly unsustainable level.

Overpopulation, overconsumption, pollution, global warming, resource depletion and land degradation are such serious problems that the survival of many species, including ours, is threatened.

Everywhere you look real standards are declining though we are usually told the opposite while incompetent and overpaid CEO's are simply looting the planet while they still can.

The heading for an article posted on the Internet is

Beware of Corporate Media Brainwashing.
Through Corporate Media Brainwashing,
the World's Elite Disguises Their New World Order Plan
as it Dumbs America Down.

The article is, in fact, a gripe about banks in the wake of the sub-prime lending crisis in the US, but it can be viewed as a reminder of what brainwashed consumer and believe any bullshit zombies we are.

19th century French lunatic asylums used to make money by having inmates perform for the public once a week. In Australia in recent years the treasurer has said year that his deliberately pessimistic national budget was in surplus but not reminded us that each time the national debt was continuing to rise.

This is the typical econobabble of economists and business leaders, stuff that would have been suitable in the public performances in 19th century French 'funny farms'.

Yet we brainwashed zombies accept such crap.

No wonder that we are in *reverse evolution* and, as we slowly grow less intelligent we are, of course, blissfully unaware of it and too busy trying to survive the 'rat race' to care even if we were.

Finally, a good and sometimes humourous example of consumer zombies can be found in the movie *Dawn of The Dead* with many scenes of hoards of zombies creeping around a huge shopping centre. In this story, however, the zombies are not looking to buy anything, they are simply looking for a meal of human flesh from a 'non-zombie', who even if just bitten will ere long become a zombie too. This 'contagion' aspect of the story reminds one of the importance of imitative learning in the very young and social learning in teenagers and adults.

As for BW zombies – what better example than Muslim terrorists? In July 2016 the Australian media began to talk of "terror health checks", that is, checking suspected Muslim activists for mental health problems. As noted earlier in this chapter, thanks to centuries of interbreeding, most Muslims are 'retards' to a considerable degree, whilst anyone following this savage, vile and primitive religion in this day and age should be certified in some way, if not several, e.g. as somewhat insane, at risk of radicalization, and thus perhaps a terrorist risk etcetera. Then, for treatment of their mental health the only sensible course would be to give them radical prefrontal lobotomies using the simple 'drilling holes from the side' method of Freeman and Watts discussed in Chapter 15.

As for reverse evolution, the increasing incidence of bullying in human societies around the world, and of sexual harassment etc., as evidenced by the growing ME TOO movement, indicate that psychopaths are becoming more common, as are most mental disorders.

REFERENCES

Adler, Alfred, *Understanding Human Nature* (1927).

Arkowitz H, Miller WR, Rollnick S, *Motivational Interviewing in The Treatment of Psychological Problems,* The Guilford Press, New York (2015).

Atkinson RC, Shiffrin RM, Human memory: A proposed system and its control processes. RW Spence, JT Spence (eds), *The Psychology of Learning and Motivation, Vol. 2,* Academic Press, New York (1968).

Atrens D, Curthoys I, *The Neurosciences and Behaviour: An Introduction,* 2nd edn, Academic Press, Sydney (1982).

Baddeley A, *Human Memory, Theory and Practice,* Lawrence Erlbaum Associates, Hove, UK (1990).

Baker P, *Decisions of Daring Achievers, Inside Out,* Perth (2004).

Ben-Menashe A, *Profits of War, The Sensational Story of the World-Wide Arms Conspiracy,* Allen & Unwin, Sydney (1992).

Bennis, Warren, *On Becoming a Leader* (1989).

Blanchard, Kenneth; Johnson, Spencer, *The One Minute Manager* (1981).

Burns, David D, *Feeling Good: The New Mood Therapy* (1980).

Burt C, The distribution of intelligence, *British Journal of Psychology* 48 (161-174) 1957.

Butler-Bowden, Tom, *50 Psychology Classics,* 2nd edition, Nicholas Brealey Publishing, London (2017).

Butler-Bowden, Tom, *50 Success Classics,* 2nd edition, Nicholas Brealey Publishing, London (2017b).

Callaghan G, Taller, Wider, *The Weekend Australian Magazine,* April 5-6, 2008, pp 13-17.

Cantwell A, *The Cancer Microbe,* Aries Rising Press, LA (1990).

Caro J, Fox C, *The F Word, How we learned to swear by feminism,* New South/UNSW Press, Sydney (2008).

Carter P, *IQ and Psychometric Tests* 2nd edn, Kogan Page, London (2007).

Cipolla, CM, *The Economic History of World Population,* 6th edn, Penguin, London (1974).

Collins AM, Quillian MR, Retrieval time from semantic memory, *Journal of Verbal Learning and Verbal Behaviour,* 8 (1969) 240-247.

Coloroso, Barbara, *The Bully, the Bullied, and the Not-So-Innocent Bystander,* 2nd edn, William Morrow/Harper Collins, New York NY (2016).

Cowie, Helen; Harriet Tennenbaum & Ffion Jones, *Emily is Being Bullies: What Can She Do?* Jessica Kingsley Publishers, London (2019).

Cozolino L, *The Neuroscience of Psychotherapy, Building and Rebuilding the Human Brain,* W.W. Norton & Co., NY (2002).

Cuthbertson I, article on TV documentary program 'Men in Danger', *The Weekend Australian,* Review p 28, March 29, 2008.

Davies B, *An Introduction to Clinical Psychiatry,* Melbourne University Press, Melbourne (1971).

Darwin, Charles, *The Expression of the Emotions in Man and Animals,* Harper Collins (Fontana), London (1999).

Di Nardo PA, O'Brien GT, Barlow DH, Waddell MT, Blanchard EB, Reliability of the DSM-III anxiety disorder categories using a new structured interview, *Archives of General Psychiatry*, 40, 1070-1074 (1993).

Drew, Naomi, *No Kidding About Bullying: 125 Ready-to-use Activities to Help Kids Manage Anger, Resolve Conflicts, Build Empathy, and Get Along,* Free Spirit Publishing, Minneapolis MN (2010).

Eagly AH, Chaiken S, *The Psychology of Attitudes,* Harcourt Brace Jovanovich, Orlando FA (1993).

Egerton Eastwick RW (ed.), *The Oracle Encyclopaedia,* George Newnes, London (1896).

Eysenck HJ, Cancer, personality and stress: Prediction and prevention, *Advances in Behaviour Research and Therapy,* 16, 167 – 215 (1994).

Fancher RE, *The intelligence men: Makers of the IQ Controversy,* WW Norton, New York (1985).

Forbes HD, *Ethnic Conflict: Commerce, Culture, and the Contact Hypothesis,* Yale University Press, New Haven (1997).

Foss DJ, Hakes DT, *Psycholinguistics: An Introduction to the Psychology of Language,* Prentice-Hall, Englewood Cliffs NJ (1978).

Frankl, Viktor, *The Will to Meaning: Foundations and Applications of Logotherapy* (1969).

Friedman M, Rosenman RH, *Association of specific overt behaviour pattern with blood cardiovascular findings, Journal of the American Medical Association,* 169, 1286 (1959).

Galton D, *In Our Own Image, Eugenics and the Genetic Modification of People*, Little Brown & Co, London (2001).

Gillespie, David, *Taming Toxic People, The science of identifying & dealing with psychopaths at work & at home,* Pan MacMillan Australia, Sydney (2017).

Goodall (van Lawick-Goodall) J, *In the Shadow of Man,* Houghton-Mifflin, Boston (1971).

Govoni N, Eng R, Morton G, *Promotional Management: Issues and Perspectives,* Prentice-Hall, Englewood Cliffs NJ (1988).

REFERENCES

Grivas, John, and Carter, Linda, *Psychology for the VCE Student: Units 1 and 2*, 4th edn, Jacaranda Press/John Wiley & Sons, Milton QLD (2005).

Insight vol. 7, part 91, Marshall Cavendish, London (1982).

Kassin S, *Psychology*, 4th edn, Prentice-Hall, Upper Saddle River, New Jersey (2004).

Kemp, Jurrian, *The Intelligent Optimist's Guide to Life: How to Find Health and Success in a World That's a Better Place Than You Think*, Berret-Koehler Publishers Inc., San Francisco (2014).

Krapp K, editor, *Psychologists & Their Theories for Students*, vol. 1: A-K, Thomson Gale, Farmington Hills, MI (2005).

Larsen RJ, Buss DM, *Personality Psychology, Domains of Knowledge About Human Nature*, McGraw-Hill, NY (2002).

Lieberman JA, *Shrinks, The Untold Story of Psychiatry*, Little Brown & Co, NY (2015).

Likert R, *New Patterns of Management*, McGraw-Hill, New York (1961).

Lilienfeld SO, Lynne SJ, Ruscia J, Beyerstein BL, *50 Great Myths of Popular Psychology, Shattering Widespread Misconceptions about Human Behaviour*, Wiley-Blackwell, Chichester (2010).

Lindzey G, Hall CS, Thompson RF, *Psychology*, 2nd edn, Worth, New York (1978).

Lovegrove, Dr Emily, *Help! I'm Being Bullied. Accent Press, Pembroke Dock, Pembrokeshire* (2006).

Lynne R, Vanhanen T, *IQ and The Wealth of Nations*, Praeger, Westport CT (2002).

Mackintosh NJ, *IQ and Human Intelligence*, 2nd ed., Oxford University Press, Oxford (2011).

Macy, Travis, *The Ultra Mindset: An Endurance Champion's 8 Core Principles for Success in Business, Sports, and Life*, De Capo Press, Philadelphia PA (2015).

296

Mamonov V, *Control for life extension: A personalized holistic approach* (2001).

Marta, Suzy Yehl, *Healing the Hurt, Restoring the Hope,* Rodale, London (2004).

McCormack MH, *What They Don't Teach You at Harvard Business School,* Fontana/Collins, London (1986).

McGuire WJ, A syllogistic analysis of cognitive relationships, in *Attitude Organization And Change,* CI Hovland & MJ Rosenberg (eds.), Yale University Press, New Haven (1960).

Meadows DH, Meadows DL, Randers J, Behrens WW, *The Limits to Growth,* Pan, London (1974).

Miller, Nick, 'New hope of escaping the dark', *The Age,* 26 August, 2017.

Mohr GA, *The Finite Element Method for Solids, Fluids, and Optimization,* OUP Oxford (1992).

Mohr GA, M----- HR, *A Microcomputer Introduction to the Finite Element Method*, Pitman, Melbourne (1986), Heinemann, London (1987).

Mohr GA, *The Doomsday Calculation, The End of the Human Race,* Xlibris, Sydney (2012a).

Mohr GA, *The War of the Sexes, Women Are Getting On Top,* Xlibris, Sydney (2012b).

Mohr GA, *Curing Cancer & Heart Disease, Proven Ways to Combat Aging, Atherosclerosis & Cancer,* Xlibris, Sydney (2012c).

Mohr GA, *Heart Disease, Cancer & Aging, Proven Neutraceutical and Lifestyle Solutions,* Horizon Publishing Group, Sydney (2013a).

Mohr GA, *The Pretentious Persuaders, A Brief History & Science of Mass Persuasion,* 2nd edn, Horizon Publishing Group, Sydney (2013b).

REFERENCES

Mohr GA, *The History & Psychology of Human Conflicts,* Horizon Publishing Group, Sydney (2014a).

Mohr GA, *Elementary Thinking for the 21st Century,* Xlibris, Sydney (2014b).

Mohr GA, Sinclair R, Fear E, *The Evolving Universe, Relativity, Redshift and Life From Space,* Xlibris, Sydney (2014).

Mohr GA, *The 8-Week+ Program to Reverse Cardiovascular Disease,* Book Venture, Ishpeming MI (2015).

Mohr GA, Fear E, *World Religions, The History, Psychology, Issues & Truth,* Xlibris, Sydney (2015).

Mohr GA, Fear E, Sinclair R, *World War 3: When & How Will It End?,* Inspiring Publishers, Canberra (2015b).

Mohr GA, *A Half Life: The Memoirs of Geoff Mohr,* private publication, Melbourne (2016).

Mohr GA, Fear E, *The Brainwashed: From Consumer Zombies to Islamism and Jihad,* Inspiring Publishers, Canberra (2016).

Mohr GA, *The Scientific MBA,* 5th edn, *Balboa Press,* Bloomington IN (2017).

Mohr GA, Sinclair R, Fear R, *Human Intelligence, Learning & behavior,* Inspiring Publishers, Canberra (2017).

Mohr GA, *The DIY Cardiovascular Cure: A Comprehensive Program to Reverse Atherosclerosis,* Amazon-Kindle (2018a).

Mohr GA, *Combating Cancer: Proven Neutraceutical & Lifestyle Solutions,* Amazon-Kindle (2018b).

Mohr GA, *The War of the Sexes, The Problems & the Solutions,* Amazon-Kindle (2018c).

Mohr GA, *Elementary Thinking for Modern Management,* Amazon-Kindle (2018d).

Mohr GA, *Mohr's Law of Hierarchies, and many other Mohr's Laws,* Amazon-Kindle (2018e).

Mohr GA, Mohr RS, Mohr PE, *The Psychology of Hope,* Balboa Press, Bloomington IN (2018).

Mohr GA, Mohr RS, Mohr PE, *New Theories of the Universe, Evolution and Relativity,* Amazon-Kindle (2018a).

Mohr GA, Mohr PE, Mohr RS, *The Population Explosion,* Amazon-Kindle (2018b).

Mohr GA, Mohr RS, Mohr PE, *Human Conflict: An Attitudinal Psychology Model,* Amazon-Kindle (2018c).

Mohr GA, Mohr PE, Mohr RS, *World Religions: From Animism to Mohronism,* Amazon-Kindle (2018d).

Mohr GA, Mohr PE, Mohr RS, *Brainwashed Zombies: Religious, Political & Consumer Persuasion,* Amazon-Kindle (2018e).

Mohr GA, Mohr PE, Mohr RS, *The Psychology of Success,* Amazon-Kindle (2018f).

Mohr GA, Mohr PE, Mohr RS, *World War 3: Global Islamic Jihad,* Amazon-Kindle (2018g).

Mohr GA, Mohr RS, Mohr PE, *Human Psychology, Learning & Intelligence,* Amazon-Kindle (2019a).

Mohr GA, Mohr PE, Mohr RS, *Real Democracy: Not Westminster-style brawling, oligarchical capitalism & corruption*, Amazon-Kindle (2019b).

Moore, Megan, *Using Social Media in the classroom: a best practice guide,* Hawker Brownlow Education, Moorabbin, Victoria (2012).

Morgan CT, King RA, Robinson NM, *Introduction to Psychology*, 6th edn, McGraw-Hill, Tokyo (1979).

National Education Association (USA), *Findings from the National Education Association's Nationwide Study of Bullying: Teachers' and Educational Support Professionals' Perspectives* (2011).

Newcomb TM, Persistence and regression of changed attitudes, Journal of Sociological Issues 19 (1963) 3-14.

REFERENCES

O'Guinn TC, Allen CT, Semenik RJ, *Advertising and Integrated Brand Promotion.* Thomson South-Western, Mason OH (2006).

Packard V, *The Waste Makers,* Pelican, Harmondsworth, London (1963).

Packard V, *The People Shapers,* Nelson, Melbourne (1978).

Parkinson CN, *The Law,* Schwartz, Melbourne (1980).

Peter LJ, Hull R, *The Peter Principle,* Souvenir Press, London (1969).

Richardson, Cheryl, *Take Time for Your Life: A Seven-Step Program for Creating the Life You Want* (1998).

Ripps LJ, Schoben EJ, Smith EE, Semantic distance and the verification of semantic relations, *Journal of Verbal Learning and Verbal Behaviour,* 12 (1973) 203-210.

Robertson I, *Sociology,* 2nd edn, Worth, New York (1981).

Rogers, Carl, *On Becoming a Person: A Therapist's View of Psychotherapy* (1961).

Rosenfeld A, *The Second Genesis: The Coming Control of Life,* Pyramid Communications, New York (1972).

Sampson A, *The Arms Bazaar,* Coronet Books, London (1977).

Sargent M, *Drinking and Alcoholism in Australia: A Power Relations Theory,* Longman Cheshire, Melbourne (1979).

Selmes C (ed.), *New Movements in the Study and Teaching of Biology,* Temple Smith, London (1974).

Shaffer JW, Graves PL, Swank RT, Pearson TA, Clustering personality traits in youth and subsequent development of cancer among physicians, *Journal of Behavioural Medicine,* 10, 441-447 (1987).

Solomon MR, *Consumer Behaviour: Buying, Having and Being,* Allyn and Bacon, Boston (1992).

Sternberg RJ, *In Search of the Human Mind,* 2nd edn, Harcourt Brace College Publishers, Orlando FL (1998).

REFERENCES

Sweeney MS, *Brain, The Complete Mind, How it Develops, How it Works, and How to Keep it Sharp,* National Geographic, Washington D.C. (2009).

Sykes CJ, *Dumbing Down Our Kids: Why American Children Feel Good About Themselves But Can't Read, Write or Add,* St Martin's Griffin, New York (1995).

Teasdale T, Owen D, A long-term rise and recent decline in intelligence test performance: The Flynn Effect in reverse, *Personality and Individual Differences* 39(4), 837 - 843 (2005).

Teasdale T, Owen D, Secular declines in cognitive test scores: A reversal of the Flynn Effect, *Intelligence* 36(2), 121-126 (2008).

Thomas M, *As Used on the Famous Nelson Mandela, Underground Adventures in the Arms and Torture Trade,* Ebury Press, London (2006).

Thomas J, Hughes T, *You Don't Have to be Famous to Have Manic Depression: The Insider's Guide to Mental Health,* Michael Joseph, London (2006).

Trump, Donald, *The Way to the Top, The Best Business Advice I Ever Received,* Crown Business, New York, NY (2004).

Ungar G, Desidero DM, Parr W, Isolation, identification and synthesis of a specific behaviour inducing brain peptide, *Nature* 238 (1972) 198-202.

Vander AJ, Sherman JH, Luciano DS, *Human Physiology, The Mechanisms of Body Function,* 6th edn, McGraw-Hill, New York (1994).

van Lawick-Goodall, Jane, *In the Shadow of Man,* Houghton Mifflin, Boston (1971).

Vernon, PE, *Intelligence and Attainment Tests,* University of London Press, London (1960).

Wagner, Richard H, *Environment and Man,* 3rd edn, W.W. Norton & Co, New York (1978).

Wattles, Wallace D, *The Science of Getting Rich* (1910).

References

Weiss ML, Mann AE, *Human Biology and Behaviour, An Anthropological Perspective*, 2nd edn, Little Brown, Boston MA (1978).

Weinberg R, *One Renegade Cell,* Phoenix, London (1999).

Youngson RM, Schott I, *Medical Blunders,* Robinson, London (1996).

Zajonc RB, Attitudinal effects of mere exposure, *Journal of Personality and Social Psychology,* 9 (2, Pt. 2), 1-17 (1968).

☺☻☹☺☻☹☺☻☹☺☻☹☺☻☹

THE BULLYING EPIDEMIC

Key topics covered in this important and timely book include:

➢ Tribal homo sapiens, the human brain & language and learning.
➢ Education and learning.
➢ Family life, the education system, the workplace & bullying.
➢ Hierarchical organizations and the psychopaths they harbour.
➢ The psychology of attitude formation and measurement.
➢ The effects of the mass media and advertising.
➢ Psychology and psychiatry. Personality.
➢ The psychology of habits. The psychology of Conflict.
➢ Psychological assessment and treatment.
➢ The Mohr Psychological Inventory (MPI).

G. A. Mohr did his PhD at Churchill College, Cambridge. He published circa 60 papers for 20 international journals and more than 30 books, including:

A Microcomputer Introduction to the Finite Element Method
Finite Elements for Solids, Fluids, and Optimization
The Pretentious Persuaders, A Brief History & Science of Mass Persuasion
Curing Cancer & Heart Disease
The Variant Virus, Introducing Secret Agent Simon Sinclair
The Doomsday Calculation: The End Of The Human Race
Heart Disease, Cancer, & Ageing: Proven Neutraceutical & Lifestyle Solutions
2045: A Remote Town Survives Global Holocaust
The History & Psychology of Human Conflict;   The War of the Sexes
Elementary Thinking for the 21st Century;   Mohr's Law of Hierarchies
The 8-Week+ Program to Reverse Cardiovascular Disease
The DIY Cardiovascular Cure;   Combating Cancer
Elementary Thinking for Modern Management;   The Scientific MBA
The Psychology of Life;   The Psychology of Depression.

Also with R.S. Mohr/Richard Sinclair & P.E. Mohr/Edwin Fear:

The Evolving Universe: Relativity, Redshift and Life from Space
World Religions: The History, Psychology, Issues & Truth
World War 3: When & How Will It End?
The Brainwashed, From Consumer Zombies to Islamic Jihad
Human Intelligence, Learning & Behaviour; The Psychology of Hope
New Theories of The Universe, Evolution, and Relativity (2nd edn)
The Population Explosion; World War 3: Global Islamic Jihad
Brainwashed Zombies: Religious, Political & Consumer Persuasion
Human Conflict: An Attitudinal Psychology Model
World Religions: From Animism to Mohronism;   The Psychology of Success
Human Psychology, Learning and & Intelligence
Real Democracy: Not Westminster-style brawling, oligarchical capitalism & corruption.